THE CHRISTIAN CHURCH:
RACIAL DISCRIMINATION,
GENDER DISCRIMINATION AGAINST WOMEN,
HUMAN RIGHTS VIOLATOR,
FINANCIAL DISCRIMINATION-
ECCLESIASTICAL GRANTS
GOVERNMENT FINANCING OF
THE CHURCHES

IN WORDS AND PUCTURES LOCAL,REGIONAL, INTERNATIONAL ORIGINAL MEDIA REPORTS

EQUAL OPPORTUNITY

VOLUME 1

BY

ANDY A. BURKETT.,MSc

JANUARY 2002

ISBN: 978-1-4033-8951-0 (sc)
ISBN: 978-1-4033-8950-3 (e)

Library of Congress Control Number: 2002095439

Print information available on the last page.

This book is printed on acid-free paper.

1stBooks – rev. 04/13/2023

Port of Spain. The Capital of Trinidad.

CONTENTS

CHAPTER THREE
DISCRIMINATION AGAINST WOMEN,
DIFFERENT GENDER BUT SAME GOAL

DISCRIMINATION AGAINST WOMEN IN THE CHRISTIAN CHURCH

INCLUDES ONLY INFORMATION ON CHURCHES WHICH I POSSESS

PREFACE.

Andy A.Burkett attended Shorter College,Wilberforce University and Atlanta University,U.S.A.

He has been in the field of research at the US Government and Business Division, Cincinnati/Hamilton County Library, Trinidad Public Library, in the government civil service Ministry of Petroleum and Mines, Ministry of External Affairs, Ministry of Foreign Affairs, Court of Appeal, Research Officer Regional Council, Community Police, North Eastern Division.

He has done a number of research papers on crime which include: "The relationship between alcohol and crime" 31pages, March 1996, "The high cost of crime to taxpayers" 20 pages, January 1998,SPEED- The automobile as a killing machine", 15 pages, January 1998, "Policing the Nation of Trinidad and Tobago",31 pages, January 2000, "Proposal for a law to deal with delinquent parents of juvenile delinquents in matters of crime" 24 pages, October 2000. He is preparing currently a "Manifesto for the control of crime, lawlessness and disorder."

On race relations he has done a 230 pages compilation titled "The Christian Church: A racial discrimination,gender discrimination against women,human rights violator and financial discrimination institution- ecclesiastical grants/ government financing of the churches." and the other titled "Racial discrimination against peoples of Indian origin from India, Bangladesh,Pakistan, West Indies,Caribbean and South America living in Canada, England,South Africa and U.S.A(part one) and Who were the first known native people of India as stated by India"s scholars and the government of India? (part two)."

In 1986 I completed this draft document with the same subject but a different format, in that it was consisting of my own analyses and opinions supported by bibliographic sources of information quoted as footnotes an I included an index. The document was 275 typed pages.

Because of its format then it could be considered my Authorship and I submitted it to be published by the Pegasus Printery in Belmont- the printery burnt with my document on plates; however I retained a duplicate of my document and never sort to publish it again.

Between 1986 and the year 2002, I continued to amass articles from local,regional and international media sources on the subjects contained in the title of this document, so that that the cumulative original sources have grown to the voluminous amount that you see exhibited here,Most of the information here are therefore are from originals in my possession and not from the internet.

I have decided therefore not to clad this document with my opinions and analyses but to allow the reader to do this themselves what the reporters or writers were saying.This is therefore a compilation. Unfortunately I can provide the reader with only information on those christian denominations which I have in my possession but I know that there does exist out there information on other denominations/churches for which I shall have to search one day to collate information on the subjects that comprise this work.

What you are about to read and see in vivid pictures will shock you! for you will find that many churches have had a history of human rights violations including genocide and other murders. With the passing of time leaders of these institutions present themselves as sanctimonious heroes of the people; their structures are un-democratic but autocratic and their great church massive buildings, huge pipe organs and enormous real estate properties have been acquired freely from the treasuries of the states and called ecclesiastical grants,

Other churches receive none but have survived on tithes and offerings of their members. Yet kings/queens, presidents, doctors ,professors,lawyers who in the secular states/countries rave sanction against un-democratic political,human rights state policies turn their myopic blind vision and support these religious mis-representations.

While this document may contain brief information on other matters, an expanded knowledge can be gleamed from pages else-where: I shall urge readers to get information on the spanish inquisitions, burning of heretics, the four crusades, genocide of indians in the Caribbean and Americas.

Know that Peter the apostle was never in Rome, no where in the new testament in all the recordings of the missionary journeys of place names that Peter had been, Rome was never recorded, he never was there nor died there instead he disappears from the pages of the new tesatment.

Paul was recorded in the new testament to have visited Rome more than once on his missionary journeys of cities named which he visited, Peter never. Peter wrote only two known books -1st and 2nd Peter. However Paul was a prolific new testament writer.

The new testament does not record Jesus naming any specific church in Matthew cpt 16, verses 13 to 19 and it was the same Peter that Jesus called Satan in verse 23, so no church has an valid basis to any apostolic succession or Peter as the first head of any church denomination.

Read Acts cpt 8 verses 27 to 39 about the Ethiopian who was under The Queen of Ethiopia when he met the apostle Phillip and was baptised by him. Did the Ethiopian christian go back to Ethiopia and start the early Ethiopian Orthodox Church?

Read about Richard Allen who started the oldest black founded church in 1787 in the U.S.A because the Methodist In Philadelphia did not allow whites and non-whites to worship together as christian brothers and sisters but segregated the non-whites, blacks to worship only in the upstairs balcony of St George Methodist as a result Richard Allen founded the A.M.E Church or African Methodist Episcopal Church. Read about Morris Brown and Denmark Vesey who started slave revolts in South Carolina in 1817 and later became the second bishop of the A.M.E Church. Read about Paul Quinn an Indian who was born in Culcutta, India, came to the U.S.A and later became fourth bishop of the A.M.E Church in 1808, Read About Sarah Allen wife of Bishop Richard Allen.

Read too about the A.M.E .Z or African Methodist Episcopal Zion Church and James Varick, Harriet Tubman, Sojourner Truth and Frederick Douglas freedom fighters of 1830. Read about the founding of the C.M.E Church.

Andy A.Burkett
18.Sunshine Ave, San Juan
Trinidad,W.I (phone/fax:638-5011)

AFRO ANGLICANISM A STEP OF FAITH

by Fr. Augustine Joseph

LOOKOUT NEWSPAPERS SEPTEMBER ISSUE 1985 Trinidad Anglican Newspaper

The name "Afro Anglicanism" was new; the conference was new. It never happened before in the history of the Anglican Communion. The fact that Anglicans of Africa and African extract met in Barbados in June to discuss the contribution black anglicans have made and are making in their christian witness, made it historic and significant. The significance could be seen from the 17 countries representing 5 continents which participated in the conference.

Anglicans of every rank and position in the church secured a place in the conference room. Archbishops, bishops, canons, priests (male and female) and laity grabbed by the quality of the presentations, discussions, organization and fellowship of the whole affair, felt, no doubt, the spirit of God among them.

They heard an inspired address by Dr. Edmundo De Sueza of the Episcopal Church of Costa Rica on the theme, "Evangelism and Justice". "Evangelism," he said, "is to speak about the concerns of life, the gospel, truth, compassion and conversion that leads to the destruction of discrimination.

Then Jesus becomes Lord because no other can be." He went on to unmask the crudities and viciousness of all world which some church leaders have allowed to parade unchecked.

Meanwhile Canon Frederick Williams of the Conference committee reminded participants of the reasons for meeting. Among other things he saw the historic assembly as a family reunions providing the basis for a transfer of sovereignty, to enable our people of colour to agree on our common ground of history, identify and culture, and to identify and oppose the structures of oppression which blurs the vision that points to the kingdom of God.

Such pertinent reminders followed by exhaustive discussions and study, kept the conference on course resulting in the release of a comprehensive document called the "Codrington Consensus" which is social, political, economic and religious in scope bringing.

It says: "We are 200 Anglicans, clergy and lay, from 17 countries and representing 5 continents and a plurality of cultures, who also recognize our common ancestry in the motherland of Africa. We are joined together by a common world view and thoughtforms which exercise common constraining and directing influences on us. We share a common sense of spirituality, of community and of beauty. We share a common history of oppression, colonialism and racism in a variety of forms, we share a common heritage which has in some ways bruised and wounded by the effects of poverty, degradation and marginalization."

Such a conference demands faith in God as we run the risk of being misunderstood by the ever present detractors. But our faith will not turn us back.

Afro Anglicanism is a step of faith attempting to give validation and recognition to our black cultural art-forms in worship and life as something God himself has blessed and now uses for the spread and advancement of his church in predominantly black societies.

If the conference was new, the social, cultural and religious roots it seeks to unearth are old but strongly imbeded in the hearts and consciousness of our people of that great country of Africa and beyond.

7

Anglicans focus on race relations

By Father
Laurence Small

The conference on Race Relations sponsored by the Church Mission of the Anglican Diocese of Barbados at the Caribbee Hotel on April 13 marked a new phase in historical, sociological and theological approach to a question which needed to be tackled, and to use the words of the diocesan Bishop Drexel Gomez "to move it from a theoretical consensus to a practical consensus.

The seminar of 65 participants from 26 ecclesiastical parishes appeared to some to be reasonable to represents a reasonable representation, while in varying degrees others called it a good beginning.

Of the 65 as was to be expected there were less than half a dozen whites whose presence and contributions to the debate were vitally important.

not moved from their former position." The Bishop himself recalled that when he first came to Barbados as a theological student in the late 1950s, the Church in the West Indies was accepting more and more black priests, but even at that stage they favoured white leadership.

Dr. John Holder

Rev. Wayne Isaacs

Senator Straughn

Racism is a strange vicious beast. It blinds before it kills.

ments.

From the foresight the gem of the exercise lay in the presentations of historian Dr. Hilary Beckles and entrepreneur Phillip Goddard. Because of other pressing duties one missed the major part of the morning session and therefore the case of Goddard owing to urgent business elsewhere he did not appear.

Content therefore to share in the entire afternoon session plus a bit of the morning fare, one concludes that the efforts of the participants though 300 years late need not be a waste of time.

The question now is 'Where do we go from here?'

Bishop Gomez says seminars of this nature are important, and while the official position of the Church is anti-racist, there are still some people in mindset have

One recalls that the most liberal bishop who was 'anti-establishment' through promoting and clamouring for black clergy then showed an inclination for white bishops in the Province of the West Indies.

On the question of bringing home to the seminar the position as it really was in Barbados, Senator Ada Straughn who was "born and bred" in St. David's, gave a historical account, through her experience of the white plantocracy, aided and abetted by the the white plantocracy. The front seats at the morning services, with the blacks only be able to sit in those pew at the night services when the whites representing 13 plantations surrounding that little. The morning services — the light for the white and the night for 'niggers' church were all conspicuously absent. The valid point made

Hilary Beckles

by Senator Straughn was ... woman.

that there was no fight, no agitation, no struggle by the blacks who appeared to have accepted what we call racism as the spirit of the age.

The senator describes the coming into their own of the blacks in the Church as evolutionary.

What evoked laughter was she said the first black priest she had seen was the Reverend S.A.E. Coleman, and that as a child she had asked if he was called "Coal-man" because he was black. Humourous now in 1991!! Reality then...!!

One of the great aspects of the afternoon session was the presentation by outstanding

theologian, author and scholar the Vice Principal of Codrington College, Dr. John Holder who traced the question of race relations from Adam, through Cain and Abel, including Moses' marriage to the Cushite woman — a black woman.

Moses the great law-giver marries a black woman. His sister Miriam and his brother Aaron "are not amused. They are appalled."

Miriam and Aaron, said Dr. Holder "cannot cope with this difference of race. It is a bit too much. The introduction of this woman from a different race into this family threw it in disarray."

Whenever Dr. Holder speaks, writes or lectures, those who hear what he has to say must give him his rightful due. An author, researcher and scholar, he is who can hold his own in any world class.

On Saturday, he dealt with the question in masterly fashion. Therefore at the risk of not being afforded space for comment on other aspects of the seminar it is requisite to include at least a couple of paragraphs from Dr. Holder's presentation.

"It is very important," Dr. Holder says, "to make this point about the Europeans wanting to make the woman (Moses' black wife) into an Arab rather than accepting her as an African. This tendency of course reflects racism at its most vicious nature.

"Not even the Biblical text is immune!

Commenting on the attitude of the European theologians, Dr. Holder continued "How dare they admit that the founder of the Jewish religion had by his side a black woman as his companion!

"How dare they," he said, "give this prominence to Africa at the

Sunday 9 January 1983   *LONDON, ENGLAND*

THE OBSERVER, SUNDAY 9 JANUARY 1983

C of E 'failed' black people

by JUDITH JUDD

THE Church of England has failed both blacks and the poor, says the Bishop of Liverpool, the Rt. Rev. David Sheppard, in a book to be published tomorrow.

The bishop, who has spent 30 years working in the inner city, says in his book 'Bias to the Poor,' (Hodder & Stoughton, £8.95), that the church can even be accused of racism. Church congregations have been unwelcoming to black and poor people, and the gap between the Church and the working class of the cities is now 'enormous.'

Bishop Sheppard said last week that a black Christian had been told by white churchmen when he arrived in Liverpool that he would be happier in an all-black church. A white worker in the city told the bishop that 'the Church always rode with power.'

In a chapter which will enrage the Church's conservative critics, Bishop Sheppard argues that churchmen must enter the political arena and campaign for social justice. Mrs Thatcher's policy of enlarging the cake so there will be more for the poor is roundly condemned.

The book says: 'I believe there is a divine bias to the disadvantaged and that the Church needs to be more faithful in reflecting it.'

It urges Anglicans to shed their respectable image and stop protecting the established order. 'The Church must risk losing its inno-

GED MURRAY

Bishop David Sheppard : Challenge to Anglicans.

Bishop Sheppard, ex-public school and Cambridge, believes that Christians have important common ground with Marxists. Even revolution should not be condemned out of hand, he says, though he does not believe it is the way forward in Britain. It may be possible, he suggests, for Christians to believe in a 'just revolution.'

He is also prepared to support such unpopular groups as dockers and print workers. The condemnation

dual may 'deny the rights of a group of people who are less articulate and influential unless they act as a group.'

The Church's respectable image is not only the responsibility of the middle class. It is also the fault of what the bishop calls the 'good working class' — working-class people with jobs who come to church and expect certain standards of behaviour.

The bishop is aware he will be accused of being 'political' and counters that

Church of England rejec[t]

bigger role for Blacks

LONDON, AP — A PLAN to give black Anglicans a bigger role in the Church of England's policy-making General Synod has been rejected.

Lay members of the Anglican state church blocked its progress by a 96-80 vote, despite a vote of 17-3 in favour by the bishops and 103-62 by the clergy.

It needed a majority of each group to pass.

Barbados-born Bishop of Croydon Wilfred Wood, the first black bishop of the church to serve in England, left Church House, Westminster, immediately after the vote.

Wood's Committee for Black Anglican Concerns had initiated the plan, but he and the seven other black members of the synod did not speak in the debate.

Next Elections

The synod has 574 members, and usually no more than two-thirds attend. The plan would have secured a minimum 24 seats for blacks after the next elections in 1990, to reflect the estimated two million blacks among England's 49 million people. Wales and Scotland have separate churches.

If 24 blacks were not elected, the black candidates with the highest number of votes would have been allotted seats.

The figure of 24 was arbitrary, Wood said earlier, adding he thought it "about right."

There are no statistics on the number of black Anglicans.

"We want God's scales of justice to be tilted in [th]eir favour," said Arch[bishop] of Bath [J]ohn Burgess propos[ing the] plan, wh[ich] would have requi[red government's a[p]proval.

Several of the 15 speakers in [the de]bate, who said they voted in favou[r when] the plan was approved at its firs[t read]ing by a straight 214-74 vote in N[ovem]ber, cautioned that they had sin[ce had] second thoughts.

The eventual vote was a secon[d read]ing.

Senior synod member Oswald [____] said legal advice had shown Parl[iament] would reject it as "inexpedi[ent]" [and] synod would be foolish to "em[bark on le]gislation which has within it th[e] [seeds of] its own destruction," he said [else]

Businessman [____] [n]ever reser[ve] Parliam[ent] [to] any party or colour and '[it woul]d se[em] reprehensible" to be ask[ed] [wh]at [community he belonge[d] [to], [and] what [____]

"We won't make res[titu]tion [f]or [the] past to those who come[,] [reti]tution [particularly from the f[ar] from a [____] by giving one group a sp[ecial ro[le]," [he] said[.]

Archbishop of York Joh[n] H[abgood] urged the synod to app[r]ov[e] the pl[an and] negotiate with the gove[rn]ment o[n what] it would accept.

"If we kill it now, that possibility [will] no longer be open to us. One gene[ration] of black people has already been lo[st] [and] unless we do something now, w[e will] lose the next generation and the g[enera]tion after that," Habgood said.

Rise of black people in key jo[bs]

a 'message of hope' says Pri[est]

BRIDGETOWN, Cana — BRITISH priest, Rajinder Daniel, says the [ris]e of black people in key jobs in the Caribbean could be a "message of hope" for those in Britain.

Rev Daniel, who visited the Caribbean recently on a three-nation [to]ur, said it was something that shou[l]d inspire British blacks to aspire to reach the top of their field.

Rev Daniel, an advis[e]r on black ministries and a spokesman for the Committee for Black affairs [in the diocese of] Birmingham, Engla[n]d, told Cana blacks in Britain face[d] two major problems: On one hand the[y] were often over-

looked when key posts were [being] [filled] and on the other they sometim[es were] spaired[.]

"I have seen (blacks) progress) [in the] Caribbean ... and this is the mess[age of] hope I will be taking back to Britai[n]," [he] said.

Rev Daniel came on a six-week [____] tour also taking in Jamaica and [Trini]dad and Tobago.

He [met] "church leaders and [ordin]ary folk" to discuss issues includi[ng how] church leadership has developed [____]

In Jamaica he also looked at [the de]vastation caused last year by hur[ricane] Gilbert and discussed how Brit[ish] [funds] were used in the rehabilitation ex[ercise]

Daily Telegraph
November 11, 1988

LONDON AND MANCHESTER **30p**

NOVEMBER 11, 1988

Synod to recruit black members

Daily Telegraph

By Jonathan Petre
Religious Affairs
Correspondent

CONTROVERSIAL proposals to ensure that the Church of England's General Synod includes a minimum of 24 black members were approved yesterday by the synod.

The opponents, who included Mr Gummer, Local Government Minister, and a black synod member, Mr Vijay Menon, from Chelmsford, argued that the proposals, which would involve "topping up" the number of black members after the 1990 synod elections, insulted blacks.

But the Bishop of Croydon, the Rt Rev Wilfred Wood, who as the church's only black bishop chairs its committee on black concerns, rejected this argument, adding that in the racially-sensitive 1960s, Mr Gummer had written a "particularly odious little book" entitled When the Coloured People Come.

"Racism bestrides our society like a collosus," he said. "It is so much the everyday experience of so many black people that to protest at every incident could become almost a full-time occupation."

Up to the last synod elections there were only three black members and now there were eight.

Synod

Continued from P1

away the dignity of black Anglicans, but to treat us as equals.

"I am British and I am proud if it. I am not in South Africa."

Mr Menon added that if the synod passed the proposals it would be "proclaiming a lie, a terrible lie" that the current electoral system contained racial discrimination.

Support for the proposals came from the Bishop of Liverpool, the Rt Rev David Sheppard, who said the synod needed "to redress the balance" to allow blacks to take their rightful place on the synod.

The Rev John Sentamu, a member of the synod's standing committee, accused Mr Gummer of "slipshod thinking".

"We are all agreed that every effort should be made to encourage more black people to stand in the synod's general election in 1990.

"Where we differ is whether we can secure adequate black presence by these means by 1990.

"The experience of black people clearly rules out such exaggerated optimism."

The proposals were carried by 214 votes to 74, with 11 abstentions.

The synod will now draft a measure which will be considered by its February meeting. It

A shoeless Dr Runcie listens to the synod debate

14. WEDNESDAY, JUNE 8, 1988. DAILY NATION. BARBADOS

OBITUARY

Priest endured many hardships

THE PASSING of Reverend de Courcey Bindley Brathwaite marked the beginning of the end of an era in Barbados' church history.

He became a priest in the Anglican communion of Barbados, at a time when it was almost unheard of for a black Barbadian to embark on a career in the ministry.

So, when the former incumbent of St. Jude's, in St. George, was laid to rest last Saturday, it was fitting that Anglican Bishop Drexel Gomez should choose as his text, a verse from Psalm 132: "Lord remember David and all the hardships he endured."

For Bindley Brathwaite, the first hardship was entering the sacred ministry when black Barbadians were not encouraged to do so, and few got through that door. He found some difficulty in getting admitted to Codrington College.

His next hardship came when, having completed his studies, the young parson could not find a curacy and settled for being chaplain to Westbury Cemetery, a job he endured for about five years before being appointed to St. Judes as vicar.

He was to enjoy 28 years of ministry at this parish, with varying success, for his strict attention to discipline and strong attachment to tradition made him a very much misunderstood person.

ARCHDEACON Malcolm Maxwell commits the body to the grave

But, said the bishop, Bindley was to endure yet another hardship, psychological in nature. For times were changing and the church itself was showing signs of change.

Accordingly, Bindley found it difficult to adjust to the liturgical and doctrinal changes that were coming about. In fact, he stuck to the tradition of the old Anglican Church of the Reformation.

The late Bindley Brathwaite placed strong emphasis on moral standards. And one example suffices, that of his attitude to the baptism of infants born out of wedlock. Not that he was against baptising them. Rather, he was making a point of morality and the casual attitude of the young towards sex-

MANY MEMBERS of the Anglican clergy were present at the funeral of the late Reverend Bindley Brathwaite.

ual matters.

The lesson to be learnt from the life and example of people such as Bindley Brathwaite is, there is a place for standards and morality in our lives, even in these days of permissiveness.

The funeral service took the form of a Requiem Mass, with Bishop Gomez as celebrant, the present incumbent, Father Austin Carrington, Archdeacon Malcolm Maxwell and other priests assisting.

Many members of the clergy,

as well as relatives, loyal congregations and friends were on hand to pay their last respects when the mortal remains of de Courcey Bindley Brathwaite were interred near the north entrance to his beloved church at St. Judes.

Church's 'White-Only'

y, August 24, 1975   THE WASHINGTON POST

Growing attendance creates space shortage at St. Philip the Evangelist Church, an all-black congregation in An

RCHES, From C1

Anderson, who has pport of the Rev. Truelove, Emma-ector, revealed that ember he would be-ng Emmanuel space without the vestry's ion.

position paper titled Joshua, Father An-charged that Em-which had no pro-or the neighborhood, come to an under-g and commitment of e for mission in Ana-or give up all rights mission and turn building to those willing to witness us."

w weeks later an uel committee of-

tion has about a dozen child-ren under 20.

In the early 1940s the church had 400 members. After World War II, dis-placed blacks from the ur-ban renewal areas down-town began moving into Anacostia. Now about half the Emmanuel members travel from Herndon, Poto-mac, Gaithersburg and other outlying communities.

They cling to the church partly because of its high,

sung mass, its cathedral ceil-ings, its brass and brocade furnishings and its dimly flickering devotional can-dles in the side chapels.

In many cases they stay because it is the only church they have ever known.

Father Truelove, 35, who became rector last Septem-ber, succeeded the Rev. Rob-ert Kell, who, as Cramer tells it, "liked to think of himself as the last living traditionalist."

Father Truelove has at-tempted to remain neutral in the controversy.

He sees his parishioners as tied deeply to the com-fort the church provides and its liturgical traditions. Many of them, he said, have "basically had no contact with blacks."

"There is an element of racism and white-condition-ing in most of us, which we've had to work through. But most of us have come to

Mrs. Scott: 'We've Always Had Struggles'

SCOTT, From C1

them," said Mrs. Scott, who lives on Ala-bama Avenue SE.

"I don't think segregation is Christian-

always had struggles. We haven't had any-thing but struggles at St. Philip. But you sort of like sticking with your own church, because I know that's how I feel about mine. Regardless of what's hap-

Tumbles in Anacostia

ANGLICAN CHURCH Washington Post August 24 1975

Photos by Linda Wheeler—The Washington P

...acostia (left) while membership declines at all-white Emmanuel Episcopal Church (right), also in Anacostia.

realize you can't make sweeping statements about blacks and whites," he said.

He said he has witnessed instances in which Emmanuel members refused to shake hands with black visitors or jockeyed for positions at the altar rail in order not to drink from the communion chalice after blacks.

Father Anderson, 38, is a manpower specialist at the D.C. office of youth opportunity services.

When he became vicar of St. Philip in 1973, the worship attendance was 25 to 35. This year the average was 125. The church has a 55-member teen-age group, a 60-member church school for younger children, and a

manuel's building won't be adequate for us," said Freeman, who works at Federal City College. His vestry believes the two churches should plan together for a suitable new building.

Father Truelove agreed: "There is no question that the Episcopal Church has to come to a better sense of what it is in Anacostia. It should not be divided.

"St. Philip has some very middle class people and values, and Chuck Freeman, for example, has done everything he can to avoid looking like he's trying to 'take us over."

But some Emmanuel members already have threatened to leave rather

than worship with blacks. Said one woman who lives in Temple Hills but refused to identify herself:

"I think it's just terrible when the colored people can take over the white people ... I never heard of St. Philip's until recently. As far as we're concerned, we don't want them ... We've had the church broken into and every time it's been colored people. They're really crude, crude people. If they come, no, I won't stay. Nor will my mother and she loves that church."

Joseph Tredway, an Emmanuel vestryman and business manager of the Washington Cathedral, lives in

Southeast. He sees the differently. "Anacosti... town people have bee... in, worked in and d... and have never been... the river ... The cha... that church is going to... eventually. It's most... without new people... blacks don't come b... they don't like our ser...

"I've been going th... years, and I feel ve... about what's happen... our church. But it... new people. It needs... to fill up the churc... make the music soun... ter. The people her... love that church and... stay, come hell or... water."

Globe & Mail, Canada

Thursday, December 19,

1996

Beginning and end of a long *ANGLICAN* journey

BY ELIZABETH ABBOTT

Elizabeth Abbott, Dean of Women at Trinity College, University of Toronto, is a parishioner at St. Michael and All Angels.

Blair and Lance Dixon, father and son and both black Anglican priests, have much to celebrate. So do we.

THE congregation of Toronto's Church of St. Michael and All Angels is hushed in anticipation as young Rev. Lance Dixon lopes up to deliver his first sermon as our new deacon. "My friends, let's be open to the idea that tradition could be wrong," he begins, bouncing lightly up and down in the pulpit like a sacerdotal Muhammed Ali. But what is this? Poetry? Yes, his poetry, titled, *Please don't call me Father.*

"Ask for my blessing, invite me for tea. Request his service, and I'll perform it

A generation ago, aspiring black Anglican priests faced a much bleaker reality. This was the case for Blair Dixon, ordained in 1966. Fortunately for us, Blair's struggles only strengthened Lance's resolve about his own vocation.

In the 1950s, Blair entered adulthood in the quasi-segregated world of New Brunswick. But it was an experience of American prejudice that was defining. As a civilian employee of the Canadian Air Force, he and a white colleague were travelling across the American South. For three days, while his complacent companion ate at restaurants that barred black diners, Blair survived on snacks in the car. He grew hungrier and hungrier, angrier and angrier.

Back home in St. John, he concluded that his community's perceived wisdom was wrong, that prejudice was *not* a private matter. It was public, and it was political. The civil-rights movement was in its infancy, and Blair became an ardent participant.

Blair also began his tortuous path to ordination. The Anglican Church in which he had been raised suffered a dearth of priests. After reflection and prayer, Blair approached Harry O'Neil, Bishop of Nova Scotia, about his vocation.

Bishop O'Neil responded with such equivocation that Blair demanded, "Bishop, are you telling me that though you need me, you won't take me?"

The bishop admitted it, blaming his board, which would not approve.

"Because of my colour?"

Bishop O'Neil was miserable but adamant. Finally he offered a compromise. If Blair would sign an agreement that after graduation he would confine himself to the foreign mission field, then he would sponsor him.

Blair, recoiling, refused this tainted offer. "Bishop, are you suggesting that I tell the Holy Spirit where he should direct me after my ordination?"

After this, Blair resigned himself to abandoning his religious calling. Then a sympathetic Air Force chaplain arranged an interview with Ernest Reid, Bishop of Ottawa. Unlike Bishop O'Neil, Bishop Reid was prepared to do battle with his board over the issue of Blair's candidacy.

In 1966, Blair Dixon was ordained. But racism was as deeply embedded in the structure of the church as in civil society, and most parishes were hostile. When an enthusiastic African-American congregation in Detroit offered him its pastorship, he leapt at it. After seven years, he and his wife returned home before their children became totally Americanized. By then some progress had been made, and an Ontario parish accepted Blair.

Two decades later, Lance Dixon has

TRINIDAD

ANGLICAN CHURCH

"CATHOLIC NEWS AND SUNDAY REVIEW," MARCH 24, 1974

BLACK CAUCUS CLAMOURS FOR A BIGGER SAY IN THE CHURCH

PRESSURE MOUNTS OVER ELECTION OF NEW ANGLICAN ARCHBISHOP

PRESSURE is mounting in Cape Town for the Anglican Church of South Africa to appoint its first black leader as its majority of African members continue to press for a greater say in Church affairs.

The so-called "Back Caucus" of the Church of the Province of South African is looking Bishop

high places to salve consciences.

Yet there have been some changes since then. The Methodist, Presbyterian and Congregational Churches now have black leaders, and the Catholic Church has become increasingly aware of black aspirations.

As far as the Anglicans themselves are concerned, the Natal

policies.

Yet from a white point of view, the Anglican Church is traditionally conservative and Establishment-minded, and many whites want to keep it that way.

Thus Bishop Zulu is not likely to become the next Archbishop of Cape Town. But Mr. Ngxlai warns: "If our requests for greater

ANGLICAN THE NEW YORK TIMES, SUNDAY, MARCH 10, 1974

CHURCH IN STRESS IN SOUTH AFRICA

Black Anglicans Press for a Leadership Role

CAPE TOWN, March 9 (Reuters) — Pressure is mounting here for the Anglican Church of South Africa to appoint its first black leader as its majority of black members continue to press for a greater say in church affairs.

The so-called "black caucus" of the church is backing the Right Rev. Alpheus Zulu, Bishop of Kwazulu, to succeed the Archbishop of Cape Town, the Right Rev. Robert Selby Taylor, who retires on Monday.

The new Archbishop, who will head the 2.2-million Anglicans in South Africa, will be elected on April 30, and though Bishop Zulu's chances are regarded as remote, the support for him is a clear indication of the growing sentiment among blacks within the church.

The leader of the black caucus, M. W. Ngxiki, a Port Elizabeth layman, says that 75 per cent of Anglicans in South Africa are black, but the leadership remains firmly in white hands. Bishop Zulu is the only black in charge of a diocese, though there are three black suffragan bishops.

Little Voice for Blacks Seen

"Blacks have very little say in the church's decision-making councils, and play a minor role in its administration," Mr. Ngxiki says.

Mr. Ngxiki recently met with Archibishop Taylor to discuss black aspirations in the church and the two men issued a joint statement denying any divisions.

But Mr. Ngxiki has now issued a statement asserting that the church is promoting apartheid, channeling funds from blacks into white church schools, and charging that

A month earlier a church commission attacked the practice in many churches of whites sitting at the front so they can take communion first, and, again, of keeping the hierarchy to themselves. It also criticized other denominations for their "tokenism," the practice of putting a few blacks in high places to salve consciences.

Yet there have been some changes since then. The Methodist, Presbyterian and Cingregational churches now have black leaders.

In the apartheid-supporting Dutch Reformed churches, the largest Christian grouping in the country, there was talk of allowing mixed worship, though it was quickly dropped.

As far as the Anglicans themselves are concerned, the Natal diocese is to begin paying its black and white clergy equal salaries this year. And canon Robert Jeffery, the Archbishop's chaplain, said Mr. Ngxiki was wrong in stating that black priests lived in sheds. He said there were instances where black clergy lived in better homes than their white counterparts.

Yet the Anglican Church is traditionally conservative and establishment-minded, and keep it

ANGLICAN CHURCH

Washington Post
March 13, 1985 THE WASHINGTON POST

Bishop Walker Nominated for Top Job

USA

By Saundra Saperstein
Washington Post Staff Writer

Bishop John T. Walker, who heads the Episcopal Diocese of Washington and is identified with liberal and ecumenical causes, is one of four candidates nominated to become presiding bishop of the Episcopal Church in America.

Bishop Walker is the first black clergyman ever nominated to head the predominantly white American branch of the Anglican church, which has about 2.9 million members, according to a spokesman.

The election of the presiding bishop, who is the top cleric of the church, will take place in September at the church's general convention in Anaheim, Calif. The convention is held every three years.

Bishop Walker, 59, was installed in 1977 as the sixth bishop of the Washington Diocese and the first black to hold that post.

He has been a leading advocate for the poor on a variety of urban issues and is known for his work with leaders of other faiths, according to a spokesman for the church in New York City, which announced the nominees yesterday. He is also dean of the Washington Cathedral.

The spokesman said the other nominees are: Bishops Edmond Browning of Hawaii, a former missionary bishop; William Carl Frey of Colorado, a leading church spokesman on peace issues, and Furman Stough of Alabama, an urban affairs advocate and chancellor of the University of the South in Tennessee.

The nominations were made by a committee of bishops, priests and lay members of the church at a meeting this week in Dallas, the spokesman said. The presiding bishop will be elected by the approximately 180 bishops expected to attend the convention in September.

The new bishop will succeed the Most Rev. John Allin of Mississippi, who has served for 12 years.

New York Times April 13, 1986   1986 April 13.

Anglicans Elect Tutu as Archbishop

New York Times

By EDWARD A. GARGAN

Special to The New York Times

CAPE TOWN, April 14 — Bishop Desmond Tutu, the outspoken opponent of apartheid and Nobel peace laureate, was elected the first black Anglican Archbishop of Cape Town this evening. As Archbishop, he will be the titular head of the Anglican Church in South Africa.

"Our church has decided that this is the person to be titular head," Bishop Tutu said. "People have to read whatever signals they want in that."

As head of the Anglican Church, the fourth largest church in South Africa, the Archbishop of Cape Town commands great authority when he speaks on social and political as well as religious issues.

The election of the 54-year-old Bishop Tutu will, in the view of many here, give him one of the most important forums in the country for his vigorous advocacy of the abolition of apartheid and the transition to black rule.

A Call for Sanctions

Last week Bishop Tutu called on foreign countries and businesses to impose punitive sanctions on South Africa in an effort to force it to eliminate its system of racial separation. There was considerable speculation that the move jeopardized his chances for being elected successor to Archbishop Phillip Russell, who is to retire in August.

But his election came in just one day, far sooner than religious experts had predicted. Indeed, Bishop Tutu said there had been none of the acrimony in the Elective Assembly that many people had expected.

"First of all, I want to indicate from all accounts the Elective Assembly was a happy occasion," Bishop Tutu said. "There was no recrimination."

Colin Wells Eglin, the leader of the Progressive Federal Party, the main parliamentary opposition to the governing Nationalist Party, said the election of the new Archbishop reflected the changing role of the church in South Africa.

"To an increasing extent," he said, "the churches in South Africa are finding it necessary and desirable to transform their religious belief into a political code or political action. This election has far greater significance than the election seven years ago. It has become part of the political dynamics of the country."

Although 80 percent of the church's membership is black, there has never been a black Archbishop. Many members of the church have been quoted as saying there was no alternative this time to the elevation of one of the church's black bishops to the throne in Cape Town.

Nonetheless, for more than a week the names of several bishops who were thought to be alternatives to Bishop Tutu were mentioned frequently. All except one is black.

Over the past decade, the Anglican Church has shifted dramatically away from its historically conservative orientation. That shift was most markedly demonstrated with the election of Bishop Tutu to head the Johannesburg diocese in February of last year.

"I regard this to be at once a courageous stand and at the same time a logical one," said Prof. Charles Villa-Vicencio, the head of the department of religious studies at the University of Cape Town. "Bishop Tutu is a man of great integrity and courage; only a week ago did he make his positions on sanctions clear. Bishop Tutu is undoubtedly one of the most authoritative voices for all Christians in South Africa, the majority of whom happen to be black."

This means, Professor Villa-Vicencio said, that Bishop Tutu will give a certain symbolic leadership to the church that it has not had before.

"One of the major churches of South Africa is going to have an articulate and forthright spokesman," he said. "The church is going to participate more forcefully in the politics of South Africa."

400 Choose New Leader

The Methodist Church, with some 12 million members, is the biggest church in South Africa. The Dutch Reformed Church, with 3.5 members, is next in size, followed by the Roman Catholic Church, with 2.4 million members. The Anglican Church has 1.6 million members.

Under a lead-gray morning sky, more than 400 representatives of the church's clergy and laity strolled across the immaculate lawn of Diocesan College, the church's elite boarding school, into a vaulted white-painted chapel. Called the Elective Assembly, the Anglicans represented parishes from across the country, although most came from this city because the Archbishop will preside over the Cape Town archdiocese.

The Assembly's deliberations were to conclude at 6 P.M., but when the

doors to the chapel were not unlocked at that time a scattering of church members around the entrance began to speculate that a decision was near. At 7:15, the doors were suddenly thrown open, light poured from the chapel into the darkness of the campus, and Bishop Tutu stepped into the cool air. Then he turned to shake the hands of each elector as they slowly filed from the church.

"I myself am overwhelmed and deeply shattered by the responsibility that God, through his church, has placed on my shoulders," the Archbishop-elect said afterward.

And then, as if to answer the unspoken fears of some church members, he continued: "It is very important to get rid of the notion that Tutu will stand out on his own account. The Archbishop is a focus and spokesperson for the synod of bishops usually. You do not see here a one-man band about to explode on the scene in South Africa.

"I suppose there will be some people who are not exactly enamored of my election. They must remember that the church does not belong to Desmond Tutu."

Nonetheless, Bishop Tutu insisted that he would not still his voice in protest against the policies of the South African Government. "I will continue to work for fundamental change in our country," he said. "We belong in one family, black and white."

11 Die in Night of Violence

JOHANNESBURG, April 14 (Reuters) — Eleven blacks died in a night of violence across South Africa, the police said.

The bodies of six men, burned beyond recognition, were found in the ruins of huts in Mooiplass in eastern Cape Province.

Five blacks were shot and killed in clashes with policemen during the night, one of the most violent in 26 months of racial strife in which more than 1,450 people have died.

Also today, the police reported that 32 charred bodies were found over the weekend in a South African black tribal homeland of Lebowa. Some of them were of people who had died when tires doused in gasoline were placed around their necks and set alight.

The police said today that they believed the victims had been suspected of being witches or wizards, but that politics could

Father Desmond Tutu, first black dean of S-Africa

Daily Times Newspaper September 18, 1973, page 7 [Nigeria]

DAILY TIMES, Thursday September 18, 1975, Page 7,

● RESPONDING to critics of South Africa, Mr Vorster, said, "If you give this chance you will be surprised where we stand. If you refuse to give this chance, you will still be surprised where South Africa stands." ●

By FELIX ADENAIKE
Our London Correspondent

FATHER Desmond M.B. Tutu, whose appointment as the first black dean of Johannesburg was announced last March by the Bishop of Johannesburg, Dr. Timothy Bavin, has left London to assume his new post.

Father Tutu's appointment has come at a time of considerable pressure within and without South Africa on the white minority regime to change its apartheid policies. And his appointment is therefore important as an anti-apartheid move by the Anglican Church of South Africa.

Father Tutu has no illusions about the conditions under which black South Africans still live in the republic. And according to him, though he was committed to seeking reconciliation among the peoples of South Africa...

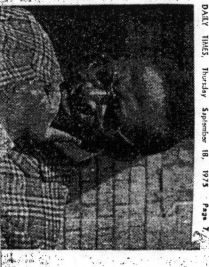

● DESPITE South Africa's much-vaunted detente policy, the Africans in South Africa continue to suffer the indignities of racial discrimination and to be denied all opportunities for human development and fulfilment ●

they are, at best, a cosmetic operation on the ugly and unacceptable face of apartheid. For the fundamental tenets and practice of apartheid remain inviolate and are at the root of racial relationships and interactions in the republic.

Mr. Vorster's policy of detente in southern Africa does not have his domestic policies as its focus. Rather, it is directed at achieving, through South Africa's good offices, majority rule in Zimbabwe, some kind of political solution in Namibia, and doing away with 'petty apartheid' at home. In the hope of placating African leaders and preserving the status quo in South Africa, In other words, Mr. Vorster does not intend to apply to South Africa, the same yard-stick that he is applying to Zimbabwe.

The obnoxious Pass Laws and the Terrorism Act under which persons can be detained indefinitely without trial, still remain. And blacks doing the same jobs as whites are still not being paid the same wage.

Two of the African leaders whose approach to the whole issue of southern Africa is universally regarded as realistic, have found it necessary to warn South Africa of the risks involved in failure to change the situation inside the republic. Presidents Nyerere and Samora Machel at their meeting in Lourenco Marques, noted that "despite South Africa's much-vaunted detente policy, the Africans in South Africa continue to suffer the indignities of racial discrimination and...

Tutu angers whites in SA

Barbados Advocate Saturday October 20, 1987

ARCHBISHOP TUTU

JOHANNESBURG, Monday, (Reuter) - A third of South Africa's white Anglicans are dissatisfied with the church, mainly because of the outspoken anti-apartheid views of its black leader, Archbishop Desmond Tutu, according to an opinion poll.

The poll by Market and Opinion Surveys, published by local newspapers today, found that political factors also led to unhappiness among 20 per cent of members of the Dutch Reformed Church, the main church of white Afrikaans-speakers.

Of the 35 per cent of white Anglicans who said they were dissatisfied, two thirds blamed Archbishop Tutu and the anti-apartheid South African Council of Churches. Another 28 per cent said the church was too political.

ANGERED BY WORDS

Whites account for only 20 per cent of the two million members of the Anglican church in southern Africa.

Right-wing whites, angered by remarks Archbishop Tutu made abroad, have called for his passport to be withdrawn. Some white Anglicans have stopped contributing to the church in protest.

Of whites dissatisfied with the Dutch Reformed Church, 35 per cent complained about a decision last year to open the previously all-white church to all races.

ANGLICAN/
CHURCH OF ENGLAND

Church of England gets first non-white bishop

LONDON (Reuter) — A priest born in Pakistan has been named as the first non-white bishop of a British diocese of the Church of England, officials said yesterday. Prime Minister John Major's office announced that Michael Nazir-Ali, 44, general secretary of the Church Missionary Society, was to become Bishop of Rochester in southern England.

Toronto star
June 28. 1994

ENGLAND, ANGLICAN

THE TIMES WEDNESDAY MAY 1 1985

New bishop: The Ven Wilfred Wood yesterday with his daughter, Nicola, aged four (Photograph: Warren Harrison).

First black bishop for the Church of England

By Clifford Longley, Religious Affairs Correspondent

The first black bishop in the Church of England is to be the Ven Wilfred Wood, present Archdeacon of Southwark, whose appointment as suffragan Bishop of Croydon was announced yesterday.

He will be responsible under the Bishop of Southwark, the Right Rev Ronald Bowlby, for 102 parishes in Croydon and East Surrey.

Archdeacon Wood is the best known black churchman in Britain, having served on the Royal Commission on Criminal Procedure, sat as a magistrate,

and been race relations officer to the Bishop of London.

He was moderator of the World Council of Churches' controversial programme to combat racism, and he sits on the Archbishop of Canterbury's commission for inner urban areas.

He is aged 49, and was ordained a deacon in Barbados and priest a year later in London in 1962. He was vicar of St Laurence, Catford, south London, and became Archdeacon and borough dean of Southwark in 1982.

The first black bishop in Britain

Anglican Church in England

by Dean Harold Crichlow

BISHOP WOOD

THE NEW SUFFRAGAN BISHOP-DESIGNATE, Archdeacon Wilfred. Wood, was trained for the priesthood at Codrington College. He was made a deacon in St. Michael's Cathedral on December 21, 1961, on letters sent by the bishop of London where he was to work. One full year after, he was ordained to the priesthood in St. Paul's Cathedral, London.

He did his curacy at St. Stephen's with St. Thomas, Shepherd's Bush, London, and was priest-in-charge of that church during a vacancy in 1966. While remaining an honorary curate, he was appointed Race Relations Officer to the bishop of London.

BUSY TIME

The 1960s were an exceptionally busy time for the Reverend Mr. Wood as he was involved in helping the British community to understand and integrate the large influx of West Indian migrants who had been invited by the British government to alleviate the shortage in many vital areas of their social services, such as nursing and transport. He had to combat a mountain of ignorance of the West Indian as a person and prejudice against him or her because of difference in skin colour.

He became vicar of St. Lawrence, Catford, in 1974 and was elected by his fellow clergy as rural dean of East

Croydon in the diocese of Southwark is well-deserved and provides the Church of England with an opportunity of witnessing more effectively to the truth of the universality of the Gospel. When asked to comment on the uniqueness of the appointment, the new bishop said:

"I don't know for sure whether I am the first black bishop for black people have been in Britain for over 100 years, but that is not the important thing. I would like to see many more black bishops in Britain. I would also like to see the diplomatic corps of Britain, the bench of judges and all other areas of influence having a large black representation.

BETTER BRITAIN

A Britain with black people

WILFRED WOOD: A first

ANGLICAN CHURCH
BLACK ROAD TO CANTERBURY

The West Indians who made Britain their home in the decade or two after the war, were somewhat disappointed with their first experience of the mother country; and not only because of the weather. In other ways too they expected more warmth than they got. They found the white British reserved or even hostile, on the whole. And the cultural shock was nowhere more felt than in church. The West Indians who came here came from fairly orthodox Christian backgrounds, being members of what are called the mainstream denominations in their West Indian incarnations; but they found the equivalent white versions of those denominations unwelcoming and unfamiliar when they tried them in Britain.

This quite quickly led to the development of a parallel religious culture, the so-called Black Churches or more accurately Black-led churches with largely Black memberships. They have become an important part of that distinctive Black culture whose exuberance and vitality finds expression in the annual Notting Hill carnival. They brought to Britain in religious terms, the insight that church worship need not be the dour, solemn ceremonial which is enough to put off all but the most devout; it can also be an experience of happiness and sheer pleasure. Southwark Cathedral has instituted an annual televised Gospel service, letting others share their enjoyment at praising God, and being uplifted thereby. The Black Christian presence in Britain is a significant enrichment of the religious life of the nation, and it is perhaps no pity that it preserved its special character on arrival, rather than assimilating too readily into the style of church worship that was already customary here.

The traditional churches did manage to hold the allegiance of some, most notably the first Black bishop in the Church of England the present Archdeacon of Southwark, the Ven Wilfred Wood. His consecration as suffragan Bishop of Croydon in July will be a symbolic moment. It will prove that the church, which has often preached on the virtues of good relations, has indeed the courage of its convictions; and when it says that all men are equal in the sight of God, it means it.

The point will not be lost, of course, that it will have a Black bishop before ever it has a woman priest; but that is another issue. The new bishop will represent in his person the truth that the very notion of a white church – or for that matter of a totally black church – is something of a contradiction, for the brotherhood of which the Gospel speaks must necessarily transcend race and all other accidentals. The initial response of West Indians to the white Christianity they encountered on arrival, the formation of their own religious institutions, was an understandable but not ideal arrangement, and a bishop is by vocation a bridge-builder, as the ancient title of pontifex reveals. The new bishop is to be Bishop of Croydon. With the usual administrative duties of area bishops, but he will also be, by his very existence, an offer of friendship between the Church of England and those newer churches.

RACE RELATIONS
IN
COLONIAL TRINIDAD
1870–1900

BRIDGET BRERETON

Lecturer in History, University of the
West Indies, St Augustine, Trinidad

CAMBRIDGE UNIVERSITY PRESS

Cambridge
London   New York   New Rochelle
Melbourne   Sydney

Race Relations in Colonial Trinidad

The principal Christian denominations in the island, the Catholic and the Anglican Churches, both had a reputation for colour discrimination. The Rev. K. J. Grant of the Canadian Presbyterian Mission reported that he knew 'the white minister of a largely black and coloured congregation of whom it was said that he boasted how he never shook hands with a black man, and his apparent failure to win and elevate would seem to confirm this strange report'.[42] We have noted the attitude of the Anglican Church to the ordination of blacks. Samuel Proctor, a black headmaster, put his case against the churches forcibly. Arguing against church services to mark the jubilee of emancipation, he wrote: 'We are indebted to the Church for less than nothing so far as freedom is concerned. The Church has always snubbed us. When a boy I was always kept at the western door. It is true I have got a little higher now, thanks to disendowment.' He did not attend the thanksgiving services, for 'no man who has seen slavery and how the negro was treated by the Church could do so. The Church taught that freedom never was ordained for the negro. . .I look upon the thanksgiving service as a *farce*. Certainly the way the Church treated the negro, she may well blush, if blush she can, for shame!'[43]

Slavery Days

in

Trinidad

A social history of the island from 1797–1838
by
Carlton Robert Ottley

First Edition published by the Author 1974
Trinidad

descent are not subject, shall be, and the same and each of them are, and is forever repealed, abolished and annulled".

In order to understand the high walls which had been erected to separate the "whites" from the "not so whites" in Trinidad, one must read into the following notice published as late as 1828 the true state of affairs. If such inequality could exist in the Church, the social and political fields must have been most unjust indeed.

The notice which appeared in the local press ran as follows: "Trinity Church Vestry Room. Dated 10th July, 1828. The undersigned will receive offers for the following pews: No. 43 for the white population; Nos. 63, 66, and 76 and 80 for the coloured population".

It is not difficult to conjure up the great social frustrations which the unjust social inequality of these free citizens caused. Discontent among the free coloured people was rampant. They wanted freedom. The Negroes also worked for their freedom. The first enjoyed economic freedom, but it was social freedom they were after. In the long run they gave up the fight entirely and withdrew from it, building up high walls to preserve their own integrity from the darker members of the population. But that was after the manumission of the Negroes. During Picton's regime they fought fiercely.

The British settlers who flocked to Trinidad after the capitulation, belonged as a rule to a class in which prejudices formed part of both their religious and political creeds, and on their arrival they were disappointed and disgusted at the great respect and esteem in which Picton held the old Spanish and French colonists from amongst whom he selected his most intimate associates. Their irritation was by no means decreased when they found that the principal posts of trust were filled by foreigners or by British subjects professing the Roman Catholic Religion. The English Party became one of the most virulent attackers of Picton.

ANGLICAN CHURCH/CHURCH OF ENGLAND

When Cazabon painted this picture in the early 1840's Trinity Church was exactly as it had been when it was consecrated in 1823 — exactly, that is, except for a spire struck by lightning and replaced by a cross. Structure-wise it was the same church that Governor Woodford had envisaged when he laid the foundation stone in 1816. It was designed by the Governor's own private Secretary, Philip Reinagle.

Trinity became a Cathedral in 1871 and twenty years afterwards it underwent substantial changes. In the period that Cazabon recorded here, it was luxuriously large, but by the 1890's it was regarded as far too small and the authorities decided to extend it. They removed Reinagle's stylish eastern end, and built a chancel extending into the open space that we see on our left. This chancel was completed and consecrated in 1895.

TODAY Trinity Cathedral (Trinity Church). Beyond the four turrets at extreme left is the only substantial change to the structure — the chancel added in 1895.

24

ANGLICAN CHURCH/CHURCH OF ENGLAND

THE HISTORY OF THE WEST INDIAN ISLANDS OF TRINIDAD AND TOBAGO

1498-1900

by

GERTRUDE CARMICHAEL

Lately Librarian to the Trinidad and Tobago Historical Society and Assistant Librarian, Imperial College of Tropical Agriculture, Trinidad, W.I.

ALVIN REDMAN *Ltd*
LONDON *1961*

The foundation stone of the new Trinity Church was laid by Woodford at the south side of the square on May 30th, 1816. The new plans were drawn up by Philip Reinagle.

Woodford also tried to establish a properly trained choir, but owing to the expense of obtaining an organist who could teach boys to sing, the project was dropped and the alternative suggestion, that the Garrison Band Master be lent to the church, was not taken up. Another experiment, that of lighting the church with gas made with pitch from La Brea, proved unsuccesful as more smoke than light was generated.

The internal organization of the Church was very different from that of today. The pulpit was in the place where Woodford's memorial now stands. The Governor's pew over the north door was reached by a " truly great staircase."

" On great occasions, Sir Ralph required the attendance of his whole staff of officials, in full dress, in his pew beside him, regardless of their religious views."

On ordinary Sundays he occupied his private pew in the north-east corner "modestly curtained". Over the altar hung a large picture, painted and presented by Mariana Birch whose father was a Colonel in the Garrison. There were four large pews in the centre of the church reserved for the Council, the Cabildo, the Garrison and strangers. In all there was accommodation for 380 white people, 120 coloured and at the west end there was a roped off space for slaves. Only 112 seats in the church were free, the remainder being rented. Pew rents appear to have been very hard to collect, as it is recorded that one churchwarden proposed that the list of defaulters be posted in the Intendent's Court as a necessary measure to force people to pay their dues.

Wesleyan Methodism was introduced into Trinidad from Grenada by the Reverend G. Talboys in 1810. There was opposition to it at first as members of the Roman Communion and followers of the Church of England held that the preaching and administration of the sacraments by the missionaries were contrary to accepted practice. These differences were overcome

Church urged to cut state link

Sunday Times [London] July 4. 1999 p96

by Christopher Morgan and Michael Prescott

AN ATTEMPT by Tony Blair to increase Downing Street's control over senior church appointments has provoked new demands for the Church of England to sever its links with the state.

Colin Buchanan, the Bishop of Woolwich, calls this weekend for the disestablishment of the church. "The possession of the Church of England by the state is so wrong in principle that it is vital we shake off our chains," he writes in today's Sunday Times.

Behind his demand for change lies a secret power struggle over the way senior church appointments are made by the prime minister, acting on behalf of the Queen.

Downing Street confirmed this weekend that John Holroyd, 64, its appointments secretary, is retiring a year early. His departure follows a two-year war of attrition, during which criticism of Holroyd by Blair's staff has grown apace.

"He is like a figure from Trollope and is the antithesis of new Labour," one insider complained yesterday. Aides said Blair was appalled at the quality of some candidates recommended by Holroyd and dismayed that he would not reveal his selection process.

Diocesan bishops are chosen from names put forward by the Crown Appointments Commission, whose meetings Holroyd attends. But other senior appointments, such as the deans and canons of cathedrals, are made from candidates chosen by Holroyd alone.

In particular, Blair has been unhappy with:

☐ Candidates put before him for the bishopric of Liverpool in 1997. He sent back both names submitted by the appointments commission.

☐ The appointment of Wesley Carr as Dean of Westminster. Even before his position was confirmed, two canons at Westminster went to No 10 to protest at Carr's nomination.

Bishop of Woolwich
News Review, page 2

Votes Reaffirm Anglicanism as Britain's Official Religion

Washington Post July 23, 1994

Religious News Service

YORK, England—The Church of England's top legislative body has rejected proposals separating church from state, striking another blow at attempts to disestablish Anglicanism as Britain's official religion.

By a vote of 273 to 110, the church's General Synod this week defeated a motion to lift direct state control over the appointment of diocesan bishops and over church legislation.

The synod, during a voice vote, also overwhelmingly rejected amendments that would have established a commission to review the constitutional relationship between the Church of England and the British government.

George Carey, the archbishop of Canterbury, firmly opposed the moves, urging the synod not to embark on "years of constitutional navel-gazing."

The British prime minister now retains the final say in putting forward to the monarchy names of candidates for bishop, and both Houses of Parliament must approve legislation approved by the general synod before it can became law.

The British monarch is the head of the Church of England, with monarchs having to pledge themselves to maintain the Anglican faith, as established by law.

The issue of "disestablishmentarianism" has been discussed in England in recent weeks after a

Bishop questions church-state bond

Newsday October 17. 1999 — Page 10

LONDON: Bishop Colin Buchanan long ago got used to being a voice in the wilderness.

But his wilderness is in the Church of England, which he wants to cut links with the state.

"An unbelieving government is a totally inappropriate organ to run the church of God," declares Buchanan, who as Bishop of Woolwich in south London is one of the more senior clerics in England's established Protestant church.

However, whenever he brings up the subject in the church legislature, "I usually get steamrollered," the bishop says.

Still, he noted cheerfully in an interview, "I haven't been incarcerated. They treat me as an annoying gadfly."

The days of arresting those who question the church-state bond first forged by King Henry VIII are over. But the questions have not stopped, and if anything have increased recently.

Planned reforms by the Labour government to the House of Lords have thrown a long shadow over other ancient arrangements that have evolved over time in Britain's unwritten constitution.

If hereditary peers are deprived of their seats in the upper chamber of parliament, as is expected to happen, what about the 26 Church of England bishops who also have seats there?

Advocates of disestablishment, as the breaking of church-state ties is called, hope the bishops' seats go next and that this leads to other reforms that break the link between church and crown.

Disestablishment is "bound to happen," says the retired former Bishop of Durham David Jenkins. But within the church this is a minority view.

There have been occasional calls for the disestablishment of the Church of England since Henry VIII broke with the Pope so he could divorce his first wife and marry Ann Boleyn.

ries, English church and society have grown together almost inextricably.

"My feeling is that our sense of national identity would be weakened more grievously than many people realise if the rich fabric in which religion and society are woven together in so much of our national life were to be unravelled," the archbishop, leader of the world's 70 million Anglicans, wrote in 1993. Spokesmen say his views on the subject have not changed.

Church officials said many people depend on the church for rites such as marriage, even if they don't attend services.

Disestablishment would effectively mean "taking the church away from the people, and giving it to those who are attending at the moment," said church spokesman Jonathan Jennings.

It would also mean giving up a great deal of influence. Bishops have always sat in the House of Lords, and the Archbishop of Canterbury crowns the monarch.

The monarch is supreme governor of the church, and appoints its bishops on the prime minister's advice.

The British parliament also has a right of veto over Church of England legislation agreed by its General Synod.

"If you leave powers lying around, somebody will pick them up and use them against you sometime," Buchanan said.

Tony Blair indicated soon after he became prime minister in 1997 that the initiative for disestablishment would not come from him. Buchanan thinks it must come from the church, not least because a financial settlement must be worked out, and it would be better for the church to arrange it "the way we want it".

In 1994, Buchanan introduced a motion at the General Synod for an end to the prime minister's role in appointing bishops and parliamentary control of church legislation. It failed by 273 votes to 110.

But there have since been small rumblings of change. In 1998 following a debate in the General Synod, a church working group

Mawer, met other churches to examine alternative national church models, but reached no conclusions.

There are also secular campaigners for disestablishment. The National Secular Society argues that Britain should let go of its "feudal past" by making the Lords a secular chamber.

"Britain is the only western democracy with religious prelates in its legislature," says the society's general secretary Keith Porteous Wood.

In any case, he says, an established church cannot last in a society where church-going is declining. "Because the Church of England is doing so badly, and we're becoming more of a multi-cultural nation, and most young people don't believe in God anyway, establishment is unsustainable."

Church of England officials say up to 1.5 million people attend their services each Sunday, about two percent of the population. They note one million people attend football games each week, yet football is considered the national sport.

Labour MP Tony Benn, who back in 1988 introduced a bill to disestablish the church, predicts it will happen eventually.

"We're the only place in the Anglican community where the church is not disestablished," Benn told *Reuters*. The church was disestablished in Wales in 1920, and in Ireland in 1870. In Scotland, the established church is Presbyterian.

Buchanan thinks disestablishment could come as a result of a crisis, like the sudden death of Queen Elizabeth. This would leave Prince Charles, a divorced man in love with the divorced Camilla Parker Bowles, to head the church — hardly an ideal situation even if the church is softening its views on divorce.

By law Charles cannot choose another religion. But he seems to have broad religious views. He said in 1996 that as king he would rather be considered a "defender of faith" rather than have the traditional title, "Defender of the Faith".

ANGLICAN CHURCH/CHURCH OF ENGLAND

14 SEPTEMBER 1997 · THE SUNDAY TIMES

Blair blocks church choice for bishop

1997

by Christopher Morgan
Religious Affairs Correspondent

TONY BLAIR has taken the unprecedented step of rejecting both of the Church of England's candidates for one of its most prestigious bishoprics.

The prime minister has risked a confrontation with the church by asking the Crown Appointments Commission, which puts forward nominees, to come up with two more names for the post of bishop of Liverpool.

While the workings of the commission are shrouded in secrecy, it is thought to be the first time in its 20-year history that a prime minister has rejected its recommendations.

Church insiders believe it is part of a drive by Blair to carry his modernising of Britain into the church. A devout Christian, he has let it be known that he wants "men of vision" leading the church into the next millennium.

He is particularly keen to find a high-calibre replacement for David Sheppard, the bishop who retires later this month. Sheppard, a former England cricketer and a charismatic figure in Liverpool, made a name for himself through his work with the late Derek Worlock, the Roman Catholic Arch-

bishop of Liverpool. Sheppard led the church's thinking on social policy.

One rejected candidate is believed to be a serving bishop in the southeast of England and a friend of George Carey, the Archbishop of Canterbury; the other is an archdeacon.

The prime minister is constitutionally entitled to reject the choices. England is the only part of the Anglican communion where bishops are not directly elected by the church and for 400 years the crown chose all bishops without having to take advice from an appointed commission.

In 1977, however, a commission was set up by the General Synod with the agreement of James Callaghan, then prime minister. It aimed to give the church more sway in the appointment of its bishops by putting forward what it considered the two best candidates. While it is rumoured that the second-choice name has been chosen on several occasions, never before have both been rejected.

Blair's stand on Sheppard's successor is thought to have been a shock to the commission, which includes both clergy and laity. The commission has recently been subject to criticism from within the church, with rank-and-file members believing the wrong choices are being made.

Last week Donald Reeves, rector of St James's Piccadilly and one of London's most prominent priests, hinted at a loss of clergy confidence in the system. "There is now a wider gap than ever between bishops and their clergy," he said.

Oswald Clark, a former chairman of the House of Laity of the General Synod and a member of the commission for a number of years, said the result has been a bland style of leadership from bishops in a time of increasing moral and spiritual uncertainty. "If you have a committee system appointing bishops you are inclined to produce bishops who are committee men," said Clark this weekend.

"If Mr Blair stops the cur-

rent trend towards blandness he will have done a great service for the Church of England."

Blair's veto comes amid signs that senior ministers were disturbed by the church's absence from the national stage following the death of Diana, Princess of Wales.

One prominent member of the government spoke of his disappointment over the Church of England's reaction to the death of the princess: "There was no spiritual focus. They did well at Westminster Abbey but that was their job."

Another senior clergyman praised Blair for intervening over the funeral arrangements and now in church appointments. "A prime minister who last week touched the spiritual pulse of the nation while the church remained virtually silent should be applauded for his decision to take his responsibilities seriously," he said.

A Downing Street spokesman declined to comment on what it regarded as a confidential process. The church is now likely to put forward new names but there is always the possibility of it resubmitting one or both of the original candidates.

Ashes for Breakfast

THOMAS J. HOLMES
in collaboration with
GAINER E. BRYAN, JR.

The Judson Press, Valley Forge

1969
USA

Foreword

WHEN TOM HOLMES SAT DOWN to begin writing this book, he suddenly bent over his desk and wept. The tide of memories, sweeping back, overwhelmed him.

He is not the kind of man who cries easily, nor is he one you would pick out of a Southern crowd as a martyr. To begin with, he is a very tall man, powerfully put together. He is friendly in the outgoing way of the neighborly Southerner —not a purse-lipped reformer, nor a hot-eyed zealot. And in him is the quiet strength and understanding of a faithful pastor who has known a quarter-century of ministry to other people's tears.

But the tears were his own, at last, as he began this simple, straightforward account of a church's ordeal, and his own.

If he had been a weak man, these events would not have happened. Had he been faithless, there would be no story. Instead there would have been just another Southern Baptist Church moving along untroubled from Sunday to tranquil Sunday while the conscience of a congregation slept.

But the Reverend Tom Holmes did have faith and strength to match the times. He believed that any who wish to worship in God's house must be welcomed, black as well as white. Many of his board of deacons and his congregation did not. What then must a pastor do?

This minister preached the truth as his faith revealed it to him. "You are lower down than any dog," a deacon told him. He preached the truth again. And again. At last they fired him.

This gentle believer had no wish to create strife. But he had no way to avoid answering his conscience. Threatened, he stood fast. Repudiated, he declined to retreat. Finally discharged, he would leave only through the front door of a church whose witness he challenged by sacrificing himself.

I saw him and his strong, lovely wife during the months of their ordeal. She told me how much she would regret moving from the pastor's residence in Macon, a house she loved. But her determination was as unswerving as his. Their faith was challenged. They would stand to the end. They could do no other.

In the scourging of a good man for bad reasons there is a Christian lesson considerably older than the crisis at Tattnall Square Baptist Church.

It is a lesson which, well told here, is going to intrude itself in time into every Sunday school room and sanctuary in the South and the nation.

Tom Holmes was not given the time to survive in his ministry, so he was driven from it. But this book tells the lesson with a clarity and a compassion that make it one of the most powerful sermons any honest believer is likely to hear in this troubled American generation. His tears were not for himself.

EUGENE C. PATTERSON, MANAGING EDITOR
Washington Post

Washington, D.C.
February, 1969

Preface

MY PURPOSE IN WRITING the story of Tattnall Square Baptist Church is to bring to full public knowledge the grievous dimensions of a tragic chain of events which created a sensation in the press of the United States and the world. The story was news because it starkly revealed the contradiction between preaching and practice by Christ's church in the critical and explosive area of race relations. Additionally, the story laid bare the ignominy of ministerial captivity by entrenched power structures within the church which have long fallen behind the thinking of the majority within the congregations — structures whose members are afraid to hear the truth and are determined to prevent their ministers from proclaiming it.

I do not write this book to romanticize my own suffering and that of my wife and family in the sacrifice of my pulpit to deeply held convictions. I do not write to vindicate a personal position that was wrestled to the ground in this controversy.

Rather, I put pen to paper to communicate a message which emerges, I believe, from the painful details of the Tattnall Square Church story. I believe that it is a message of prophetic quality, of both judgment and hope, of breaking down in order to build up.

I address this book to the men and women in the pew and to my brethren in the ministry who together, under God, hold the keys to the church's authority, fellowship, and witness.

Tattnall Square Baptist Church, when I was its pastor, was a typical urban church of the Baptist denomination in the deep South. It differed only in degree from most white congregations of other denominations and other areas of the country. The response that it presented to the critical problem of racial reconciliation confronting churches everywhere was typical. Other congregations need to see their situation mirrored in the dilemma of Tattnall Square Baptist Church. They need to identify and acknowledge their own guilt in the continuance of racial attitudes which are tearing our society apart because these prejudices have not been exorcised from the very house of God.

The tragedy of this church is the nearly universal disgrace of the churches — they might have led the way to community, but, alas, they would not!

The message of this book is that there is yet time for the church to be the church in the modern world. It can yet fulfill its divine commission of reconciliation between God and man, and between man and man. The courageous stand of the Master's minority in Tattnall Square Church, indigenous to the same culture as the majority, points the way to progress and hope in the present crisis. Those who are committed to Christ must stand and suffer, if need be, regardless of the consequences to themselves or the possible shattering of a false peace, in order to be the salt that saves society from decay.

Only as the people of God affirm the basic personhood of all men can they heal the breach between class and race within the fellowship of Christ's church. Only then will they recover the spiritual force to turn the tides of public opinion and conduct into the Christian stream within the nation.

10

I wish to express appreciation to my wife, Grace, to Dr. Rufus C. Harris, President of Mercer University, and to Mr. Eugene Patterson, who was editor of *The Atlanta Constitution* when the events recorded in this book were occurring. Their encouragement was the dominant factor in my undertaking what has proven to be a very arduous and sometimes painful task of writing and reliving this tragic experience.

Especially am I grateful to Mr. Gainer E. Bryan, Jr., for his collaboration in the writing, rewriting, and editing of this book and for the professional skills that he brought to the task.

My thanks go also to Dr. Benjamin W. Griffith, Jr., of the Mercer faculty, to Mr. Hugh C. Carney, Atlanta attorney who has been my friend since college days, to Mrs. Bernice McCullar, Atlanta author, and to Dr. Oliver M. Littlejohn, Dean of the Southern School of Pharmacy, for their invaluable assistance in reading the manuscript and offering helpful suggestions. To my secretary, Mrs. Louise Meier, I owe a debt of gratitude for typing the manuscript and for the many other services she has rendered.

And to those heroic persons who joined their pastor in this witness, I can think of no more fitting personal tribute than that which Paul paid the Philippian Christians:

"I thank my God for you all every time I think of you; and every time I pray for you, I pray with joy, because of the way in which you have helped me in the work of the gospel, from the very first day until now." (*Good News for Modern Man*).

THOMAS J. HOLMES

1

THE SEPTEMBER SUNLIGHT glinted from the ebony face of Sam Oni, African student, as he walked the short block from old Sherwood Hall, men's dormitory, to the church on the corner of the Mercer University campus. A look of calm determination was highlighted in the finely chiseled features of this tall, muscular twenty-three-year-old man from faraway Ghana.

Oni felt himself bound on a historic mission. He was a convert of Baptist missionaries to his country. He had come to Mercer, the Georgia Baptist university, because a missionary and Mercer graduate had guided him there. He was preparing himself for a public service career in his native Ghana.

Tattnall Square Baptist Church, to which he was headed, was one of the churches that had sent the missionaries to his land. This church had voted in the summer of 1966 not to seat Negroes at its worship services. When the pastor and his two assistants had continued to preach and to declare that the house of God should be open to all persons, the deacons had recommended to the church that pastoral services of the three be terminated.

Word of these developments came to Oni in California

13

where he had spent the summer in study. When he returned to Mercer for his senior year, he felt compelled to go to Tattnall Square because of his unique involvement in the campus and church situation. It was Sam Oni, product of Christian missions, whose application for enrollment at Mercer had broken the impasse between a progressive school administration and a conservative constituency and brought about the integration of the 133-year-old university three years earlier.

During his three years' residence at Mercer, Oni had become familiar with the spiritual schizophrenia of the church in America over the race issue. Shortly after he had arrived at Mercer, the deacons of this very Tattnall Square Baptist Church, dedicated to the service of campus and community, had advised their minister to tell Sam that he was not wanted in their sanctuary. He had been accepted for membership in Vineville Baptist Church of Macon, but only after a grim debate and a plea by their courageous minister that Oni was not an ordinary local Georgia Negro. He was a peculiar Negro, the minister had told the congregation, a unique Negro, one who had come to know the Lord through their own praying, their own gifts, and their own efforts on the mission field.

Sam Oni was going now to Tattnall Square to tell the members that their segregationist policy was torpedoing their own mission program in Africa.

The young foreign student, neatly dressed, knowing impeccable English, fluent French, and three tribal languages, approached the red brick church on the corner of the Christian university. There he was stopped rudely by the ushers of the segregated congregation. They had been instructed to turn all Negroes away, and to these Georgia middle-class white men Sam Oni was just another "nigger." They blocked his way. He asked for the privilege of talking to the deacons or reasoning with them, but the ushers wanted no part of Sam Oni. In their view he had been a troublemaker ever since he had integrated the university and brought integration pressures on the campus church.

BAPTIST CHURCH

When Oni politely insisted that he be admitted, he was seized by two deacons of the church. One applied a headlock on him, and the other dragged him down the steps. Oni kept his cool and did not fight back. He endeavored to reason with his adversaries from the sidewalk.

"Go to the church where you are a member, or some other church," a deacon ordered.

"No," said Oni.

Meanwhile the chairman of the deacons had called the police, who were conveniently nearby with a patrol car. Two policemen appeared in their summer gray uniforms, pistols on their belts, and led the African student to their car. They placed him inside and kept him there until he agreed to leave quietly — while the people inside the church sang the hymn by Frank Mason North:

> Where cross the crowded ways of life,
> Where sound the cries of race and clan,
> Above the noise of selfish strife,
> We hear Thy voice, O Son of man!

Thus was an African Christian rebuffed in trying to enter the house of God to warn his fellow Christians of the disastrous effect of their actions on their own witness. Thus did a white missionary Baptist church reject a child of its own missions. Oni said later, "I couldn't help but remember that Scripture verse which says, 'He came unto his own, and his own received him not.'"

These were the happenings *outside* of the church on the corner of the Baptist university campus the morning of September 25, 1966. They were matched by what occurred inside, which Oni was not able to stop. The congregation voted, 250 to 189, to oust their three ministers.

By these actions the church members denied God's universal ideal stated in Isaiah 56:7 and restated by Jesus Christ in Matthew, Mark, and Luke, "My house shall be called a house of prayer for all peoples" (RSV).

The next day the dismissal of the ministers and the rejec-

BAPTIST CHURCH

tion of the African student made headlines throughout the United States and around the world.

To hard-bitten newsmen that was standard man-bites-dog news copy, although the church majority was blind to the inconsistency of their action.

The ministers resigned that Sunday night as ordered, having fought their fight and finished their course, but Sam Oni was not giving up yet on Tattnall Square Baptist Church. "My faith has almost been shattered," he told newsmen at a press conference that afternoon, but he vowed that he would try again next Sunday to attend services and communicate his message to the church.

On October 2, the determined African again was denied admission, but communicate he did — to the church and to the world. He preached a poignant sermon at the foot of the church steps, and the scene and message were carried on national television!

The young man approached the church entrance alone. Two men were waiting at the bottom of the steps. One was an off-duty policeman, a deacon of the church, and the other was an inactive member whom the policeman that day had recruited to help him. Each was more than six feet tall and weighed over two hundred pounds; the deacons had feared that Oni would return this time with a mob. As in his first appearance, however, he refused to let other students join him. This must not be a demonstration, he felt, but a personal stand by a missionary convert from Africa who could not forsake the faith he had been taught by missionaries sent by churches like this one.

The hands of the church "ushers" were not extended for a friendly handshake. Rather the men stood jut-jawed and grim. Their arms were folded across their chests, and when Oni tried to walk around them, they sidestepped to stop him. When he sought to go between them, they blocked him by closing together. Glancing down from their superior elevation, they repeated their statement that the church had decided by majority vote to seat white people only. It was their right, all perfectly legal. After all, can't a Baptist church vote to do whatever it wants to do?

It was then that the rejected African delivered his brief sermon. In calm and measured tones he said, in essence, "Do you not see the inconsistency of what you are doing? You send missionaries to my land to tell me about the love of God, and then when I come to your land I do not find this same love in your hearts. Does God not love in the same way here? Do you not care if my people go to hell?"

Police officers were called again to the church to take Oni away, but when they asked if anyone in the congregation would take out a warrant against him, no one would step forward to do so.

The officers did not talk to Oni that time, and he left saying he would not make any effort to attend the church again. "I have made my point and there's no point in going back," he told reporters. He added, "The world will see what is going on — the empty mockery in that holy of holies."

THE WASHINGTON POST *June 21. 1995*

Ministers James B. Henry, right, and Gary Frost, pray after a
Southern Baptist Convention vote to apologize for past racism.

An Apology for Racism

Southern Baptists Regret 'Acts of Evil'

By Gary L. Carter

ATLANTA—The overwhelmingly white Southern Baptist Convention, born of the split between North and South over slavery, apologized to blacks yesterday for condoning racism for much of its history.

The vote in favor of the resolution received a standing ovation from 20,000 members of the nation's largest Protestant denomination during their annual convention.

The resolution denounces racism, repudiates "historic acts of evil such as slavery" and asks for forgiveness. It commits the 15.6 million-member church to eradicating vestiges of racism and notes that the denomination failed to support the civil rights movement of the 1950s and '60s.

Gary L. Frost, the only black in the faith's leadership, accepted the apology on behalf of black Southern Baptists.

Convention over the question of whether slave owners could be missionaries. The resolution acknowledges that "many of our Southern Baptist forebears defended the 'right' to own slaves" and that in "later years the Southern Baptists failed, in many cases, to support, and in some cases opposed, legitimate initiatives to secure the civil rights of African-Americans."

In 1989, the denomination first declared racism a sin.

The apology resolution, which was approved overwhelmingly after only a few minutes' debate, states:

"We apologize to all African-Americans for condoning and-or perpetuating individual and systematic racism in our lifetime. . . .

"We ask for forgiveness from our African-American brothers and sisters, acknowledging that our own healing is at stake . . .

"We hereby commit ourselves to eradicate racism in all its forms from Southern Baptist life

ASSOCIATED PRESS

Ministers James B. Henry, right, and Gary Frost, pray after a
Southern Baptist Convention vote to apologize for past racism.

An Apology for Racism

Southern Baptists Regret 'Acts of Evil'

By Gary L. Carter
Associated Press

"We pray that the genuineness of your repentance will be reflected in your attitude and your actions," said Frost, a pastor from Youngstown, Ohio. He and the denomination's president, James B. Henry, embraced at the podium after the vote.

Supporters of the resolution hope it will open the door wider to evangelizing among blacks and other ethnic groups.

The Southern Baptist Convention was created in 1845 in a split with the American Baptist and ministry.

"I think it's an admirable resolution, and I would hope that it would not merely be a resolution that is on paper," said the Rev. Clifford Jones, president of the General Baptist Convention in North Carolina, a predominantly black Baptist denomination.

About 1,800 of the 39,910 churches in the Southern Baptist Convention are primarily black, said spokesman Herb Hollinger. He said there is no official count of black members.

New York Times Newspaper 23 September 1986, page A14

Deacons at Michigan Church Vote to End a Ban on Blacks

REDFORD TOWNSHIP, Mich., Sept. 22 (UPI) — Deacons at one of the state's largest Christian congregations have voted to end a 60-year-old policy of banning blacks from joining their church.

By a vote of 29 to 7, deacons at the Temple Baptist Church approved a decision Saturday to scrap an unwritten policy that kept blacks from joining the parish.

Church elders said the 9,500-member congregation will be informed of the vote at next Sunday's services. The congregation will then have the opportunity to vote to approve the decision of the deacons. About 70 blacks attend church services at Temple but are not considered members.

"I have been here two-and-a-half years and have been working to change attitudes," said the Rev. Truman Dollar, pastor of the church. "It appears we're almost there."

THE NEW YORK TIMES, MONDAY, APRIL 14, 1975

30 Black Students Barred By Alabama White Church

TUSCALOOSA, Ala., April 13 (UPI)—About 30 black students from the University of Alabama were refused admittance to a white church today and the police were called to maintain order.

The Rev. Dorsey Blake said he had accompanied the members of his college class in the "Black Religious Experience in America" to the Alberta Baptist Church as "part of my program to supplement classroom experience with authentic experience."

Mr. Blake said that his group had been told by a man, apparently an usher, "that the church did not seat colored and there was a nigger church around the corner."

1994

Georgia Baptists Call Racism a Sin

Washington Post Nov-Dec 17, 1994

MACON, Ga. — The Georgia Baptist Convention has declared that racism is a sin and that many of its congregations have been steeped in it for 125 years.

In a resolution passed Wednesday on the last day of the convention's 1994 gathering, delegates called for a "ministry of reconciliation" between black and white Americans.

The resolution also confessed that "since the War between the States, many of our congregations have been bathed in racism by intentionally and unintentionally excluding blacks from worship, membership and leadership."

It challenges Georgia Baptists to "seek reconciliation between black and white Americans by seeking forgiveness for the sins" of the past and present.

Page 16 EVENING NEWS, Monday, November 8, 1976

The *NEWS* saw...

Carter to quit church because of race row?

BAPTIST

ST. SIMONS ISLAND, Georgia, Mon:
PRESIDENT - ELECT Jimmy Carter may be forced to consider resigning from his local Baptist church because of a race row involving its White pastor, his spokesman said here.

Mr. Carter will be at the church in his hometown of Plains, Georgia, next Sunday when the congregation votes on a decision by the Board of Deacons to bar a black preacher and sack the pastor, the Reverend Bruce Edwards, for sup-porting the admission of Blacks.

Asked if Mr. Carter, on a working holiday here, would resign if the congregation backed the deacons, his spokesman, Mr. Jody Powell, told reporters: "It's a decision he is going to have to make for himself."

The Carter family has been almost alone among the church's White congregation in supporting Black membership and have endorsed Pastor Edward's stand.

The row stems from attempts by a Black preacher, the Reverend Clennon King, to worship in the church for the past two Sundays.

After being refused the first time, he returned yesterday, and attended the men's Bible class. But when the group adjourned for Sunday service Mr. King stepped outside to read reporters a statement and was locked out.

On the first occasion the Deacons of the church suspended services for the day.

Mr. Carter owes his election victory over President Ford last week to a large Black vote.

Carter's Church May Dismiss Pastor For His Role in Dispute Over Black

THE NEW YORK TIMES November 2, 1976

By WAYNE KING
Special to The New York Times

ATLANTA, Nov. 1—The membership of Jimmy Carter's Baptist Church in Plains, Ga., will be asked sometime next week to ratify a decision by the church's deacons to dismiss their pastor for his role in a dispute over whether to admit a black activist minister to membership.

Mr. Carter, an inactive deacon, said at a news conference today in Sacramento, Calif., that he felt the incident yesterday, in which the church was closed rather than admit the minister, the Rev. Clennon King of Albany, Ga., was "politically inspired."

That assessment seemed generally to be shared by a number of black leaders and others across the country who have supported Mr. Carter.

The Democratic Presidential nominee has said repeatedly that he opposes the dismissal of the Rev. Bruce Edwards, who has been pastor of the church in Plains for almost two years.

Mr. Edwards told reporters in Plains today that he would fight the dismissal recommendation, made by an 11-to-1 vote at a meeting last night of the church's 12 deacons. The 30-year-old minister added, however, that his pastorship of the church "might be ending" regardless of the outcome of the move to oust him.

Mr. Edwards conceded that he had been in error yesterday when he said at an impromptu news conference in front of the locked church that the 1965 resolution adopted by the congregation barred "niggers and civil rights agitators." Copies of the resolution passed out to reporters used the word "Negroes."

The minister acknowledged today that the wording in the printed resolution was correct, and said he had made the mistake because the word "niggers" had been used at a meeting of the deacons last Tuesday night, affirming the intention to enforce the resolution if Mr. King attempted a "confrontation" at the church.

It was not immediately clear whether

Associated Press
The Rev. Bruce Edwards, pastor of the Plains, Ga., Baptist Church, talking to reporters yesterday.

the deacons' recommendation to dismiss Mr. Edwards resulted from his strong public opposition to the bar against blacks or whether it was based solely on the misquotation of the wording and the resulting embarrassment to the church. Whatever the case, the decision to dismiss or retain a pastor must be made by a vote of the congregation.

The deacons have refused to discuss the matter until Thursday.

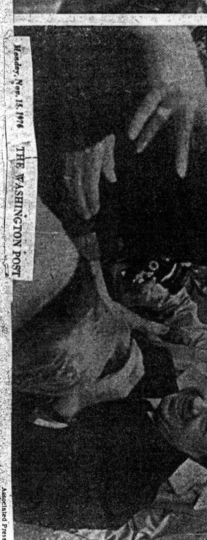

Associated Press

Monday, Nov. 15, 1976   **THE WASHINGTON POST**

he'll return to seek membership in Plains Baptist Church, and Jimmy Carter shakes hands after vote to open doors to all "who want to worship Jesus Christ."

Carter's Church Ends Ban on Admission of Blacks

Washington Post November 15, 1976

By Edward Walsh
Washington Post Staff Writer

PLAINS, Ga., Nov. 14—The members of President-elect Jimmy Carter's Baptist church voted today to end their ban on the admission of blacks to worship services and church membership.

With Carter in the congregation urging the change, the church members voted 120 to 66 to open their doors "to all people who want to worship Jesus Christ."

By a closer vote, 107 to 84, the congregation also decided to retain the Rev. Bruce Edwards as pastor. Edwards' resignation had been sought by the church's 12-member board of dea-

cons because of his opposition to the ban on admission of blacks.

At the end of the nearly three-hour meeting of the full congregation, Carter, smiling but looking tired, emerged from the small, white frame church building that is just a few blocks from his home. With him was his wife, Rosalynn, her eyes marked by tears.

"I was proud of my church. God's church," he said to reporters who had huddled together in a chilly rain outside the church during the meeting.

Saying the doors of his boyhood church are now "open to anyone who wants to worship Jesus Christ," Carter added:

"I'm completely satisfied with the

church's action. I am proud of the church members. I believe our church will now be unified. The pastor is pleased and the church congregation has spoken very clearly."

Asked specifically whether the vote today means that blacks can become full members of the church as well as worship there, Carter replied, "Yes, it does. There will be no exclusion of anyone from both worship or membership on the basis of race."

The man who precipitated today's meeting and the crisis atmosphere that surrounded it, the Rev. Clennon King, was outside the church building throughout the meeting.

It was King, an occasional Republican candidate for office and the black

minister of a non-denominational church in Albany, Ga., about 40 miles from here, who sought admission to the Plains Baptist Church two weeks ago on the Sunday before election day.

He was denied admission on the basis of a 1965 resolution that barred Negroes or any other civil rights agitators from attending church services or becoming church members. Shortly thereafter, the deacons also sought Edwards' resignation.

After today's meeting, King approached Hugh Carter, a cousin of the President-elect and clerk of the church, who was standing on the

See CHURCH, A4, Col. 1

Integrating The Segregated Hour

N.Y. AMSTERDAM NEWS   Saturday, November 27, 1976 — A.9

By Dr. Samuel K. Roberts

The vote has been taken at the First Baptist Church of Plains, Georgia and the membership has informed Black Americans that they are now free to worship in the modest, white framed edifice which houses a congregation of less than 300, all of whom are white by virtue of a 1965 resolution which barred "negroes and other civil rights agitators." The vote on whether to rescind this resolution was, of course, the result of the furor caused when the Rev. Mr. Clendon King, a Black minister from Albany, Georgia attempted to gain membership in the church only a few days before the Presidential Election.

Had Clendon King knocked on the door of any other of the thousands of white Southern Baptist churches in the South where local custom has discouraged the presence of Blacks he, like the church in Plains, would have remained in relative obscurity. But because the church happened at that time to be the spiritual home of the then Democratic nominee for the Presidency, Clendon King's rap on the door of the church in Plains had a ring of history in it. Yet surprisingly, his virtual one-man campaign to integrate the church remained essentially that — a one-man affair. No Freedom buses came to Plains

out that Carter and his family were among the six people who voted against the 1965 resolution. They counseled Black Americans to not let the situation in Plains divert them from supporting the man whom many believed offered a more sympathetic administration than the Republican nominee. Thus they showed, in the estimation of this writer, an amazing degree of political sagacity on the eve of the election. How could Clendon King's potentially explosive gesture fail to galvanize support in the national Black community? The answers to this question, I believe, are worthy of discussion.

First, the man himself may have been a factor. Rev. King does not enjoy a reputation in the state of Georgia for sound judgment, having announced his own candidacy for the Presidency. One could even question his sense of responsibility if the charges brought against him in Illinois for non-support of his six children are true. These, however, are not necessarily sufficient reasons to take him to task for his specific acts in Plains. One does, however, have to wonder at the judgement of a man who declares that the people who closed the doors of their sanctuary in his face are "still the sweetest white people on earth."

But there are other reasons of greater import than Rev. King's own behavior patterns, however controversial they may be, that may help explain why the affair remained a relatively isolated one.

One further reason is this: the texture of American religion has been changed radi-

thermore, a sizeable number of upwardly, mobile Blacks no longer operate with the assumption that joining a "white" church is the capstone to their ascendancy. What all of this has meant is that the standard for normative American religious behavior is no longer to be found exclusively in the "white" church. Thus if King expected support from the vast majority of the Black community he miscalculated, and his miscalculation is explained by these historical and sociological changes.

Finally, it was apparent to many observers at the time of the affair and in retrospect, to still others, that King's action, however noteworthy, simply did not symbolize the aspirations of Black Americans at this particular juncture in American history. This is not to say that Blacks have become less interested int he church or that they are no longer concerned with the ethical mandates of the Christian faith and the implications of those mandates on the local church level. Neither is this to suggest that Blacks are somehow impervious to the great hypocrisy practiced by the vast majority of American churches on Sunday morning during what Martin Luther King called "the most segregated hour of the week." Rather, what is being suggested is that at this Presidential campaign, Rev. King's attempt to integrate a white church tha did not particularly desire his presenc appeared to many Blacks as a symbolic ally bankrupt act reminiscent of a bygon era. Symbolic acts are by their ver

The Washington Post

THURSDAY, NOVEMBER 11, 1999

BAPTIST CHURCH

Two Congregations Seek 'Racial Reconciliation'

Washington Post November 11, 1999

By HAMIL R. HARRIS
Washington Post Staff Writer

It's 11 a.m. Sunday, the most segregated hour of the week in many churches.

But the Rev. Jean Robinson-Casey of University Baptist Church in College Park is on a mission to change that.

"Our goal is for this community to see that University Baptist Church believes in being one in Christ," Robinson-Casey said. "Most churches are either European American, African American or Hispanic. What we want is a diverse community that God called us to have through Jesus two millenniums ago."

At Robinson-Casey's urging, University Baptist, a predominantly white church, recently reached out to Zion Baptist Church, a 135-year-old African American congregation in the District, for a "service of racial reconciliation."

At the Oct. 31 service at University Baptist in College Park, a mul-

tiracial choir performed a cultural mix of songs, and a pulpit dialogue was held on racial stereotypes. Robinson-Casey said she thought the service was a good start, something that she has a highly personal stake in seeing succeed.

Robinson-Casey's presence in the pulpit already has broken down some barriers. An African American, she is assistant pastor

Above, Tommy Williams, of the Zion Baptist Church Choir, listens to the sermon during the service. Left, 3-year-old Mariana Smith, of Fort Washington, sleeps in the arms of her mother, Kendra Smith.

See UNITY, Page 3, Col. 1

12 • SATURDAY, APRIL 1, 2000 • TRINIDAD GUARDIAN

Trinidad Guardian
Equality for Baptists

FAR more than any other religious sect; the Spiritual Baptists have had the hardest row to hoe to achieve official recognition. The orthodox Christian churches have enjoyed a comparatively easy time from the earliest days of European occupation of Trinidad and Tobago. On the other hand, the Hindus and the Muslims had to wait until the middle of the 20th century to get their due when their officials were given legal authority to conduct religious ceremonies, the right to build their own schools, and the proclamation of their holiest days as public holidays.

The Spiritual Baptists are a Christian sect, but were long held at more than arm's length by the orthodox churches. After all, this was a British colony where up to the early years of the 19th century, Africans and their descendants who followed this faith in Trinidad and Tobago were slaves, labouring uncomfortably at the bottom of the social ladder and ignored if not scorned by those who regarded themselves as their betters.

The Afro-Trinidadians sought refuge and solace in developing and conducting their own rites in a fashion they had brought with them across the Middle Passage. But the laws of the colony did not permit them to practise their faith in public. The beating of drums, the ringing of bells were forbidden. The churches had to go more or less underground.

Four years ago, the UNC Government announced Shouters Liberation Day as a public holiday, a gesture that was more than symbolic. For to give what they regarded as practical effect to their religious concerns, the ruling party had appointed Archbishop Barbara Burke a member of the Senate on the Government side.

Now, as with the other religious sects, the Spiritual Baptists are to get their own primary school. Prime Minister Panday turned the sod on Thursday to signal his and his Government's support for the proposal to build the school at the African Spiritual Park at Orange Grove Estate in Maloney.

Secure Place

The Spiritual Baptists sect is not a monolithic organisation as, say, the Roman Catholic Church. Reports suggest they are divided into more than a dozen sub sects, each with its own leaders and ways of carrying out its own versions of religious ceremonies.

No doubt there are Spiritual Baptists who yearn for unity among the various sub sects on the basis that a collective approach to their concerns may bring religious and social advantages in both the short and long term and that in any case it is a goal worth seeking. But it is not a process that should be forced and the responsibility for mending fences or reducing whatever contentions may exist should be left to the various leaders.

2 WESTINDIAN WORLD   Friday, June 16th to Thursday June 22nd 1978   ENGLAND   June 16-22

COMMENT

METHODIST CHURCH

THE BLACK CHURCH

If ever there was a case of double standards and hypocrisy then surely there could be none as blatant as that which is this week being put forward by the Methodist Church, formerly the Methodist Missionary Society in their annual report.

The report is critical of the growing number of black churches in Britain and accuses them of being ghettoes with "ghetto congregations and ghetto mentality", denying the catholicity of the church.

Exactly what they mean by "ghetto mentality" is not quite clear but one thing is, and that is black people can never win in the eyes of the "authorities" who know what is right for us.

What the report fails to note is that white established churches are responsible for the formation of black churches. As in all other strata of society black people were cold shouldered by the very same people who are now pointing the accusing finger.

Black churches are increasing in numbers every day while on the other hand the established places of worship are either being sold off to private developers or turned into bingo halls. The reason being that white worshippers are more readily found in the pub than in the pew on a Sunday.

It is darn right hypocritical that the society, in an effort to woo back black worshippers to prop up their fading congregation, should use the black church as a scape goat.

The reality of the matter is that the black church like its congregation is of the ghetto. They were put there forcefully with all the tact in the world and are now trying their best to get the hell out by their shoe string.

This statement from the General Secretary of the mission Dr. Collin Morris is as obvious in its context as having a boil on ones backside:

"Any monochrome congregation (whether white, or black) in a multi-racial society, is a denial of the catholicity of the Christian Church.

"It is easy to understand how the so-called black churches — a term I find as offensive as 'white' church — came into existence. No doubt some of their members were discriminated against or were chilled by the formalism of too much of our worship. But ghetto churches are hardly likely to help in the struggle to prevent our society polarising into ghetto communities."

What the good Doctor, who is described as a leading churchman, fails to point out is that black churches have never cold shouldered any person because of race or colour. Their gatherings are vibrant and full of warmth and brotherly love.

If he is afraid that the black man is becoming too organised, and too powerful then he should say so. There is nothing wrong with black people worshipping with black preachers, and contrary to popular belief, no one race, or colour have a monopoly on God neither should it matter where one chooses to worship be it a palace or a pigsty.

Friday, August 11th to Thursday, August 17th, 1978 *London, England*

6 WESTINDIAN WORLD *Newspaper August 11-17, 1978, England*

METHODIST CHURCH

I know for a fact that Churches in England and Wales, with predominantly Black membership are proud of the Westindian World's response report on Friday June 16th about the Methodist Church's insult to our churches.

The white churches are playing a game which one slaps you, then another pats you; one insults you and another consoles you; one kills you and another raises a monument in your honour.

At the same time, the attack is good, in that it should drive home the lesson to the Black church leaders, some of whom are lackeys to the white church establishment, that building their future on relationship and promises of the white man (whether he is in the pew, pulpit or pub) is building on sinking sand.

Some of the Black Church leaders and members, cannot conceive of a future of development, without their white ecclesiastical guides, interpreters and patronisers. They will compass sea and and land to, attend their meetings and conferences simply because the whites are organising it, and when they get there, they beg for building, money, education, acceptance and love.

The Black members of our churches deserve better from their leaders than the subservient and inferior attitude which they presently suffer.

At the same time the Lord of our Black members and friends, have given our leaders a mandate to be strong. That mandate is their regular Church attendances and financial contribution. Let our leaders take the example of Christ.

"Who for the joy that was set before him, endured the Cross and despise the shame . . ."

Ben Cunningham, (General Secretary)
Afro-Westindian United Council of Churches

METHODIST CHURCH SLAMMED

WESTINDIAN WORLD

Friday, June 30th to Thursday, July 6th, 1978

WESTINDIAN **world**

June 30th to July 6th, 1978
LONDON, ENGLAND

Friday, June 30th to Thursday, July 6th, 1978

Criticism of black led churches made in the annual report of the Methodist Church Overseas Division were repudiated by the staff of the London based Zebra Project which fosters co-operation between black and white Christians, last week.

The staff of the project which is based at the Bow Mission and of the Overseas Division, rejected allegations in the report that the black led churches were creating 'ghetto con-gregations', 'hoarding talents' that should be shared with other

Arguing that the Over-seas Division's report is our of touch with the current situation, the statement ends: "The 'Zebra Project' and 'other projects have been encouraging real links between the black led and white led churches for several years.

The Afro-West Indian United Council of Churches (AWICUC),

is largely financed by under its chairman, the Rev. D.V. Pemberton, is making firm moves in the direction of fellowship.

The recent report from a joint working party 'Coming Together in Christ', makes it quite plain that there is a desire in many hearts to share together in the overall mission of the church in Britain.

L to R: Mr. Habibur Rahman (UK Islamic Mission) Rev Fred Rollinson (C of E) Father Victor Camilleri (Roman Catholic — Community Relations Officers — Tower Hamlets) Rev Lloyd Booker (All Saints Apostolic).

A deputation from the Society for Religious Peace and Family Unity presented a letter of protest at the headquarters of the Evangelical Alliance, Chelsea. The protest concerns a secret conference "Challenge by the Cults" sponsored by the Deo Gloria Trust in conjunction with the Evangelical Alliance.

Racism still

New York Amsterdam Newspaper

plagues Methodisn

March 26, 1983. page 2

NEW YORK AMSTERDAM NEWS
2340 Eighth Avenue
New York, N.Y. 10027 678-6600

Racism, "regrettably," still is "alive and well in United Methodism," according to a national leader of the church.

tion's Commission on Religion and Race, but he thinks much work still must be done. "If there are those who have concluded that we can now leave our efforts to combat racism, and move to some new issue, they are clearly mistaken," he said.

Dr. White, general secretary of the commission, based his report to the agency's spring meeting on a poll taken recently among 482 church leaders. Included were bishops, conference council on ministries directors and other leaders, ethnic caucus representatives, laity, clergy and members of the Commission on Religion and Race. The 326 responses showed, he said, that "There is not a level in the church" where racism does not need to be confronted.

Later in its meeting here, the commission adopted a report from its Black Concerns Committee that asked the General Council on Ministries expressly to include strengthening and developing ethic minority local churches in the denomination's mission priority for 1985-88, with specific funding included. GCOM will complete work later this year on recommendations for a quadrennial priority for submission to the 1984 General Conference.

Dr. White said the survey conducted by his agency, and a national poll released during the same period, found that a "perception gap" between white and Black Americans "loomed large." and realities, Dr. White continued. "It is crucial," he asserted, "that white United Methodists, whatever their theological disposition, . . . understand what it means

Some "considerable strides" have been made toward racial inclusiveness, the Rev. Woodie W. White told the denomina-

to be an ethnic minority in a predominately white denomination and nation. White United Methodists must willing and encouraged to share hones and openly their perceptions, fears, hop and anxieties."

It is estimated that less than five perce of the United Methodist Church's about ! million members in the United States a Puerto Rico are ethnic minorities. Tl local church, Dr. White said, "is the pla where so much dialogue is missin Pastors and laity must place this as a hi priority among their many programs a ministries."

In the country as a whole, "There is sense of frustration in many ethr minority communities," the 48-memb Commission on Religion and Ra (CORR) was told. "There is the belief th the nation — the government — has turn its back on these communities.

"Programs which were just beginning have some impact on ethnic minori communities are being dismantled, la passed assure greater opportunities a increased participation by ethic minorit are being abolished. What a trage indeed, if the ethnic minority constituen would now be abandoned by the church.'

Although CORR asked that a visil emphasis on strengthening ethi churches be continued in the n quadrennium, both Dr. White and a com mittee monitoring this quadrenniun priority on minority congregations point to problems in its implementation in t current quadrennium when it is priority in the church's mission.

THE TIMES MONDAY FEBRUARY 25 1985

METHODIST 1985

Sense and censure about race

By Clifford Longley, Religious Affairs Correspondent

It may be counted as one of Christianity's successes, since the war, that is has modified, and diminished the natural racism of the English people to the extent that many non-white immigrants have been absorbed peacefully into the community. It might well not have happened; and there could have been awful consequences.

It is ironic, therefore, that most of the country's religious bodies, when they talk of race, do so indignantly and often with shame. Racism is rife, they tend to say, both in society in general and in the churches. The "white" churches lament that they were unwelcoming when the first West Indians called on them, and bear it as a mark of continuing failure.

They are as censorious about other people's "racial" attitudes as Puritans once were about sex, as if racialism has become the great sin of our time. The latest Methodist report, *People, churches, and Multi-Racial Projects*, has much of that tone to it. It does less than credit to what has been achieved, and to the churches' considerable contribution to it.

The Methodist report contains plentiful evidence that racial prejudice is still having emotionally and materially wounding effects on its victims; and as much evidence that all over the country church groups are trying to counter it. The unasked question, which has to be faced before any perspective can be achieved, is whether racial prejudice is eradicable, and if not then how much of it should set the alarm bells ringing. Is Britain "very" or only "slightly" racist? Methodists seem to think "very"; but their report sets out a theological approach, which is questionable because it is idealistic.

It proceeds from the unspoken assumption that if racism is a sin, it is unique among sins in being totally banishable. That supposition unconsciously directs attention towards how it should be banished; rather than how it should be forgiven, and committed less often and less gravely. It is not treated as a spiritual sickness.

It is remarkable how little attention is ever given, in writing, to the inner detail of this particular sin: who commits it, how it arises, what the temptations are, what part it plays in the general malady of the soul. Methodists, at least, should be good at that sort of thing.

It would be constructive to take it seriously as a sin, rather than to deplore that it ever happens. A great many decent people, some of them no doubt Methodists, must commit it from time to time without much malice; but because it is such an unmentionable vice, they are probably not aware of it.

It also tends to be branded unforgivable as if society was divided neatly into two groups, the racists and the non-racists. Racists are spoken of not as people to be healed but people to be defeated.

That there is racism in the church is taken as ground for self-hatred, not for humility. What is lacking in much church discussion of racism is any sense of "Let him who is without sin cast the first stone". But that would have to be the starting point of any course of treatment.

There is a self-righteousness about anti-racism which undermines its powers of persuasion. Church groups borrow that tone from secular groups, thus operating within an ideological rather than a theological framework. A recent Roman Catholic report on Britain's immigration laws, demanding that they should be recast on an entirely non-racist basis, was guilty of the same ideological distortion.

There are in fact no non-racists, just as there are no non-adulterers who may cast the first stone. So there can be no totally non-racist societies, just as there can be no totally just societies. It is surprising that Christian groups in particular, with their strong conception of mankind's fallen state, should fall into the trap of utopianism.

Both the Methodist Church and the Roman Catholic Church have good records in the practical steps they have taken to encourage racial harmony, although both churches naturally have ginger groups who insist they have not done enough. When they come down to practical detail, they do not see the banishment of racism in those idealistic terms, but seek realistic ways of improving human relationships.

Thus their theology is "out of sync" with their practical behaviour; and it is their practical behaviour which has the ring of truth to it. In society at large, when it comes to the test, there is an almost unlimited reserve of racial decency which makes it rather unjust to condemn the British on this score. The astonishing response to the Ethiopian famine brought that to the surface. A truly racist society would have turned its face away: the Ethiopians are, after all, black.

People, Churches and Multi Racial Projects (Methodist Church Division of Social Responsibility, Central Buildings, London SW1; £2.50).

16 WESTINDIAN WORLD   Wednesday, July 3, 1985

Church today

West Indian World Newspaper July 3. 1985. page 16

Minister claims church is racist

England

THE NEWLY inaugurated vice president of this year's Methodist Conference, Mr Leon Murray, has said that racism exists within both central and local government bureaucracies.

Said Mr Murray: "It is an unwritten law in central and local government institutions that if you are black or brown, no matter how good your qualifications, you are unlikely to be employed by any of these government institutions.

Speaking at his inauguration in Birmingham last Friday, Mr Murray added: "With this great bombardment of discrimination and prejudice, the black community feels threatened and the only society left for them to turn to did not want them. "The Church was that society – surely the Church, which for centuries sent missionaries to their countries would accept them. But it can now be said, they came unto their own, but their own did not accept them.

"Between 1949 and 1970, the Church or the majority of the Church did not want to know about the suffering of the black community in Britain. Between 1950 and 1970, the mass exodus of the white members from the inner city Churches took place.

"Those left in the inner city churches were old, or very young and poor, or black and very poor. These three groups lacked the resources to rebuild the Churches, hence today we have the inner city problems, and the blacks are said to be the problem – at least that is how many think about the cities today.

"Many of the evil governments of the world are propped up by Britain, and Western Europe, North America and the Soviet Union and her friends in Eastern Europe; it just depends which camp you are driven into."

METHODIST CHURCH

IE TIMES THURSDAY OCTOBER 27 1977

Black churches 'will put white Christianity to test'

By Our Religious Affairs Correspondent

Relations between established white churches in Britain and the new black Christian churches will be the crucial test of the sincerity of white Christianity, according to a booklet published by the Home Mission division of the Methodist Church.

Roswith Gerloff, pastor of a Lutheran church in Oxford, and arises from a doctoral thesis she is doing on black churches. She estimates that there are about 40,000 members of the new churches, and that two or three times that number attend regularly. They have about 650 churches or meeting places, and are either independent or belong to one of several loose groupings of independent black churches.

So far they do have no formal relationships with indigenous churches in Britain, although the British Council of Churches has a working group drawn from both sides examining possible forms of cooperation.

The churches were mainly derived from churches already established in Africa, the West Indies, or the United States and most of them have a pentecostal or evangelical emphasis. They are the only institutions offering unrestricted black leadrship possibilities to immigrant communities, and they offer one of the best means of communcation to the West Indian communities in Britain.

"Black-led churches must become accepted as partners within the community of British Christians," Miss Gerloff says.

Some of the conditions for affiliation to local councils of churches may be unconsciously discriminatory. Experience of black worship leads to the conclusion that it is usually a far more whole-hearted endeavour than white worship. She describes it as "total worship".

Partnership in Black and White (Methodist Information Office, 1 Central Buildings, Westminster, SW1, 35p).

JUNE 5, 1988

NY Times 5 June 1988

Bishop Fred Holloway Of Methodist Church

WILMINGTON, Del., June 4 (AP) — Bishop Fred G. Holloway, the first bishop of the West Virginia Area of the Methodist Church, died here Wednesday after a long illness. He was 90 years old.

The Methodist churches in West Virginia, most of which were in rural areas, were under the jurisdiction of Pittsburgh until 1960 when the national church voted to make West Virginia a separate area. There were 200,000 Methodists in the state when Mr. Holloway was named bishop.

In February 1965, Mr. Holloway announced that the 1,600 white Methodist churches and the 25 Negro Methodist churches in West Virginia would be united under a common administration. West Virginia was one of the first states to make the plans public to combine the two groups.

Mr. Holloway retired as bishop in 1968, the same year his church merged with the Evangelical United Brethren Church to become the United Methodist Church.

He was born in Newark and graduated from Western Maryland College in 1918. He attended Westminster Theological Seminary in 1918 and 1919 and graduated from Drew University in Maryland in 1921.

His first church assignment was in Wilmington and he served in Baltimore and Cherrydale, Va.

Mr. Holloway also served as president of Western Maryland College from 1935 to 1947 and president of Drew University from 1947 to 1960.

MOTHER BETHEL

A.M.E. Church — Philadelph a, Pennsylvan.
1787- :

Mother Bethel African Methodist Episcopal Church, the oldest church in Af.ican Methodism, was founded by Richard Allen in 1787 at 6th Street below Pine Street, in Philadelphia, Pennsylvania. As a result of mistreatment on the part of the officers of Old St. George's Methodist Church in 1794, the first church was dedicated by Bishop Francis Asbury.

The present building, constructed in 1890, is the fourth on the same site, which represents the oldest continuous plot of real estate owned by Blacks in America. In 1965, under the pastorate of Dr. Charles E. Stewart, the Department of the Interior, United States Government, designated Mother Bethel, a National Historic Shrine, and in 1974, under the pastorate of Rev. Joseph L. Joiner, the same Department designated it a Historic Landmark.

Richard Allen

Founder of African Methodism

Early African Methodism

The African Methodist Episcopal Church has a history which is both unique and glorious. It is unique in the fact that it was the first major religious denomination that sprung from sociological rather than theological or doctrinal concerns, in the western world. It was the response to the "Africans" need for self expression and full involvement in the service of the worship of God and society as a whole. It was the answer for a people seeking recognition as human beings of dignity and self-respect.

Richard Allen and Abaslom Jones founded the Free African Society in 1787. This society was to become the African Methodist Episcopal Church in 1816 when Allen and others came together in a formal way to solve religious problems and to work for a better social order.

The catalyst for the organization of the Free African society was the practice of St. George's Methodist Episcopal Church in Philadelphia, in 1787, to segregate its colored or African members from its white members. The Africans were assigned to the gallery of the church. One Sunday as these Africans, as they were called, knelt to pray outside of their segregated area they were literally pulled from their knees and told to go to the place assigned them. These Negroes responded by saying, "wait until prayer is over and we will go and trouble you no more." Their leader Richard Allen opposed segregation but he equally opposed racial hate. He mentioned in his memoirs many whites who helped him in his cause.

Allen learned that other African groups were encountering the same conditions as the Africans in Philadelphia. After much study and consultation, five churches came together in a general convention and became the African Methodist Episcopal Church with Allen as its first Bishop.

The church grew with the nation and was a pioneer in the field of education. It established the first Black University in the nation. Young black people were educated in a climate of caring and challenge. Presently, there are seventeen colleges and seminaries that have their roots in African Methodism.

The African Methodist Episcopal Church first came to Southern California in 1872 and presently many prominent blacks are among it's members. The African Methodist Episcopal Church continues it's two-hundred year tradition

METHODIST CHURCH

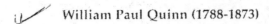
African Methodist Episcopal Church

William Paul Quinn (1788-1873)

The fourth Bishop of the A.M.E. Church, William Paul Quinn was born in Calcutta, India on April 10, 1788. Admitted into the Conference in 1816, Quinn was ordained a deacon in 1818 and ordained an elder in 1838. Defying slavery, he organized churches in Missouri and Kentucky and was a missionary that pastored and organized churches in the "Western Mission." The General Conference elected him Bishop on May 19, 1844 after he submitted his report on the churches he established.

In 1848 Bishop Quinn presided over the General Conference and delivered the first written Episcopal Address for any conference. After the death of Bishop Morris Brown in 1849, he became the Senior Bishop of the A.M.E. Church and served for 24 years and 8 months, until his death on February 3, 1873 in Richmond, Indiana.

Daniel A. Payne (1811-1893)

The sixth Bishop of the A.M.E. Church, Daniel Alexander Payne was born to free colored parents in Charleston, South Carolina on February 24, 1811. Payne can be credited with the A.M.E. Church's attention toward trained ministry. The first Bishop to have had formal theological seminary training, Payne developed a course of study for all A.M.E. preachers as an alternative to the seminary. Payne, who had served as a schoolmaster in Baltimore, set the educational goals for the A.M.E. Church. He encouraged the A.M.E. pastors to organize schools in their community as a part of their ministry. Ordained an elder in the Lutheran Church, in 1837 he was admitted to the Philadelphia Annual Conference in 1842. On May 7, 1852 Payne was elected a Bishop at the General Conference in New York City. As Bishop he presided over the1st, 3rd, 2nd, and 7th Districts. Founder of Wilberforce University, he became the first Black President of a college in the U. S. A. where he served for 13 years. It was the first institution of higher education founded by African Americans in the U. S. A. The theological school's establishment at Wilberforce is also credited to Payne. In 1865 he organized the South Carolina Conference. As an author, Bishop Payne spent twenty years gathering information for his book "History of the A.M.E. Church." His

the African Methodist Episcopal Zion Church

GREATER WALTERS A.M.E. ZION CHURCH
8400-22 South Damen
Chicago, Illinois 60620

William Alexander Hilliard, Host Bishop

Norsie L. Meeks, Host Presiding Elder

George W. Walker, Host Pastor

Mother A.M.E. Zion Church, New York City, Dr. G. W. Mc-Murray, Pastor.

The World Book Encyclopedia

Copyright © 1988, U.S.A.
by
World Book, Inc.
Merchandise Mart Plaza, Chicago, Illinois 60654

Allen, Richard (1760-1831), founded the African Methodist Episcopal Church (A.M.E.), the first black denomination in the United States.

Allen was born a slave in Philadelphia, and grew up on a plantation in Delaware. He later bought his freedom, and moved to Philadelphia in 1786. Allen helped form the Free African Society, a service group for blacks, in 1787. He soon came to believe that blacks should have their own churches, and founded the Bethel African Methodist Episcopal Church in 1794. He was ordained a minister in 1799. In 1816, Bethel ended its link with the Methodist Church. That year, Allen helped establish the African Methodist Episcopal Church, uniting Bethel with other A.M.E. churches. He became bishop of the new church.

New York Public Library.

Richard Allen.

Edgar Allan Toppin

See also Jones, Absalom.

African Methodist Episcopal Church (A.M.E.) is one of the largest Methodist denominations in the United States. The church was founded by a group of black Methodists who withdrew in November, 1787, from the St. George Methodist Episcopal Church in Philadelphia, protesting segregation. Blacks at that time made up a large percentage of the Methodists in America. Two free blacks, Richard Allen and Absalom Jones, led the withdrawal. Blacks at that time were called Africans. The church name was chosen to indicate it was formed by people of African descent. However, the church has never had a policy of discrimination and has members of all races.

Twenty bishops serve the church in the 50 states, Canada, 14 African countries, the Caribbean, and South America. The church operates six senior colleges and two junior colleges. It has about 1,150,000 members.

Critically reviewed by the A.M.E. Church

See also Allen, Richard.

African Methodist Episcopal Zion Church (A.M.E. Zion) is a large Methodist denomination in the United States. It was formed in 1796 by a group of blacks who withdrew from the John Street Methodist Episcopal Church in New York City. The John Street church had both white and black members. Many leaders of the abolitionist movement of the 1800's were members of the A.M.E. Zion Church. They included Harriet Tubman, Sojourner Truth, and Frederick Douglass.

A general conference is the supreme administrative body of the church. Between meetings of the conference, the church is administered by the Board of Bishops. The denomination operates Livingstone College in Salisbury, N.C., and two junior colleges. Its missionaries are active in North and South America, Africa, and the Caribbean region. The church has about 1 million members.

Critically reviewed by the A.M.E. Zion Church

HANDBOOK OF DENOMINATIONS

in the United States
by
Abingdon Press. Frank S. Mead
New York. 1965

Christian Methodist Episcopal Church
Known until 1954 as the Colored Methodist Episcopal Church, this church was established in 1870 in the South in an amicable agreement between white and Negro members of the Methodist Episcopal Church, South. There were at the time at least 225,000 Negro slave members in the Methodist Episcopal Church, South, but with the Emancipation Proclamation all but 80,000 of these joined the 2 independent Negro bodies. When the general conference of the Methodist Episcopal Church, South, met at New Orleans in 1866, a commission from the Negro membership asked for a separation into a church of their own. The request was granted, and in 1870 the organization of the Colored Methodist Episcopal Church was realized. They held this name until the meeting of their general conference at Memphis in May of 1954, when it was decided to change it to the Christian Methodist Episcopal Church.

Their doctrine is the doctrine of the parent church; this denomination adds a local church conference to the quarterly, district, annual, and general conferences usual in Methodism. Seven boards supervise the national work, each presided over by a bishop assigned as chairman by the College of Bishops. The general secretaries of the various departments are elected every 4 years by the general conference. There were 444,493 members and 2,523 churches in 1961.

Sarah Allen.

The Washington Post   SUNDAY, JANUARY 15, 1995

But from the rafters of Memphis's Clayborn Ball Temple A.M.E. Church could be heard another refrain—a voice not heard there since 1968, but resonating all the same in its ghostly persistence.

"The masses of people are rising up. And wherever they are assembled today . . . the cry is always the same: 'We want to be free.' "

The Rev. Martin Luther King Jr., who would have observed his 66th birthday today, visited **Clayborn Ball Temple** on Hernando Street at least twice during his trips to Memphis. The church was the starting point of sanitation-worker marches he led there in 1968. Its sanctuary was virtually destroyed during riots after King's assassination in Memphis on April 4 of that year.

The church isn't a tourist attraction; most visitors to the city who are interested in the civil rights movement go instead to the National Civil Rights Museum on Mulberry Street. But visitors to Memphis who make the effort will find that the church is one of several lesser-known

See MEMPHIS, E6, Col. 6

A plaque below the balcony of Room 306 at the Lorraine Motel memorializes the spot where the Rev. Martin Luther King Jr. was slain in 1968.

PHOTOS BY BILL BOWDEN

Clayborn Ball Temple, the start of the 1968 sanitation worker marches led by King.

Memphis's
Clayborn Ball Temple A.M.E. Church

METHODIST CHURCH

THE WASHINGTON POST   MONDAY, MARCH 4, 1985

John Lewis;
the Rev. Jesse Jackson; Joseph Lowery and wife, Evelyn; and Coretta Scott King march across the Edmund Pettus Bridge in Selma, /

Spirit of Selma Resurrected 20 Years Later

By George Lardner Jr.
Washington Post Staff Writer

SELMA, Ala., March 3—With an escort of Alabama state troopers, sheriff's deputies and city police leading the way, nearly 3,000 civil rights marchers walked across the Edmund Pettus Bridge today in exuberant commemoration of "Bloody Sunday" here 20 years ago.

It was a remarkable blend of past and present. Except for the marchers, the downtown streets were largely deserted. There is still a black Selma and a white Selma, and white Selma stayed home.

But at Brown Chapel AME Church, where it all started, Joe Smitherman, the city's white mayor who also held that office in 1965, showed up to acknowledge the wrongs done in the past and to present keys to the city to the leaders of today's march,

𝕿𝖍𝖊 𝖂𝖆𝖘𝖍𝖎𝖓𝖌𝖙𝖔𝖓 𝕻𝖔𝖘𝖙   Saturday, August 27, 1983

1983

Rallying 'Round The Cause

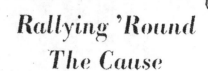

The Rev. Jesse Jackson, left, speaks to a packed house last night at a rally and religious service at the Metropolitan AME Church, 15th and M streets NW. The event was part of the preliminary activities for today's 20th anniversary of the 1963 March on Washington.

WASHINGTON POST   Saturday, August 27, 1983   ... R   **B5**

Photos by Craig Herndon—The Washington Post

Metropolitan AME Church, 15th and M streets NW.

A20 TUESDAY, JANUARY 21, 1997 THE WASHINGTON POST

THE SECOND INAUGURATION OF BILL CLINTON

Clintons attend an interfaith prayer service at Metropolitan AME Church. About 2,200 people crowded into the M Street NW church for the service.

BY JAMES A. PARCELL—THE WASH

Page 2L TRINIDAD GUARDIAN, Tuesday, November 5, 1996

tional news

US·ELECTIONS
Clinton stays well ahead

IN CHURCH: President Clinton addresses the congregation during church services at St Paul's AME Church in Tampa, Florida, Sunday. *AP wirephoto exclusive to the Trinidad Guardian.*

A4 MONDAY, SEPTEMBER 26, 1994 · · ·

By Ruth Marcus
Washington Post Staff Writer

THE WASHINGTON POST

At U.N., Clinton Discusses Lifting Bosnia Embargo

Meetings Come at a Critical Time, Potential Turning Point in Crisis, Envoy Albright Says

Earlier, Clinton was joined by New York Gov. Mario M. Cuomo at the Bethel AME Church in Harlem, where the president urged voters not to be misled by critics who "bad-mouth those who are trying to move the country forward."

President Clinton, with New York Gov. Mario M. Cuomo, left, and the Rev. O'Neil Mackey Sr., right, sings hymn Sunday during church services in Harlem.

ASSOCIATED PRESS

Legal Supplement Part C to the "Trinidad and Tobago Gazette", Vol. 19, No. 229, 17th July, 1980

No. 8 of 1980

Fourth Session First Parliament Republic of Trinidad and Tobago

SENATE

BILL

AN ACT to provide for the incorporation of certain persons as Trustees of The Church of Jesus Christ of Latter-Day Saints (Trinidad and Tobago).

Latter-day saints

Page 8 TRINIDAD GUARDIAN, Wednesday, January 10, 1990

LIKE Senator Louise Horne, we are surprised at the ease with which the Church of Jesus Christ of the Latter Day Saints - The Mormons - have been able to register themselves as a religious organisation in our county.

You will have seen them, no doubt, the ubiquitous duos of young males, dressed in white shirts and ties, dark trousers and sunshades, walking always in twos, and ready to convince anybody that the Mormons are the divinely inspired messengers for our age.

Back in the seventies, they first attempted to set up their church in this country but, as a result of strong objections raised by Senator Louise Horne and others, they failed to gain the required foothold. Subsquently, we felt our people would only read of their activities in the foreign press.

But it seems that they were not prepared to take no for an answer and are back in full force to show us the way of the Mormons. Having regard to their basic beliefs and religious practice, however, we must wonder what attraction a little Third World country such as ours could have for them.

Racist Belief

The Mormons are a religious group emanating from Salt Lake City, Utah, which holds views that are distinctly different from the traditional faiths established in our country.

They claim to have outlawed polygamy in 1890, but there are still "pockets of tolerance", according to Edgar P. Kaiser author of the book, *How to respond to the Latter-Day Saints.*

But what is even worse is their foundational and racist belief that dark-skinned people are lesser beings who are not allowed to hold any positions of importance in either their church (where they are not allowed to be anything but rate-paying worshippers), or the wider world.

Surely, if that is a basic tenet of their faith then they have disembarked at the wrong destination, for this country comprises at least 90 percent of people with non-white complexion, including citizens of African and East Indian descent.

The Church began when a certain Joe Smith, their founder, claims to have received direct communication from no lesser person than an angel called Moroni, who also came with two golden plates, on which were written the tenets of their religion.

The angel subsequently took back the golden plates and sealed them away, so that odinary mankind was deprived of any opportunity to verify Mr Smith's version of the events leading up to the birth of his religion.

Their re-entry to this country tells us that they wish to leave with us some of this great wisdom to which Mr Smith was privy and, by so doing, improve the quality of life and spirituality that exists here.

But, while we are always in the market for good and noble gestures, we must wonder about the relevance of these missionaries from Utah. If the principles enshrined in our beloved anthem run counter to some key doctrines of the Mormons, how then can we be comfortable with their proselytising in our midst? What new spiritual insight can they impart to us?

We proudly claim that every creed and race should find an equal place in this society, but the goodly Mormons would have none of that. They have been taught, from their doctrinal texts, that people with dark skins are cursed by God and cannot hold a responsible place in the church structure.

Shouldn't they, then, just leave Trinidad and Tobago alone?

Far from being a xenophobic society, Trinidadians may well be among the world's most hospitable people; and if the Mormons would like to learn from a nation that believes in the equality of the races, in the dignity of the human being regardless of his colour, and his equal standing before his creator then they are welcome to visit us.

If they are here to convert us to their esoteric form of religion and to their racist beliefs, then we must tell these latter-day saints thank you, but no thank you.

Their view that dark-skinned people are really accursed spirits who rebelled against God and have been made to return to the flesh so that they could be recognised by all the other good and clean spirits leaves us to wonder whether Mr Smith had enough time to read the golden plates in detail, and might have, in either awe or haste, misread the thing entirely.

Marching Out

The President of the Inter Religious Organisation (IRO), Anglican Bishop Clive Abdulah, has said that the Mormons are a racist group. He noted also that they are not members of the IRO, and argues that "they have come out of a tradition which is contrary to the message of the Christian Church."

We believe Bishop Abdulah is speaking for the entire Christian community in our country and we expect that the Mormons would get the message.

Christians, however, must fear that since the Mormons have already deployed what appears to be hundreds of their footsoldiers throughout the length and breadth of the country, they will soon be making more than just the noise of footsteps, and it might be quite difficult to wish them goodbye.

Perhaps we should pray for the day when these saints would go marching out.

MORMONS / CHURCH OF JESUS CHRIST OF LATTER DA

THE INTERMEDIATE BARBADOS REZ [TOBAGO] Fargo House, Cenador

Page 8 MONDAY 20TH MAY – 1985

GOD NO LONGER RACIAL

Barbados has now come under the influence of the Church of Jesus, of the Latter Day Saints of Mormons.

Last December, they had a member-ship in Barbados of 150. But by the end of February membership grew to 200.

Surprisingly, of the 34 work permits granted by the Barbados immigration 18 went to the Mormons. This is quite disproportionate when other churches with hundreds of members only have two or three or no foreign expatriate ministers.

These men of God come in full force, when Tom Adams was colla-borating with Reagan under the guise of democracy.

Well, Mormonism is similar to segregation as was practised in the U.S. It is no different from Apartheid, as practised by the Dutch Reform-Church in South Africa.

And in one of their songs which tells the history of the Mormons, one would read these lines.

"The Church of Jesus Christ was formed to purge the world of sinning to civilize many people Lords and Nobles, tramps and nigg-ers."

But since Negroes are 5/8 of a man according to U.S. history "we'll see the niggers coming to join us!"

But today after the niggers seem to have a high political profile God told these Latter Day Saints in 1979 in a vision, that he stopped being

racial, so niggers can join the priest-hood and are no longer zombies! yet, he is a God that changeth not!

The Informer is appealing the

Voice of the people

Sad commentary on religious ignorance

PASTOR AMRESH SEMURATH,
Reformed Evangelical Church.

— TRINIDAD GUARDIAN February 5, 1990

THE EDITOR: As a nation that holds to the principle of freedom of worship, we will be on shaky grounds to argue that the Mormons should never have been allowed in our country. After all, one of the greatest boasts is our religious tolerance and our so-called undefined religious unity.

It is for this reason, I argued against the Senate's rejection of the Menenonite's application for registration.

On the other hand, it is a sad commentary on our religious ignorance and the work being done by religious teachers that a group like the Mormons who have and continue to teach and practice religious apartheid against non-white races can come into this country and plant roots and begin to flourish.

Let me state very clearly that Mormons are not unbelievers in the sense though they profess to believe in Him. Their beliefs are in total contradiction to what the Bible teaches.

Cursed Of Cain

Mormons have always held that non-white races are the cursed, inferior or dark perpetuated human and is a marriage to Egypt, a so-called descendant of Cain.

But they have reserved a special curse for those races with black skins. And as far as they are concerned, people of African descent are at the very bottom of the ladder. Consider the following quotes:

"As a result of his rebellion, Cain was cursed with a black skin," (Apostle Bruce R. McConkie). "A black skin is a mark of the curse of heaven placed upon some portions of mankind." (Juvenile Instructor, Vol 3, p.157)

Joseph Smith said the skins of Indians became 'dark, according to the mark which was set upon their fathers, which was a curse upon them because of their transgression.' (Book of Mormon, Alma 3).

'Inferior Race'

"Not only was Cain called upon to suffer, but because of his wickedness he became the father of an inferior race. A curse was place upon him and that curse has been continued through his lineage and must do so while time endures.

"Millions of souls have come into the world cursed with a black skin and have been denied the privilege of Priesthood and the fullness of the blessings of the Gospel. These are the descendants of Cain. Moreover, they have been made to feel their inferiority and have been separated from the rest of mankind from the beginning," (Joseph Fielding Smith).

In an address entitled "Race Problems — as they affect the Church" Apostle Mark E. Petersen declare: "that Africans, Indians, Japanese and Chinese are all the descendants of Cain and curse. Those who willfully sin with their eyes open to this wrong will not be surprised to find that they will be separated from the presence of God in the world to come. This is spiritual death... It does not matter if they are one-sixth negro or one-hundred and sixth, the curse of no priesthood is still the same... To inter-marry with a negro is to forfeit a 'Nation of Priesthood holders.'"

Penalty Of Death

Brigham Young stated in the journal of Discourses, vol. 10, page 110, "Shall I tell you the law of God in regard to the African race? If the white man who belongs to the chosen seed mixes his blood with the seed of Cain, the penalty, under the law of God, is death on the spot. This will always be so." As a matter of fact, Mormons teach that the drop of non-white blood is enough to disqualify a person from being among the chosen seed.

Okay, Mormons are attempting to change their teachings concerning black-skinned people by misrepresenting what their great prophet Brigham Young said. Young also stated that blacks cannot receive the full blessings and priesthood "until the last of the posterity of Abel had received the priesthood, until the redemption of the earth." By changing the teachings of Young, are Mormons saying that he was a false prophet?

Chosen Seed

In the meantime, Mormon writer, John L. Lund wrote in 1967 (The Church and the negro, pp.54-55) "Brigham Young made a very strong statement on this matter when he said... shall I tell you the law of God in regard to the African race? If the white man who belongs

to the CHOSEN SEED (emphasis his) mixes his blood with the seed of Cain the penalty under the law of God is death on the spot. This will always be so."

"God has commanded Israel not to intermarry. To go against this commandment of God would be to sin. Those who wilfully sin with their eyes open to this wrong will not be surprised to find that they will be separated from the presence of God in the world to come..."

Important Discovery

The second issue concerns the Book of Abraham. I quote from 'former Mormons, Jerald and Sandra Tanner, the latter being a great-great-grand-daughter of Brigham Young.

They wrote, "The Book of Abraham was supposed to have been written on papyrus by Abraham about 4,000 years ago. According to Mormon writers, this same papyrus fell into Joseph Smith's hands in 1835. He translated the papyrus and published it under the title "The Book of Abraham.'

The Book of Abraham was accepted by the Mormon church as Scripture and is now published as part of the "Pearl of Great Price" — one of the four standard works of the church.

If the papyrus were really written by Abraham, as the Mormons claim, its discovery was probably one of the most important finds in the history of the world... Dr Sidney B. Sperry, of Brigham Young University, observed: "If a manuscript were to be found in the sands of Egypt in Egyptian characters with the title of 'The Book of Abraham,' it would cause a sensation in the scholar-

ly world. Our people do profess to have such a scripture containing but five chapters which were written by Abraham..." (Ancient Records, testify in Papyrus and Stone, 1938, p.39).

Lost Papyri

For many years, Joseph Smith's collection of papyri was lost. But on November 27, 1967, the Mormon owned Deseret News announced "their re-discovery. It even declared: "included in the papyri is a manuscript identified as the original document from which Joseph Smith has copied the drawing which he called 'Facsimile No. 1' and published in the Book of Abraham."

While Mormons rejoiced the same Dr Sperry and a Dr Nibley, both Mormon scholars, warned Mormons that trouble was ahead and that the church has been caught flat-footed by this discovery; Joseph Smith was not versed in Egyptology and could not translate the so-called Book of Abraham through scholarly labours.

Smith Discredited

His way our was to falsely claim inspiration to translate. Thorough research, which Mormons cannot dispute, has shown that the Book of Abraham is really the Egyptian "Book of Breathings" which is an outgrowth of the Egyptian "Book of the Dead." They are both high-ly superstitious books supposedly written by the god, Thoth. Joseph Smith has been completely discredited as a fraud.

Furthermore, Mormon President, David O. McKay has stated that the Book of Abraham is their only 'scriptural basis" for their doctrine against non-white races, and particularly those of African descent. It is time for the people of this nation to begin closing the doors of their homes to Mormon missionaries.

Let the Bible speak for itself now. "For you are all sons of God through faith in Jesus Christ. For all of you who were baptised into Christ have clothed yourselves with Christ. There is neither Jew nor Greek, there is neither male nor free man, there is neither male nor female; for you are all one in Christ. And if you belong to Christ, then you are Abraham's offspring, heirs according to promise." (Gal. 3:26-29; see Eph.2: 11-22).

"To him who loves us, and released us from our sins by His blood, and He has made us to be a Kingdom, priests to His God and Father; to Him be the glory and the dominion forever and ever. Amen."

Wednesday, January 17, 1990 7 | The Jamaica Record

MORMONISM: Giving the curse blacks a 'bligh'

By
REV. CLINTON
CHISHOLM

"Shall I tell you the law of God in regard to the African race? If the white man who belongs to the chosen seed mixes his blood with the seed of Cain, the penalty, under the law of God, is death on the spot. This will always be so." The words of Brigham Young, "prophet, seer, revelator" and 2nd president of the Mormon Church (Journal of Discourses, Vol. 10, p.110).

Speaking about the status of blacks and the standing of blacks with reference to the Mormon priesthood, the said Mormon "revelator" declared, "Cain slew his brother...and the Lord put a mark upon him, which is the flat nose and black skin."

Black skin is cursed skin

Brigham Young's views are quite consistent with general Mormon beliefs and with unrevealed Mormon scripture. According to such beliefs and scriptures, the black

In the same Book of Mormon, Alma 3:6, we find the words, "And the skins of the Lamanites were dark, according to the mark which was set upon their fathers, which was a curse upon them because of their transgression...."

Similar anti-black statements can be found in other Mormon scriptures (see in Pearl of Great Price, Book of Moses 7:8 and Book of Abraham 1:21-27).

Now many people have been duped by the so-called revelation from Mormon president Spencer W. Kimball in June, 1978.

Mormons retain racist doctrine

*Advocate Newspaper
May 5, 1985
Barbados*

By Terrence Coppin

THERE are Mormons in the land, and they are causing the occupants considerable concern. In our neighbours' countries too, the Mormons are causing more than a little stir. The leaders are taking counsel together on the subject of the doctrines being propagated by the people who call themselves the Church of Jesus Christ of Latter-day Saints.

In Barbados, the first Mormon baptisms took place in April 1978. Since then the number of local adherents to that strange faith has risen, according to the Mormons themselves, to about 100. They practise their religion in two congregations, in rented premises. They have plans, and the land, to build their own temple.

Last October in an interview, a Mormon spokesman who was in Barbados on a missionary stint from the United States, home of Mormonism, said that there had been no unfavourable response to their presence in Barbados, but they had encountered some problems with obtaining property to put up their building.

There has been a reversal of that situation, for the Latter-day Saints have come under sharply critical scrutiny during 1985, and they are told in unmistakable terms that they are not welcome by many individuals and religious groups.

Barbados has a plethora of religious sects and denominations, and there are so many of them that one old man has put the number in excess of 300. Perhaps there have been that many in his long lifetime. But however great the number, it is an indication of a tolerance among the local populace for whatever the wide world has to offer, and an openness that sustains and at the same time endangers the country as an international tourist destination.

It is in part that unquestioning attitude to the thousands of visitors from North Atlantic countries who pass through this land every year that has allowed the Mormons easy entry. And it is also partly the desire to keep Barbados attractive to all and sundry short-stay sojourners with money to spend here that keeps open the gates of this supposed haven of freedom that is home for the descendants of a people who suffereed the oppression of slavery and racism.

The substance of the unfavourable response to the Mormons, over the past few months, is the widespread claim that the Latter-day Saints organisation is a racist one. Religious leaders have said it, radio journalists have said it; and so too have newspaper columnists. Although I have not heard any of them say it, I suppose politicians have too. During the past week, in the Press, the Mormons have denied the accusation.

The Mormon statement said: "We are not racist. We now do, and always have, accepted people of all races for baptism into the Church as equal candidates for salvation in the Kingdom of God. For a time in our Church, as was true in many Christian churches for much of their history Blacks were not allowed to hold the Holy Priesthood. However, The Church of Jesus Christ of Latter-day Saints never considered this to be a denial of their ultimate ability to enjoy all the blessings of God in His Kingdom.

"One fact often overlooked by these detractors of our faith is that, from the beginning of our Church, members have been taught that at some time Blacks would receive the Priesthood...We repeat: We are not racist. We would not be here today if we were."

The charge that the Mormons are racist derives from at least two aspects of their religious doctrine and practice — their teachings concerning the significance of dark skin, and their exclusion of Blacks from the priesthood. On both counts their statement that they are not racist falls flat. First, let us examine the priesthood issue.

The Mormons themselves say that "Priesthood is the authority to act in the name of God." They also say, since June 1978 only, that all positions in the Mormon Church are open to people with dark skins. At the same time they maintain that the exclusion of dark-skinned people from the priesthood" prior to that date was right, and divinely ordained. There can be no doubt, therefore, that the Mormon position is that some dark-skinned people have been unworthy to act for the god of the Mormons simply because they (the dark-skinned) happen to be the colour of what the Mormon scriptures describe as "a dark and loathsome, and a filthy people, full of idleness and all manner of abominations."

The above estimation of Africans and their descendants, and of American Indians too, is just as much a part of present-day Mormon teaching as it was when articulated during slavery days in the United States by Mormon founder Joseph Smith.

The only way the Latter-day Saints can convince any right-thinking person that such a racist view of dark-skinned people is not theirs is to reject these statements of their "prophet" Smith and other like-minded "prophets" since him. This they are unlikely to do, because their religion is based on the "revelations" that came to these "prophets."

Strange as it may seem, the majority of Barbadians in the Mormon flock are dark-skinned, as I have been led to conclude from a visit to one of their Sunday assemblies. These Barbadian Mormons, like all other Mormons, are required to accept the doctrine that their god brought dark skins into being as a badge of identification for the wicked 'Lamanites' and 'Sons of Cain' and all their descendants. A Barbadian once active in the Mormon church told this to me. He could not long entertain that racist belief, so he ceased to promote the Mormon cause.

But those dark-skinned Mormons who continue in that faith must have some need that is filled by believing that the dark skin is the mark of loathsome wickedness from which they need to be redeemed. This is an unhealthy attitude, and cannot be one that the anti-racist Barbadian community would wish to promote, for it amounts to an inferiority complex among Mormon believers not favoured with the "white" skin.

As long as the Church of Jesus Christ of Latter-day Saints, so called, continues to teach that the colour of a man's skin, whether the man is now dead or alive, is a determinant of that man's goodness or worthiness for any earthly or heavenly privilege, then that church is racist, and should be out of the kingdom of Barbados. The same goes for the god of that Church

MORMON CHURCH

Evening New

No. 10112. Port-of-Spain, Trinidad and Tobago. *Evening News*

Evening News March 13, 19 74

MORMONS STILL

BARRING BLACKS

SALT LAKE CITY, Wed: PRESIDENT Spencer W. Kimball, leader of the world's Mormons, says he does not expect the church to lift its ban on full participation for blacks.

President Kimball became head of the 3.3 million member church of Jesus Christ of Latter-Day Saints on December 31 after the death of Harold B. Lee. His comments came in an interview broadcast yesterday on the NBC "today" show.

The church gives its priesthood to all faithful male members 12 years or older unless they are of black, African descent. The church says only that this is God's will.

Despite the controversy the policy caused, church presidents over the years have stood behind it in the absence of any revelation it should be changed.

The church leader was asked whether he had prayed about the issue. "Yes, indeed, and about every important issue of the church," he replied.

Asked whether he anticipated a change, he said, "No," I do not anticipate it. If it should be done, the Lord will reveal it and we believe in revelation.

"And we believe the leader of the church is entitled to that revelation and that it would come if it's necessary and it's proper."

President Kimball said he was concerned about charges of bigotry against the church.

"We know there are many honest people who have honest opin...

Which One Is Doing The 'Hustle'?

PORTLAND, ORE: Morman high priest Douglas A. Wallace violated a century-old taboo of the Church of Jesus Christ, Latter Day Saints, when he baptized and confirmed Larry Lester, a Vancouver, Wash., Black, as the first Black in more than 100 years as a priest of the church. Officials at church headquarters in Salt Lake City, Utah, declared the ordination "null and void." Mormons don't allow Blacks to rise to the priesthood.

Mormons Oust First Indian in the Hierarchy

SALT LAKE CITY, Sept. 2 (AP) — The Mormon Church has excommunicated the only American Indian who ever achieved a leading position in its hierarchy.

The excommunication of the church official, Elder George P. Lee, a 46-year-old Navajo, was announced Friday in a one-paragraph statement. It followed his assertion that Mormon leaders were racist and that the church's president was too feeble to make decisions.

The excommunication is the first in 46 years imposed against a Mormon general authority, one of 85 men who administer the Church of Jesus Christ of Latter-day Saints.

The church's statement said Mr. Lee had been expelled for "apostasy and other conduct unbecoming a member of the church." A church spokesman, Don LeFevre, said he would not elaborate on the statement.

'Them or Jesus Christ'

In an interview, Mr. Lee said the action was based on basic doctrinal disagreements with church leaders about the role of Indians in the religion and from his contention that the leadership was racist, materialistic and bent on changing the meaning of Mormon scripture.

"It got to the point where I had to fol-

low them or Jesus Christ," he said, "and I chose to follow Jesus Christ. I told them they are the ones that are apostatizing — teaching false doctrine."

Mr. Lee was made a member of the First Quorum of the Seventy in 1975. It is a leadership group responsible for administering the affairs of the 6.7-million-member church under the direction of the Council of the Twelve Apostles and the church presidency, which is made up of the president and his two counselors.

Members of the leadership are known as general authorities.

In an hourlong meeting on Friday

with Ezra Taft Benson, the 90-year-old president of the church, Mr. Benson's two counselors and the 12-member quorum, Mr. Lee read a 23-page, handwritten letter in which he accused fellow churchmen of distorting doctrine to satisfy their racial bias, relegating Indians to second-class status and denying them their rightful place in the faith's theology.

Prophesies Are Clear, He Says

"While physical extermination may have been one of the Federal Government's policies long ago, your current scriptural and spiritual extermination is the greater sin," Mr. Lee wrote, "and great shall be your condemnation for this."

The church says American Indians are the descendants of ancient peoples described in the Book of Mormon, pub-

32 News ★ Your briefing on · church activities

Sunday Sun News paper Barbados 1985

Sunday Sun, April 21, 1985

1985

Mormonism: A racist religion

by Jeff Grisamore

RACISM AGAINST black people has characterised the history of the Church of Jesus Christ of Latter-day Saints, or Mormons. The founder of the Mormon church, Joseph Smith, said "Had anything to do with the negro, I would confine them by strict law to their own species."

Joseph Smith's apartheid views led early Mormon leaders to support slavery.

Joseph Smith, in 1838 when asked, "Are the Mormons Abolitionists?" He replied, "No . . . we do not believe in setting the Negroes free."

Smith's successor as Mormon president and prophet, Brigham Young, said "You must not think from what I say, that I am opposed to slavery. No! The negro is damned and is to serve his master." Young described slavery as a "divine institution."

Racial prejudice and support of slavery by the Mormon founders was accompanied by strong anti-black teaching in the Mormon church. The Mormon position on Blacks was clearly stated in a letter written by the First Presidency on July 17, 1947: "From the days of the Prophet Joseph even until now, it has been the doctrine of the Church, never questioned by any of the Church leaders, that the Negroes

are not entitled to the full bless- ings of the Gospel.

Mormon Apostle Bruce Mc- Conkie wrote that "Negroes are not equal with other races . . ."

Former Mormon President, Joseph Fielding Smith, called black people "an inferior race." he called their black skin a race. Taylor maintains, is the "black covering, emblematic of eternal darkness."

"Black skin is a mark of the curse of heaven placed upon some portions of mankind," ac- cording to Mormons. Brigham Young taught that, "Cain slew his brother . . . (Abel) and the Lord put a mark upon him, which is the flat nose and black skin . . . that curse will remain upon them.

The Bible does record God's curse on Cain for killing Abel in Genesis 4:3-11, but no mention is made of the curse being a flat nose and black skin.

After the flood, described in Genesis 6, destroyed mankind Cain, Moreover, they have been made to feel their inferiority and have been separated from the rest of mankind from the begin- ning:

"Inter-racial marriage has been strictly forbidden in the Mormon church. Brigham Young taught that the penalty of Mormons marrying negroes was "death on the spot." Mormons believed that "one drop of Negro blood" dis- qualified people from the Mor-

upon Cain was continued through Ham's wife, as he had married a wife of that (black) seed. And why did it pass through the flood? Because it was necessary that the devil should have a representation upon the earth . . ." The negro answer. We must not inter- marry with the Negro. If I were to marry a Negro woman and have children by her, my children would all be cursed as to the priesthood. If there is one drop of Negro blood in my children, as I have read to you.

Because of the alleged curse of God on black people, the Mormon Church has historically denied them the right to join the Mormon priesthood. Apostle McConkie stated, "Negroes in this life are denied the priesthood; under no circumstances can they hold this delegation of authority from the Almighty."

Mormon president Joseph Fielding Smith wrote that "Millions of souls have come into this world cursed with a black skin and have been denied the privilege of Priesthood . . . These are the descendants of Cain . . . every faithful, worthy man in the Church may receive the holy priesthood; without regard for race or colour."

After 148 years of banning black people from their all-white priesthood in 1978 amidst in- creasing social pressure, the Mormon Church made a change. present Mormon Prophet, Spencer W. Kimball, said the card "has heard our prayers and by revelation has confirmed that . . . every faithful, worthy man in the Church may receive the holy priesthood; without regard for race or colour."

In claiming a new revelation from God, Mormons avoid blame for their previous racist teachings and make God out to be the racist. They contended that until 1978 the Law of God

mon priesthood.

Mormon Apostle Mark E. Petersen, now second-in-line to be Mormons God has heard their prayers and changed his mind about negroes. In so doing they place the responsibility of their racism on God to avoid the guilt and embarrassment of their 148-year old anti-black doctrine.

The Mormon explanation of the curse on blacks, and the resulting consequences of black inferiority, has not been changed or renounced. Mormons seek to deny and cover up their pre- judice history. The documented evidence clearly reveals that Mormonism is a historically racist religion.

References

1 — Joseph Smith in *History of the Church*, vol. 5; p. 218.

2 — Ibid. vol. 3; p. 29.

3 — Brigham Young quoted in *The New York Herald* newspaper of May 4, 1855 cited in *Dialogue* magazine, Spring 1973, p. 56.

4 — Brigham Young quoted in *History of Utah*, A.L. Neff. Recorded interview between Abolitionist Horace Greeley and Brigham Young at Salt Lake City on July 13, 1859, p. 618.

5 — Letter from the First Presidency, quoted in *Mormonism and the Negro*, by John J.

Memo from a Mormon:
In which a troubled young man
raises the question of his Church's
attitude toward Negroes

LOOK MAGAZINE October 22nd 1963 Newly out, USA

WITH THE POLITICAL rise of Gov. George Romney of Michigan, a Mormon, and the thrust of the Mormon Church into the urban life of our nation, the position of the Negro in the Mormon Church is gaining new attention. There has been a good deal of confusion surrounding this question for some time. Non-Mormons have been confused. As a life-long Mormon, I have been, too.

The Mormon Church taught me that the Negro was not equal to the white in terms of religious rights and opportunity, that the Negro was cursed with loss of God's priesthood and the evidence, or mark, of this curse was his dark skin. Consequently, the Negro could not hold the priesthood in the Mormon Church and was thus unequal to the white in a very important sense. But the reasons for this doctrine, and the scriptural evidence behind it, has always seemed unconvincing to me.

Post *Washington Post newspaper* M 2 WEDNESDAY, JUNE 11, 1997, C9

ASKETBALL

1997   USA

MICHAEL WILBON

Rodman Is the Bulls' Problem

SALT LAKE CITY A team can always tolerate Dennis Rodman when his production is greater than his disruption. He can be late for practice and games, he can pick up technical fouls with foul behavior, he can act like a complete fool if he grabs 19 rebounds and makes the other team crazy.

But since he's not hitting the boards, since he's not playing particularly inspired defense, and since he's now firing up stupid three-pointers, while proving himself incapable of making a simple layup, there's only one thing for the Chicago Bulls to do with Dennis Rodman: Bench him for Game 5, and perhaps beyond.

He's useless now. Maybe his knee is hurt worse than he's let on. More likely, at age 36, he has too much mileage from playing and living the way he has. Regardless, seven rebounds per game, which is what he's averaging in the NBA Finals, isn't enough to put up with all Rodman's wacked out behavior, his two trips to Las Vegas.

Here's the big difference between Michael Jordan driving to Atlantic City with his father for a little gambling after going down 0-2 to the Knicks in 1993 and Rodman's excursion flights to Vegas Sunday night and again Monday afternoon: Rodman isn't Jordan.

Rodman might have been the real MVP of the Finals last year, but we've seen enough this postseason to know that Rodman is about done as a legitimate basketball player. He won't go outside to guard Greg Foster because he's selfishly looking to

in, Phil can't beat his head in . . . It's frustrating when you can't get to him. But I'm past that frustration."

So Jackson ought to consider sitting Rodman now, or risk waving bye-bye to a fifth title.

(I should point out my view on Rodman has nothing to do with the insult he directed at Mormons on Saturday, which the Anti-Defamation League has criticized. What Rodman said was ugly and uncalled for. But so is something else.

In the Book of Mormon: Another Testament of Jesus Christ, 2 Nephi 5:21-24, as a black man I was rather distressed to find: "Wherefore as they were white and exceedingly fair and delightsome, that they might not be enticing unto my people the Lord God did cause a skin of blackness to come upon them . . . And thus saith the Lord God: I will cause that they shall be loathsome unto thy people, save they shall repent their iniquities . . . And cursed shall be the seed of him that mixeth with their seed . . . And because of their cursing . . . they did become an idle people, full of mischief and subtlety . . . And the Lord God said unto me: They shall be a scourge . . . they shall scourge them even into destruction . . .

Now, let me say that everybody I've encountered in several trips to Utah, Mormon or not, has been as friendly and hospitable as you could possibly expect, sometimes beyond the call of duty. I've met plenty of Mormons, including men such as Jazz owner Larry Miller and 49ers quarterback Steve Young who are more racially tolerant and progressive than

the Bulls, who've won four championships in six years, are completely uncomfortable with this new concept of being played dead-even so deep into the playoffs.

"It's been pretty devastating," Scottie Pippen said. "We're not playing the kind of basketball we need to play to survive this series."

And Pippen is not alone in his assessment. Usually upbeat reserve Jud Buechler said before Tuesday's practice, "Everyone in this organization is on edge."

There simply hasn't been this much doubt surrounding a Jordan-led Bulls team since 1990.

Even Jordan, who was quick to assert he's still confident about winning the series, talked very seriously about the need for his team to show up Wednesday for Game 5, "Refocused, reenergized, with more purpose, redefined, fire rekindled . . . We have to go practice and find a way to get our game back. Sure, there's a sense of urgency. We haven't been in this situation for a long time. Maybe this is exactly what we need for some people to elevate their attitudes. This is the time you better search within yourself."

The talk is serious because the Bulls are in a predicament they've not experienced. Yes, they lost two games in Seattle last year but only after winning Game 3 there to take a 3-0 lead. But here, the Bulls have no illusions about being in control, even with Games 6 and 7 scheduled for Chicago on Friday and Sunday. They lose so seldom

Religion

Time Magazine August 7, 1978

Mormonism Enters a New Era

But America's biggest native faith remains a kingdom apart

It was July 24, 1847 when Pioneer Brigham Young gazed down at the desolate Salt Lake Valley and declared: "This is the place." His Latter-day Saints, hounded out of three states, had found their homestead. Last week in Salt Lake City, 200,000 people celebrated the Pioneer Day legend with a mammoth parade. At the head of the procession was Brigham Young's latest successor, Spencer Woolley Kimball, 83, president of the Church of Jesus Christ of Latter-day Saints. Behind him were brass bands, floats, fiddlers, and such lesser dignitaries as Scott M. Matheson, the Governor of Utah.

Just as the Saints once made the desert bloom through honeybee-like enterprise, so have they made their church into the biggest, richest, strongest faith ever born on U.S. soil. It has grown fourfold since World War II to 4 million members, including 1 million outside the U.S. Church income is rumored to exceed $1 billion a year, though Kimball insists it is "much less than that."

Despite Mormonism's obvious success and the comforting image evoked by Donny and Marie or the Tabernacle Choir, outsiders (known as Gentiles) still find something disturbing about the faith. Though Mormons are no longer as isolated as they once were in Young's mountain kingdom, they nonetheless seem to exist behind an invisible barrier. Once a Mormon temple is consecrated, no outsider may enter to see the secret rites or oxen-borne baptistries. Ecumenical entanglements with conventional Christian groups are forbidden. The Mormon religion, with its modern-day prophets and scriptures, can seem odd indeed to nonbelievers.

The most offensive tenet vanished in June in a "revelation" promulgated by Kimball, who is regarded as God's unique "Prophet, Seer and Revelator." Henceforth, headquarters announced, "all worthy males" may enter the priesthood, a lay office normally attained by all young men in the clergyless church. Previously the Mormons had denied the office to "Africans." The change will give blacks celestial benefits. Priests can "seal" their marriages for eternity in the temple. This, in turn, means they can aspire to the highest level in the multitiered Mormon heaven after they die. Thus Phone Repairman Joseph Freeman, 25, who became the first known black in the priesthood in the 20th century, was able to seal his marriage. Several dozen U.S. blacks are expected to follow Freeman's example.

Kimball's revelation freed the faith from a gnawing problem. Missionaries faced constant questions about Mormon racism. "Church young people were mortified," says University of Utah Historian Brigham Madsen. "They would not put up with it any longer." The N.A.A.C.P. went to court to end bias in Mormon Boy Scout troops. A dissident member even dared picket the 28-story headquarters building that dominates the Salt Lake City skyline. The revelation also solved the dilemma of who is eligible to use the new temple in racially mixed Brazil.

How did the word come? By one account, 13 Apostles (top leaders) experi-

Costumed girls at Nauvoo, Ill., ceremonies
Women priests? "Impossible."

Photographs by David Burnett—Contact

BomB
February 10
1984
Trinidad

Bomb views

Security
Minister
John
Donaldson

Bomb 10 Feb 84

BLOWS
AS WHITE PREACHER ATTAC[KS]
BLACK PREACHER

YET ANOTHER Open Bible-styled holy war is raging in the country.

This time it involves the largest of the small-time churches, the New Testament Church of God, which has over 50 church buildings and 70 congregations.

At the core of the problem are three "expatriate preachers" who came on a Caribbean holiday four years ago and have refused to go back to their native United States.

The white Americans have occupied a posh residential property at Lange Park, Chaguanas, which is paid for by locals and have hijacked the coffers of the church, a disgruntled churchman said.

Over the coming days, followers of the New Testament Church of God will be collecting signatures to petition Minister of National Security, John Donaldson to deport Reverend Robert Clagg, his wife, Reverend Georgina and their sidekick Reverend Raymond Shockley.

Rev Chunilal Peach.. alleges that he was beaten and humiliated by three American preachers

was shocked at the treatment he got from the people who came here as overseers to the church.

He said Rev. Robert Clagg held on to him and said "You f... ing nigger; you zombie; you uncivilised man. What do you know about religion? What can you teach me? Get out of here."

Neighbours had to shut their doors and send their kids to bed when the preaching tourists started their bacchanal. Rev Peach has reported the matter to the Chaguanas Police and he said damage to his vehicle was $5,000.

The Police told the BOMB they are investigating the case.

Reports coming from the church said the Claggs operate a travel agency and get gifts and an allowance from the Church in Trinidad, all contrary to the special work permit granted them.

Barataria church.

Black Sellers, American preacher was debarred by the Claggs from preaching here as a guest of the New Testament Church of God in Montrose.

Local ministers said Rev Sellers is a better preacher than the Claggs, but as he was black he had to be kept out.

A well-respected minister that the church is will com- dirty line cupboard Today on Nat Minister to revo permits o Shockley out of her sundown.

Whites only church relaxes race rules

CAPE TOWN, Tuesday (Reuter) — South Africa's powerful whites only Dutch Reformed Church voted today to open membership to all races.

But the synod of the Nederduitse Gereformeede Kerk (NGK) retained the current structure which provides separate churches for different race groups, although permitting non-whites to apply for membership of the 'mother' church.

The NGK has been under increasing pressure from reformed churches abroad and mixed race worshippers in a rebellious 'daughter' church to relax its strict whites only rule.

Professor Pieter Potgieter, of the theological faculty of Bloemfontein University, said when yesterday's debate on apartheid resumed today that the decision meant people of all races would now be welcome.

"We are saying that the NKG does not want and will not tolerate race discrimination," he said.

The church, whose worshippers include most cabinet ministers, has traditionally reflected the views of the National Party which has ruled South Africa since 1948.

Yesterday the synod took a middle line in nationalist political terms, rejecting liberal and hardline amendments alike.

Page 2 TRINIDAD GUARDIAN, Thursday, January 17, 1980

1980

200 people walk out of church

JOHANNESBURG, Wed:
A MIXED congregation of nearly 200 people walked out of a suburban Johannesburg church this week when the minister refused to hold a funeral service because there were blacks and Indians present.

An impromptu service led by the undertaker was then held at the graveside.

The widow of a white factory worker, Mrs. Robina Smith, said the minister at the NHK Dutch Reformed Church had stormed in and abruptly demanded that the 100 or so blacks and Indians present must leave.

"Something exploded inside me and I left the church in protest and my three sons and everyone else followed," she said, adding: "We told this unmannered and inhumane minister that the blacks and Indians were most definitely going to stay."

Most of the people present were fellow workers of her husband.

A spokesman for the NHK, one of three branches of the Dutch Reformed Church, said it was the church's policy that different race groups attended different services and it was exceptional for a person of one colour to attend a service held for people of another colour. The Dutch Reformed Church is South Africa's largest white religious group. (Cana-Reuter)

RACE

By REV. HAROLD SITAHAL
(Moderator of the Synod of the Presbyterian Churches in Trinidad and Grenada).

THE DRAMATIC intrusion of the non-white members of the Dutch Reformed Chu of Sou Africa immied ely before the beginning of the opening Communion Service of the 21st General Council of the World Alliance of Reformed Churches in Ottawa from August 17 to 27 set the tone or flavour of the meeting.

The central and burning issue was going to be the question of apartheid (or separate development as the white South Africans euphemistically referred to apartheid.'')

At the opening Communion Service at which 300 or more people were present, a statement was read from the pulpit by one of the black South African delegates (an East Indian Pastor of the Indian section of the Dutch Reformed Church of South Africa)

The statement affirmed that the black South African participants at the General Council meeting were not going to participate in the Sacrament with the rest of the congregation of delegates and visitors from many parts of the world.

WISEST METHOD

The reason given was that there were also sitting in, and about to participate in the Sacrament, members of the white Dutch Reformed Church of South Africa.

The act of non-participation on the part of the black South Africans was in protest to the reality which obtained in South Africa where members of the Dutch Reformed Church of South Africa who were non-white (both African and East Indian as well as coloured) were not allowed by decree of the white church to participate in the Lord's Supper with white members.

REV. HAROLD SITAHAL
...attended meeting.

The white members of the Dutch Reformed Church of South Africa defended the State policy of apartheid claiming that it was the wisest method to adopt in the development process of their multi-racial society.

One of the white theologians of the white Dutch Reformed Church insisted that his Church was against racism. Yet, he pointed out that in any situation where different races lived together in any country, as they do in South Africa, one

In fact non-whites are to this day prevented from worshipping or sharing in the Lord's Supper in white Dutch Reformed Churches in South Africa, except by special invitation.

Many whites and other members of Reformed Churches in other parts of the world, including North American and Europe, also abstained, in support of the black group of South African representatives.

Later on, during the proceedings of the General Council, the white South African representatives insisted that it was the wrong way to deal with the issue.

DOMINATES CANADA CHURCH

TRINIDAD GUARDIAN, September 23, 1983

the social, economical and political, as well as cultural and religious problems of South Africa.

The result of this kind of defence by the white South African Church is that the Dutch Reformed Church of South Africa is divided into four racially diverse communions.

One for the white members and three other divisions for the native Africans, coloured and East Indians, respectively.

SAME TIME

The pastors and members of the black churches can attend any black church, but not the white church. The white members are free to attend any church.

White Pastors, however, who have opted to serve in black churches exclusively, in defiance of the policy of separation of the white church, are defrocked and denied their ordination privileges in the white churches.

Two such pastors were present at the General Council meeting.

But, one might ask, what is so unique about the General Council of the World Alliance of Reformed Churches and its predominantly coloured South African churchman, Dr. Allan Boesak, directed a concerted attack on the White Church and State policy of South Africa, namely, apartheid or separate development.

The significance of the W.A.R.C. issuing its own word lies in the fact that the Dutch Reformed Churches in South Africa which, at the same time, are closely associated with the South African white minority Government, hold and have cherished membership in the World Alliance of Reformed Churches.

At the same time, the non-white Reformed Churches in South Africa also hold membership in this body. So at the General Meeting in Ottawa, the discriminated-against black, East Indian and coloured Churches, as well as the discriminating white churches, were both represented.

Fed by the anger, hurt and pain of being the objects of discrimination by...

occupation with the question of apartheid in South Africa? Haven't other bodies leveled attacks on the system?

It was pointed out among other things that, "separate development" involved such programme as the "homeland" policy of the white minority South African Government.

YOUNG PEOPLE

The "homeland" programme involved the uprooting of native Africans and resetting them in often undesirable, low-productivity exclusively non-white areas where there are little or no industries. Young and old are included in this inhuman programme.

It is also well-known that black young people in South Africa who protested against inferior separate schooling have been persecuted.

Both white church and Government, the Black and East Indian brothers led by a prominent coloured South African churchman, Dr. Allan Boesak, directed a concerted attack on the White Church and State policy of South Africa, namely, apartheid or separate development.

It became evident to the General meeting in Ottawa that the time had come for meaningful action on one of its member Churches which was obviously defending, sometimes on theological grounds, the practice of apartheid.

Thus two very meaningful and definite actions were taken which meant a serious blow to apartheid.

The first was that the white Dutch Reformed Churches of South Africa were, by majority vote, suspended from the privileges of memberships in the World Alliance of Reformed Churches, until such time as they renounced the state policy of apartheid and took positive steps to have it eradicated.

The White South African members responded in consternation claiming that this was un-Christian.

The other decisive act by the Council was the election of Dr. Boesak, a coloured South African and Pastor of the coloured Dutch Reformed Church of South Africa as Chairman of the General Council of the World Alliance of Reformed Churches.

OVERSEAS

Dispute on apartheid threatens to split church in South Africa

THE TIMES SATURDAY MAY 10 1980

From Nicholas Ashford
Cape Town, May 9 *1980*

An unseemly squabble has developed within the Dutch Reformed Church, one of the pillars of white rule in South Africa, which not only threatens to jeopardize the church's position at two forthcoming international conferences in Britain and France, but also could result in a split in the church itself.

The dispute is about the church's support for apartheid policies and is between the white Dutch Reformed church, on the one hand and its Coloured (mixed race), black and Indian daughter churches.

The three daughter churches, which between them have well over one million adherents, have followed for years a line of unquestioning obedience to the white mother church, despite its attempts to provide biblical justification for apartheid.

Recently, however, a growing number of Coloured, black and Indian clergy have been openly questioning their churches' association with a church which practises racial discrimination against them.

"I believe that we must break links with the white Dutch Reformed church" says Dr Allan Boesak, a prominent Coloured theologian and chaplain at the (Coloured) University of the Western Cape. "We are confronted by an absolutely fundamental theological problem. How can we remain associated with a church that not only practises apartheid but argues that it can be justified by the bible?"

ernment's shift in attitude towards the Acts.

At the end of the meeting a cautious compromise statement was issued saying that the churches would have no objection in principle should the Government reconsider the Mixed Marriages and Immorality Acts. It was also agreed that none of the four churches would elaborate to the press.

However, within hours of the meeting Dr E. P. Kleynhans, the Moderator of the white Dutch Reformed Church, gave a radio interview contradicting the joint statement. This angered the daughter churches. The Coloured and Indian churches demanded that the Moderature (the executive church council) of the white church should publicly reprimand Dr Kleynhans.

The Coloured and Indian churches were to have taken part in a joint church delegation which is to attend talks with the United Presbyterian Church of America in London next month and then the Reformed Ecumenical Synod in France in July. The Reverend E. J. Manikkam, the head of the Indian Church, has withdrawn. "For 30 years the white Dutch Reformed Church has played with apartheid," he says. "Now they must state where they really stand."

The Coloured church has agreed to remain in the delegation after being told of plans to hold a new meeting of the four churches later this year to reconsider the Mixed Marriages and Immorality Acts.

This decision, however, has led to a split within the Coloured church between the church's white Moderator, the

A black mirror to the white church in South Africa

A COLOURED South African minister, a man without vote or privilege in the apartheid state, has been elected president of the World Alliance of Reformed Churches — which makes him spiritual father of Prime Minister P.W. Botha.

And along with the election of Dr Alan Boesak late last year, the alliance delivered an even more bitter blow to Afrikanerdom by declaring apartheid a heresy and suspending the white Dutch Reformed Church of South Africa from membership "until such time as they repent."

The irony of the election of Boesak, says the Bishop of Johannesburg, Dr Desmond Tutu, proves that God has a sense of humour. But it underlines the deep divide in South African society. Apartheid even splits the official church.

"It is not simply a political philosophy but pseudo-religious ideology," Boesak says. For the past 100 years the Dutch Reformed Church has been divided racially, with separate churches for blacks, coloureds and Indians dominated by the white "mother" church.

"I have never in my whole life been allowed to preach in a white Dutch Reformed Church," Boesak said in a British television interview. "I cannot go to a white Dutch Reformed church without express permission of the local church council — and then only on special occasions."

Many commentators saw Boesak's election by the alliance as a humiliation of the official South African church. Boesak, however, has a forthright answer. "If a church wants to identify itself with the breaking up of family life, which in South Africa is caused by design, by law — if a church wants to align with a law that says people who are different colours, white or black, cannot marry although they love one another, and though the church says love is born' of God — if a church wants to align with a government that would mercilessly shoot down children in the streets because they dare to protest for the sake of a better future — if the rejection of those policies is seen as a humiliation of the church, then I would say let them go through that humiliation."

Naude broke away from the Dutch Reformed Church. As a key member of the Afrikaner establishment, his questioning of the biblical justification. of apartheid rocked the church to its foundations.

Naude established the Christian Institute and, together with the SA Council of Churches, set up a project on Christianity in apartheid society to examine South African life and how to develop a new and acceptable social order.

But to Afrikanerdom, Naude was a traitor. The Christian Institute was outlawed and he was banned. Indicative of the government's vindictiveness towards him was the recent extension of his banning order for another three years, a restriction that will last until he is 70. As Boesak says, if Naude were freed now, at this time of turmoil and self-doubt, he would have more influence on young Afrikaners than the Prime Minister.

The other major development which heightened church-state conflict has been the emergence in the 1970s of radical black churchmen. Alan Boesak was one. Like so many of his race, he grew up in poverty, with first hand experience of the cruelties of the apartheid system.

As an embittered student Boesak met Naude. "By his lifestyle he drew me very close to him. I learned to love the man, and he was one of the people, who brought a new kind of reality to my life." It was Naude who persuaded Boesak to fight to liberate his church from the bondage of the white church.

Another person to emerge was Bishop Desmond Tutu, president of the South African Council of Churches (SACC). Tutu, like Naude, has been restricted by the government. Under his leadership the SACC has dispensed millions of dollars to defend anti-apartheid activists on trial and care for the families of political prisoners. Now the council has become the target of state action with a commission of inquiry — or political inquisition — appointed to probe its affairs.

Tutu has unashamedly espoused liberation theology.

The Church and Aparthei

By Betty Ann Bowen

I WAS quite astonished and disappointed to have visited the displays of various countries organised by the International Women's Day of Prayer here in Jamaica, and to see that there were two separate booths on South Africa; one manned by a black South African and essentially depicting, through magazines and booklets, the plight and the suffering of the oppressed masses, while the other, manned by a white South African, had prominently posted on the wall a message that read, "Come to South Africa, it is great!"

We here in Jamaica must be careful that we don't become complacent about the South African issue, for the strugggle is far from over, and in fact is perhaps in its most difficult stage. In particular, we have to be vigilant in the way we allow South Africans to visit our country, and even when it involves the Church, we must check out the facts carefully.

While many South African churches have come a long way in the struggle against apartheid, the majority of white church members still hold firm to the belief of the inferiority of the Black Man, and deeply support the Calvinist views of the dominant Dutch Reformed Church.

Afrikaners see themselves as true to their faith in promulgating and perpetuating apartheid. The Bible's authority is constantly invoked to authorize land expropriation and white social and economic ascendence. One passage they often quote, Psalm 105 instructs. "...He brought forth his people with joy and His chosen with gladness: and gave them the lands of the heathen: and they inherited the labour of the people. Segregation and discrimination find their justification in advice given to the Corinthians which reads: "be ye not unequally yoked together with the unbelievers: for what fellowship hath righteouness with unrighteouness? Wherefore come out from among them and be ye separate saith the Lord, and touch not the unclean thing and I will receive you."

Afrikaners see themselves apartheid, their state, as well as their acts as part of the fulfilmen of a divine scheme. To them God is the architect of all history and imbues it with ultimate meaning. The Afrikaners' settlement in South Africa was divinely ordained an their history of survival and triumph a miracle. D.F. Malan, th principal helmsman of apartheid who became Prime Minister when the Afrikaner National Party came to power in 1948, spoke for Afrika nerdom when he observed:

Afrikaner Minister Tells of His Long Road of Conversion From Apartheid

By ALAN COWELL
Special to The New York Times

THE NEW YORK TIMES, SUNDAY, NOVEMBER 10, 1985

The Rev. Nico Smith with a group of handicapped children outside his church in Mamelodi, South Africa.

The New York Times/Mark Peters

MAMELODI, South Africa — He was 4 years old, the Rev. Nico Smith said, when he learned his first lesson of apartheid: You talk to blacks, his mother told him, only when you have an order to give to them, a command to impart.

The lesson, he says now with a rueful smile, seemed to take root and blossom.

When the Afrikaner National Party came to power in 1948 on a platform of racial separation, he recalls with the same smile, he rejoiced.

He studied in Pretoria and joined the Dutch Reformed Church, which found scriptural justification for apartheid. He was called into the ranks of the secretive and powerful Afrikaner fellowship called the Broederbond. He became a professor in the theology department at the University of Stellenbosch in the Cape, a cradle of Afrikanerdom. In terms of the orthodoxy of his forebears, he had arrived.

Ordained in Black Church

These days, he seems to have arrived somewhere else completely. He has withdrawn from the Broederbond and resigned his professorship to be ordained in the black "daughter" branch of the Dutch Reformed Church that apartheid theology created for black worship.

"During his childhood, he said, "blacks were not considered as people — they were just implements — an attitude which I believe was strengthened by the policy of separate development.

The building of more and more segregated townships and the removal of blacks to so-called tribal homelands were "very convenient for white people."

Verdict on apartheid

THE system of apartheid by which South Africa was governed for more than three decades has been finally exposed in all its bloody and coercive ruthlessness by the findings of the Truth and Reconciliation Commission which handed in its final report to President Nelson Mandela last Thursday. Although the horrors of the racial separation policies of the South African government became generally known to the outside world, the Commission's report still makes surprising, even shocking, reading for the sheer viciousness of the white-supremacist regime and the extent to which it was supported by the supposedly independent institutions of the country.

The Commission, headed by Rev Desdmond Tutu, was set up by President Mandela in July 1995 and has fulfilled its mandate by producing a comprehensive and indepth study of apartheid, a system of government that is considered one of the great evils of the twentieth century. The integrity of the report is unquestioned as it exposes the brutality of both the State and its opponents, including Madikizela Mandela's so-called Football Club and the African National Congress with the same uncompromising impartiality.

For this newspaper, the most depressing findings of the report is the abject failure of the South African media, its judges and the Christian Church to oppose and condemn the systematic human rights abuses being committed by those in power. The mainstream English language media adopted a policy of appeasement towards the state, largely censoring itself, while the Christian church "promoted the ideology of apartheid in a range of different ways that included Biblical and theological teaching".

The Commission rightly rejected the argument of judges that they were impotent in the face of the exercise of legislative powers by a sovereign parliament. The commissioners noted: "Parliamentary sovereignty and the rule of law work hand in hand and are premised on a political system which is fundamentally representative of the people subject to that parliament. This situation never applied to South Africa."

In any case, the judges had a choice. A concerted stand by a significant number of them "could have moved the government formally to curtail the jurisdiction of the courts thereby laying bare the degeneracy of its policies more devastatingly". For those who continue to regard Madikizela Mandela as some kind of heroine, and there are many in Trinidad and Tobago who still do, the findings of the report will be chastening indeed. The committee found that the Mandela United Football Club was really a private vigilante unit engaged in acts of murder, torture, assault and arson against its critics who were capriciously branded as informers. The Committee found that Madikizela Mandela herself was responsible for committing such gross violations of human rights. The commissioners also found former President PW Botha, who presided over the racist regime for several years, accountable for gross violations of human rights, including

PRESBYTERIAN CHURCH
PHYLON

THE ATLANTA UNIVERSITY, *Georgia USA*

Review of

RACE AND CULTURE *December 1979*

| VOLUME XL | CONTENTS | NUMBER 4 |

By JULIA KIRK BLACKWELDER

Southern White Fundamentalists and the Civil Rights Movement

WITHIN MONTHS after the *Brown versus Board of Education* decision in 1954, *Christian Life*, a widely circulated evangelical publication, reported that "Since the Supreme Court's verdict against racial segregation in schools, America's churches have realized that the thorny problem of discrimination cannot be avoided."[1] The *Brown* ruling did trigger extensive and divisive discussions of racial issues within many Protestant denominations, but the smaller Protestant sects passed through the years of the civil rights revolution with little dissension or disharmony. Within the South, predominantly white denominations whose membership was heavily but not exclusively fundamentalist were deeply divided on racial issues beginning in the 1950s. Smaller and wholly fundamentalist sects felt the impact of the civil rights movement later and much less intensely.

During the 1950s the Southern Presbyterian Church faced a critical struggle over denominational desegregation with fundamentalists leading the segregationist forces. In contrast, two largely white fundamentalist sects, the Church of God, headquartered in Cleveland, Tennessee, and the Assemblies of God with central offices in Springfield, Missouri, did not confront racial issues until the 1960s, and the absence of a vocal desegregationist element among them was matched by an absence of segregationist rhetoric. Among Presbyterians the controversy over church desegregation spread to the larger issues of the civil rights movement while Southern fundamentalist sects rarely addressed secular civil rights questions.

The 1954 General Assembly of the Southern Presbyterian Church adopted a resolution that all racial divisions within the Church should be abolished and touched off more than a decade of infighting over racial issues. Coming on the heels of the Supreme Court's verdict on segregated schools, the Assembly's mandate encouraged segregationist Presbyterians to mount a single campaign on the issues of church and school. During the years of racial controversy some white congregations voted to dissociate themselves from the Church, but a larger number chose to remain within it while resisting denominational pressures for desegregation.

During the 1950s the *Southern Presbyterian Journal* became a forum for resistance to desegregation. *Southern Presbyterian Journal* was founded in the 1940s to promote fundamentalist theology within the

[1] *Christian Life*, XVI (December, 1954), 36.

Southern Presbyterian Church and to protest the Church's membership in the National Council of Churches. Journal founder L. Nelson Bell maintained that Christians might in good conscience refuse to comply with desegregation, writing that although some Christians accepted integration "There are others — and they are as Christian in their thinking and practice as any in this world — who believe that it is un-Christian, unrealistic and utterly foolish to *force* those barriers of race which have been established by God and which when destroyed by man are destroyed to his own loss."[2]

Bell's rationale for considering segregation nondiscriminatory, and his basis for claims that he was not a segregationist, was a narrow distinction he drew between "forced" segregation and "forced" integration which he opposed and "voluntary" segregation and integration which he supported. In attacking "forced" segregation Bell wrote, "To abolish laws which discriminate against any citizen is something which we believe Christians should work for."[3] He related an incident in which four blacks were required to eat behind a partition in an Atlanta airport restaurant in compliance to Georgia segregation laws. The episode was presented in illustration of involuntary segregation, but voluntary segregation was neither illustrated nor clearly explained. Bell stated that "many Negro leaders are keenly aware of the problems brought about by desegregation and largely prefer that alignments continue on a voluntary basis."[4] Bell did not identify any black leaders who assumed this posture.

In 1957 *Southern Presbyterian Journal* adopted "voluntary segregation" as its official policy, its Board of Directors declaring such an arrangement to be "for the highest interest of both races."[5] An indication that segregation did not function voluntarily among some Southern Presbyterians was a policy statement adopted by the Board of Trustees of the Presbyterian Retreat Center at Montreat, North Carolina. The Board agreed that "Negro adults be entertained in the Fellowship Hall and Cafeteria but that Negro delegates in Young People's Leadership School could not be entertained."[6] Both black adults and black young people were denied use of the center's lodging facilities. The segregation position, first drawn in 1950, was reaffirmed following the 1954 General Assembly desegregation resolution. L. Nelson Bell and some other *Journal* staff served on the Montreat Board of Trustees or owned private cottages surrounding the retreat complex. Following criticisms of the Board's policy statement in *Presbyterian Outlook*, the *Journal* defended

---

[2] "Christian Race Relations Must Be Natural, Not Forced," *Southern Presbyterian Journal*, XIV (August 17, 1955), 4. In 1959 *Southern Presbyterian Journal* shortened its title to *Presbyterian Journal*.
[3] "Some Needed Distinctions," *Southern Presbyterian Journal*, XVI (June 5, 1957), 3.
[4] Ibid.
[5] *Eternity*, VII (October, 1957), 16.
[6] *Southern Presbyterian Journal*, XIII (August 17, 1954), 4.

the action, declaring "We believe that the Trustees of Montreat have been eminently Christian in their viewpoint and action."[7]

During the 1950s and 1960s the *Journal* criticized the National Council of Churches and the Southern Presbyterian Church for their support of desegregation of the church and the larger society. The *Journal* published resolutions adopted by individual Presbyterian churches declaring their intentions of remaining segregated despite General Assembly policy. Beginning in 1957 the *Journal* carried segregationist articles which were less temperate than Bell's statements. In one such essay Mississippi clergyman G. T. Gillespie wrote that "to many of us this sweeping decision of the higest court in virtually taking over the control and regulation of the schools of the nation seems to be a clear violation of the Constitution itself. . . ."[8] Gillespie's writings, which have been much publicized by both the apologists and opponents of segregation, also charged that the Supreme Court had rendered its verdict on improper evidence prepared by Communist and socialist sympathizers. Gillespie urged Americans to launch a massive drive for reversal of the decision. Another article in the *Journal* similarly appealed to a conspiratorial view of the rights movement, asking "If the NAACP is not Communist why do Communists publicly approve every NAACP action?"[9]

As the civil rights movement grew more militant during the 1960s, the focus of white resistance shifted from rationalizations for maintaining segregation to criticism of civil disobedience. An article in the *Journal* acknowledged the theoretical validity of civil disobedience if civil law were in conflict with God's law. However, the article concluded that "In our present situation and under our present laws and even in spite of the fact that they may at times be unjustly administered, it does not seem likely that any case of civil disobedience is justified."[10]

The *Journal's* condemnation of civil disobedience was inconsistent with its earlier resistance to compliance with desegregation orders. A Bible study lesson in the *Journal* attempted to resolve the conflict with the familiar assertion that the Supreme Court had exceeded its powers in rendering the 1954 verdict because the decision was actually a form of legislation and because public schooling is a state and not a federal responsibility. The lesson advised readers that "Many Christians, therefore, in resisting the Decision, do so on the basis of sound principles."[11]

Unlike the Southern Presbyterian Church, the Church of God and the Assemblies of God did not directly confront racial issues until the 1960s. When the editor of the Church of God's monthly journal, the *Church*

---

[7] L. Nelson Bell, *Southern Presbyterian Journal*, XIII (September 15, 1954), 3.
[8] G. T. Gillespie, "A Southern Christian Looks at the Race Issue," *Southern Presbyterian Journal*, XVI (June 5, 1957), 7-8.
[9] Joseph S. Jones, "The Ku Klux Klan, the NAACP, and the Presbyterian Church," *Southern Presbyterian Journal*, XVI (July 31, 1957), 7.
[10] Samuel T. Harris, Jr., "The Problem of Civil Disobedience," *Presbyterian Journal*, XXVI (December 6, 1967), 10.
[11] Morton H. Smith, "Bible Study for Circle Bible Leadership on 'Jesus and Citizenship'," *Southern Presbyterian Journal*, XVI (July 3, 1957), 21.

of God Evangel, was questioned in 1957 as to the position of the Church on segregation, he replied:

> No formal position has ever been made concerning it. None to my knowledge has ever been needed, for the relationship between the races is respectful, dignified and brotherly in the Church of God. The colored work of the Church is a vital part of it, with equal rights and requirements. In our recent General Assembly (as in all of them) there were delegates of many races present, and participation by all on the program. Yet there is no untoward fraternization between our members of different races.[12]

Segregation within the Church of God had been reinforced through the 1927 incorporation of black churches into a separate conference and the establishment of an office to handle church programs for blacks and evangelization among blacks. The Church has issued a monthly denominational publication, *Church of God Gospel Herald,* specifically for black members. Until 1959 blacks were not served by Lee College, the sect's educational facility in Cleveland, Tennessee. When the first Bible institute for blacks was held, it consisted of a four-week course conducted by Lee College instructors at rented quarters in Jacksonville, Florida. Despite the Church's emphasis on evangelizing blacks, no full-term education for blacks was offered during the 1960s.

During the 1960s the Church of God began to react to the civil rights movement. At its 1964 General Assembly the Church passed a "Human Rights" declaration. While affirming the concept of equal constitutional rights for all citizens and stating that "no Christian can manifest a passive attitude when the rights of others are jeopardized,"[13] the resolution was not a desegregation mandate and reference to segregation or other specific civil rights issues was avoided. The Church continued its policy of maintaining a separate administrative office to serve blacks although black churches were no longer segregated into a separate conference after 1965.

The Assemblies of God, like the Church of God, was able to avoid sect-wide confrontation of racial issues during the 1950s. Although fundamentalist sects were slow to confront racism within the church, it is apparent that church members were concerned about racial issues. Readers of fundamentalist publications frequently expressed interest in the racial identity of biblical characters. A subscriber to *Pentecostal Evangel,* official voice of the Assemblies of God, expressed concern over attempts by some black Christians to teach that Jesus was black. An *Evangel* staff member responded that "Jesus was a Jew as to his humanity, a descendant of David." Regarding the origin of the black race, the *Evangel* stated, "it is probable that the Negroes descended from Ham. But we must remember that various nations descended from Ham." In

[12] *Church of God Evangel,* XLVII (January 21, 1957), 15.
[13] *Church of God Evangel,* LIV (August 31, 1964), 34.

Priest racism in Britain against blacks

TRINIDAD GUARDIAN, Saturday, November 6, 1982 Page 5

BRIDGETOWN, Fri., (Cana)

A LEADING Barbadian Roman Catholic clergyman, fresh from a two-month pastoral stint among Britain's large black community, says regional Governments should show more concern for the problems facing West Indians living there.

"...The cry from many West Indians (is) that little interest is shown on our side of the Atlantic to what is happening there."

Rev. Fr. Harcourt Blackett, co-administrator of the Roman Catholic Diocese here, told Cana.

OFTEN UNWELCOME

Fr. Blackett said though racism was real, the current situation was a stark improvement over the circumstances that prevailed in the 1950s, when blacks were confined to particular areas for housing, and even in the church, where they were often unwelcome.

"Even today, some churches just tolerate the fact that blacks are there. In the past, the priest might simply have told you not to return because you were disturbing his congregation."

The Roman Catholic

Catholic Church hierarchy still mostly white

Jamaica Record March 26 1990. page 3A

By Laura Sessions Stepp

The Catholic Church in the United States, which has struggled for several years with public allegations of racism, got more bad news this week: Blacks interested in becoming priests or nuns drop out of their religious training at a higher rate than other races.

Also, while Hispanics, blacks and other non-white groups make up more than half the Catholic population, whites will continue to dominate church leadership in the near future.

These findings and others on church vocations were presented this week by the Centre for Applied Research in the Apostolate of Georgetown University.

More than 200 people listened to the results of surveys of religious communities throughout the United States and of Jesuit schools and colleges in New York state. Later they heard black, Hispanic, Asian and native American speakers talk about their frustrating, often lonely experiences in the 53-million member U.S. church.

There were a few positive surprises in the data, according to research fellow Sister Eleace King, such as a relatively large proportion of Asian women training to be church leaders. But the news from minorities, particularly black Catholics who make up roughly 4 percent of the Catholic population, was not good. Among the findings:

Black males constituted 7 percent of 2,279 students enrolled in high schools that prepare students for the seminary, 2 percent of those enrolled in seminary colleges and 1 percent of those getting higher degrees in theology.

not as dramatic. The proportion of black women who had taken temporary vows was the same as those in the first stage of training - 3 percent. Hispanic women made up 11 percent of those in the first stage, 5 percent in the final, and white women comprised 78 percent of the first stage, 83 percent of the final.

A survey of the attitudes of young men in Jesuit schools in New York state toward the priesthood and toward their church revealed some interesting differences among ethnic groups:

When asked whether mandatory celibacy was a serious obstacle to going into the priesthood, 83 percent of the whites, Hispanics and Asians said yes, compared with 48 percent of blacks. Blacks rated the white church culture, high admission standards and inadequate knowledge about priestly life as other key obstacles.

More than half the respondents said they had never been asked by a Catholic adult to consider the vocation of priesthood - a finding noted by King as untapped potential. "Significantly," the report said, "black respondents are much less likely (22) to have been asked than is the case for Hispanics (31), Asians (30) or whites (37)."

The Jesuits got a jolt when the students were asked if they felt close to their Jesuit teachers and administrators. Only 14 percent of the black students answered yes, followed by 36 percent of the Hispanics, 26 percent of the Asians and 46 percent of the whites.

The Rev. Francis Gillespie, the centre's president and Jesuit, said that Jesuit leaders in New York have seen the results of the survey and are attempting to reach out to ethnic groups, particularly blacks.

Black priests attack racism

BY VICTORIA STREATFEILD
AND REBECCA FOWLER

Britain's black priests have accused the Roman Catholic Church of racism. They claim their careers have been impeded because of their colour and that black parishioners are often ignored by their priests.

Three of the church's nine black clergymen, including Patrick Kalilombe, the first black Catholic bishop in Britain, have condemned the church's "racist" attitudes. They say their experiences have discouraged blacks from joining their ranks.

The priests said they have had to endure racist gibes from fellow students at their seminaries and from parishioners. They also claimed churches allowed couples to demand white priests at weddings and that black Catholics were told to worship only with "their own kind" by fellow parishioners.

"Being black makes you marginal in the church. You are not ever visible," said Kalilombe, who arrived in Birmingham from Malawi 12 years ago. "It is as if I don't exist at bishops' meetings."

He believes the fact there are only four black priests and four black deacons, compared with about 60 black priests in the Church of England, reflects Catholics' negative attitudes to race relations. While the church preaches against racism abroad, Kalilombe claims it is unable to deal with it at home.

The first black priest of West Indian origin to be ordained in England two years ago is among those calling for change. Father Howard James, 34, said: "People have been hurt terribly. Racist statements have been made and lay people feel they have been ignored by priests." James said he came up against racism soon after starting his studies for the priesthood in 1985. On one occasion when he wanted some milk, a member of staff at his college suggested he would use it to wash his colour away.

James, who said he also encountered priests and laity who treated him with great respect, hoped the situation would improve after the 1990 Congress of Black Catholics. It ended with the Catholic bishops of England and Wales supporting the 20,000 black church members and pledging to support race relations training.

But James believes that overall attitudes have not changed. "The record of the church is disgraceful," he said. "It is up to all of us, parents, teachers children and priests to do something about this."

A third black clergyman, who did not wish to be identified, told of his dismay after finding out that his church allowed parishioners to prevent him officiating at their wedding because they wanted a white priest. Only one of the five colleges for priests took up the idea of race relations workshops after the 1990 congress, and even then it was quickly dropped.

Other Christian communities believe Catholics must act quickly. The Rev David Haslam, Anglican chairman of the Churches Commission for Racial Justice, said: "The spotlight must be on the Catholic church because it is the largest. It must do more." The Catholic Church in England and Wales last week accepted that racism was a problem among its members, but denied it was not being dealt with. "The issue of integrating black people into the church and into the priesthood is a weighty topic," said Nicholas Coote, assistant general secretary to the bishops' conference. "The Catholic church is taking it seriously."
— The Sunday Times

Church Racism Poses Problem for Black Catholics

THE WASHINGTON POST

By Marjorie Hyer
Washington Post Staff Writer

Loretta Butler's voice quavered a bit as she described the painful incident of so long ago.

"It was in the late '40s .... My friend and I were on vacation in Southern Maryland," said Butler, a retired teacher. "We went to a little Catholic church—I don't even remember the name."

But she remembers the humiliation as the two young black women were sent to the back pew and made to wait until all the white people had been served before they received communion.

"It was one of the times when I didn't know how I could continue," she said.

But Butler clung to the church that had been her mother's and grandmother's. For a time she gave up her teaching job to join black and white Catholics who used nonviolence to banish segregated seating in Washington parishes.

While the roped-off "blacks only" pews and other blatantly discriminatory practices have disappeared from Catholic parishes, black Catholics feel they still lack full acceptance in the church.

The dramatic announcement by the Rev. George A. Stallings Jr. that he will establish his own church today to combat racism in the Catholic Church has stirred both sympathy and controversy among the more than 80,000 black Catholics in the Washington area and others throughout the country.

There is little disagreement among whites and blacks that racism exists in both the church and the society of which it is a part. But just how many blacks will follow Stallings out of the church remains to be seen.

The Roman Catholic Church, said Brother John Payne, who was born and raised a Catholic, "is a terribly racist institution."

BY ELLSWORTH J. DAVIS—THE WASHINGTON POST

Loretta Butler recalls joining other Catholics to end segregation in parishes.

Black Catholic Bishops Cite Bias in the Church

Washington Post November 14, 1985 p. A 15

By Marjorie Hyer
Washington Post Staff Writer

The 10 black bishops of the Roman Catholic Church in this country have challenged their brother bishops to stamp out racial prejudice, saying it continues to make black Catholics "feel unwelcome" in their church.

Just as some whites feel that "black neighbors, black co-workers and black classmates will be disruptive of their value system and their familiar patterns of life, some white Catholics feel that it will be equally disruptive to share the Scriptures, the bread of life and the cup of salvation [holy communion] with black Catholics," said Bishop Joseph L. Howze of Biloxi, Miss.

White Catholics may "feel sorry" for blacks or "even feel guilty about their plight," Howze said, but whites do not welcome blacks to their churches. Consequently, "many black Americans still feel unwelcome in the Catholic Church."

Howze, the senior of the 10 black bishops and the only one to head a diocese, presented their joint statement Tuesday at a closed-door session of the National Conference of Catholic Bishops, which agreed to make the statement public yesterday. About 1.2 million of the nation's more than 52 million Catholics are black, Howze said.

Howze disputed the "prevailing myth" that the remainder of American blacks are members of Protestant churches. Many, he said, "are simply unchurched."

In order to reach them, the black bishops asked help in developing "black Catholic styles of public worship," evangelistic efforts in black communities, racially sensitive recruiting of black men and women into religious work, and more blacks in leadership roles involving white as well as black Catholics.

They cited the example of Episcopal Bishop John T. Walker of Washington, who is black. He "was not chosen because of the number of black Episcopalians in Washington," they said, but "because he has qualities that are needed to head the Episcopal Church in this area."

Only hours earlier, the national bishops' conference had elected Auxiliary Bishop Eugene Marino of Washington as secretary—the first black bishop elected to a major leadership post.

In other actions the bishops moved toward possibly toughening their controversial 1983 pastoral letter on nuclear warfare, which said that the nation's policy of nuclear deterrence is "morally acceptable" only if the nuclear powers pursue disarmament and weapons-reduction agreements.

Six activist bishops, led by Auxiliary Bishop Thomas Gumbleton of Detroit, said, "In the judgment of many people, these strict conditions for the moral acceptance of deterrence are not being met."

In executive session, the bishops agreed to name a committee to study the deterrence situation and recommend, at next year's meeting, whether to change their stance.

New York Times September 10, 1985

Bishops Seeking Larger Role for Black Catholics

By CARLYLE C. DOUGLAS

The black American bishops of the Roman Catholic Church called yesterday for increased black influence and representation in the church hierarchy.

In a daylong symposium at St. Charles Borromeo Church in Harlem, they also spoke of the benefits that

"black spirituality" could bring to the church and of the need for liturgy that reflects black culture.

The bishops met at the invitation of John Cardinal O'Connor, the Archbishop of New York, to mark the first anniversary of the pastoral letter issued by the church's 10 black bishops.

Bishop Emerson J. Moore of New York picked up on that theme. He said that "many black Catholics as individuals have met resistance" when seeking to join white parishes. "Racism as sin must always be on the agenda of Catholics."

"What We Have Seen and Heard." Almost without exception, the speakers, including Cardinal O'Connor, said not enough progress had been made in addressing the concerns of black Catholics as set forth in the letter.

'Very Little' Done

In brief remarks to a predominantly black audience of about 300, Cardinal O'Connor said that, in the last year, "very little" had been done to bring about the changes sought by black Catholics.

"For too many years, we have thought about what we whites could do for you blacks," he said, and have not considered that "we are ministering together." He called on the symposium participants to speed the process of change and said he hoped to make the symposium an annual event.

A spokesman for the New York Archdiocese later characterized the symposium as "a historic meeting underlining Cardinal O'Connor's commitment to Black Catholics and the Black community."

In the keynote address to the group, the Rev. Edward X. Braxton, director of the Catholic Student Center at the University of Chicago, called on the church to strengthen its evangelical efforts among blacks, about 1.3 million of whom are Catholics.

years that church schools have been disappearing from inner-city areas.

Father Braxton also suggested that the church establish leadership training programs with the aim of bringing blacks to "the highest levels of leadership in the Catholic Church."

Seven of the 10 black bishops who issued the pastoral letter last year also spoke at the meeting.

Bishop James P. Lyke of the Cleveland Diocese stressed the "gift of spirituality" that blacks offered the church. But he noted that there were currently only about 300 black seminarians the 700 black sisters among the various orders of nuns.

"We have to dispel the myth that black Catholics belong to a white church," he said.

Bishop Eugene A. Marino of the Archdiocese of Washington, D.C., who talked about the effect of racism on evangelization, was one of the most enthusiastically received speakers. "We cannot talk about the problems of reaching the unchurched and forget about the many who act with racism toward those already in the church," he said. "Racism is a grievous offense against the love of God."

Clergymen outside St. Charles Borromeo Roman Catholic Church in Harlem yesterday before mass. At right, in rear, is John Cardinal O'Connor.

The New York Times/William E. Sauro

New York Times Sept 10, 1985

ROMAN CATHOLIC

Black priest breaks from RC church

WASHINGTON: A rebel black priest defied the Roman Catholic hierarchy and established an independent African-American church to combat what he called institutional racism.

More than 2,000 people packed a chapel at Howard University law school for a dissident service that included African drums, rattles, bells, incantations and a 30-member chorus.

The Rev George Stallings, 41, said he did not want to break with Rome in setting up what he called the *Imani* temple, African-American Catholic congregation." Imani means "faith" in Swahili.

But he acted in spite of warnings he would be suspended from the priesthood and possibly forced out of the established church.

"The Catholic Church is a white racist institution," he thundered from the pulpit. Black Catholics "can't wait any longer" for the church to meet their needs and celebrate their cultural heritage, he said in his homily.

Cardinal James Hickey, Archbishop of Washington, said he was deeply saddened by the service, which he called a setback for race relations.

"Father Stallings has seriously weakened his relationship with the Catholic Church," Hickey said in a statement.

Stallings, who attended the North Ameri-

DETROIT CATHOLICS WARY ON CLOSINGS

Protests Set Against Church Consolidations — Black Priests See Benefits

NEW YORK TIMES, WEDNESDAY, OCTOBER 5, 1988

By JOHN HOLUSHA
Special to The New York Times

DETROIT, Oct. 4 — With 43 of the Roman Catholic churches here designated by the archdiocese for closing, people at some of those churches were planning resistance today while a group of black clergy were saying the consolidation could provide added resources to help the city's majority black population.

Several hundred Catholics, meeting Monday night, agreed to stage protests, fasts and to explore the possibility of bringing a lawsuit against the Archdiocese of Detroit to block the planned closings. They agreed to send a letter to the Archbishop, Edmund Cardinal Szoka, saying that the closings had "brought shock, scandal anger and even disgust" to the affected parishes.

Most of the churches designated to be closed are predominatly white.

But the black clergy said the proposed change in the church structure in the city presented an opportunity for the Catholic Church to remedy some past wrongs, in which churches composed of white ethnic groups discouraged blacks from joining.

Wyatt Jones Jr., director of the Archdiocese of Detroit's Office of Black Catholic Affairs, said at a news conference today that blacks had not been encouraged to join many of the older Catholic Churches in the city, even as their numbers increased.

Mayor Agrees With Clerics

The Rev. Clarence Williams, a priest at St. Anthony's Church, said that in the past: "Blacks were not welcome. Blacks who tried to get into the high school were paid to go elsewhere."

The Mayor of Detroit, Coleman A. Young, who is black, echoed the clerics' comments about past rejection of blacks by Catholic ethnic parishes. "A big percentage of the Catholics in Detroit and all around this area are ethnic members, coming from various language groups," The Detroit Free Press quoted him as saying. "And many of them have refused to reach out and admit blacks openly."

The black clerics said they favored some church closings and consolidations, but they said blacks as a group needed to be part of the process of deciding which churches should be closed and which should be retained. Father Williams criticized the way the decision to close 43 of archdiocese's 112 churches was announced last week on television without consultations with the affected parishes.

"The church has a credibility problem in the black community," he said. "The recommended closings and the manner in which it was done confers the feeling that the Catholic Church is for whites only."

RACISM DEPICTS MAN
AT HIS CRUDEST

TITLE: *Racism: A Philosophic Probe* ✓

AUTHOR: *Father Chukwudum Barnaboas Okolo, Ph.D.* ✓

PUBLISHERS: *Exposition Press, Inc. Jericho, New York.*

PRICE: *$6.00 (N4.00) hard back.*

RACISM is the child of the slave trade organised by West European and American imperialist governments. The European slave trade marked the beginning of the dehumanisation and deculturalisation of the black race.

Dr Okolo's book is an immense contribution to the seemingly endless debate on the racial question. It is written in a language and tone easily understood by the general reader. It should definitely broaden the reader's general knowledge of the world's most volatile problem, racism, as seen from the point of view of a Nigerian clergyman of high academic standing. well

It should, of course, serve its probable objective as a textbook for students of the social sciences.

In his preface to the book, Dr. Okolo attacks the myopic and pessimistic view that racism is an 'inevitable burden and an inescapable curse'. He re- at peace with itself, it exploits and degrades

He refers to incidents in American churches where white members would vacate a seat if a black member sat close to them, and also where church members would refuse to go for services if a black priest officiated.

The author indicts the whiteman for his racial bigotry, his failure to recognise the problem as it and take effective mea- his unbridled "will to po-

— **By D. WILSON**
University of Ibadan

Race, Sex and My Failed

Len Cooper is a Washington writer, and a pressman at The Washington Post. By Len Cooper

IT IS MY FIRST day at St. Meinrad Archabbey and College Seminary. More than 500 men live here, and through the window of my tiny, musty room it looks like most of them are outside, moving beneath the evergreens that seem to reach toward some final stillness.

Some have lived here for a few days, some for most of their lives. Just now, they are taking advantage of the waning daylight that is mocked by the dry-weather lightning flashing in the distance.

I am 22. It is 1976. I have come here to Indiana to become a priest and then I want to go back home to Birmingham, Ala., and live the rest of my life christening babies, hearing confessions, burying the dead. For me the Roman Catholic priesthood not only promises to fulfill my spiritual hopes, but it also means freedom—it can raise me socially and loosen the bonds that accompany being black.

Three of the four beds in the room have already been claimed by my roommates, whom I have not met. One will regularly offer his arguments on the inferiority of the black race, one will have frequent

For now, the sun has almost set as I sit on the windowsill: alone, depressed, scared and wondering if coming here was a bad decision after all.

I watch men walking toward the campus lake with towels on their shoulders. Just yesterday I quit my job in Birmingham as a lifeguard at the neighborhood pool in East Thomas Park. Here, at least, is something I know I can do, a place to fit in. I find my Speedo swim suit, goggles and towel. I run barefoot down the stairs and past the moss-covered cemetery to the lake. A dozen or so young men are playing a game they call "greased-

watermelon" football. I stand on the shore with mud squishing between my toes, watching two teams try to score goals with a Vaselined melon. I get asked to play. I am delighted.

My troubles and acute homesickness vanish as we tussle for control. Then the melon squirts out in my direction, all mine, a chance to score one for the team and pick up a few points with the guys. I dash for the goal, the opposition converges on me—but so does my own team. They are dunking me up and down, and laughing. Suddenly, I can feel hands reaching for my crotch. Surely this is an accident or some kind of hazing. Then the truth is unmistakable and I am struggling to break their hold.

I push the red and green pieces of broken melon away, but they ignore it—it's me they're after. Now they're holding me under, way longer than is reasonable. I'm choking. I force my way to the top, throwing

FIRST PERSON:
Spiritual Ambitions

punches and missing with all of them. Grabbing my towel and

THE rest of my family was Baptist, and my mother sang in the choir. I had converted to Catholicism when I was in high school. My conversion was easy. I found the statues, the smell of incense from the thurible and the Latin chants most attractive. The girls in the Catholic church seemed prettier, with their light, even-toned skin and long, flowing hair. In my family's church, the young girls who were unfortunate enough to get pregnant out of wedlock were forced to come before the congregation and apologize for their transgressions. (The boys in question were free of the humiliation.) Not so with the Catholics. And the Catholics didn't pass the collection plate for the third, fourth and often fifth time as the Baptists did.

I was also becoming part of what I saw as an elite circle.

The lighter-skinned and better educated blacks who went to my Catholic church were richer and better-connected socially than the parishioners in the church I left behind. The white priest's social circle consisted of whites from other parts of the city. Those closest to him in the congregation were included in that circle. That was where I wanted to be.

For me, along with many of my Catholic friends, the church was a means of escape.

As time progressed I often attended the sacrifice of the mass daily. My role in my home parish, Our Lady Queen of the Universe, encompassed spending weekends trimming the hedges, mowing the lawn, polishing the floors of the sanctuary and making certain that all was in order for the the Sunday mass. I did not seek to be applauded for my efforts by the congregation. This was my outward expression of love and devotion to a God and church I placed above everything. To serve God for the measure of my days was my only desire, my focus, my all.

In the months that followed the incident in the lake I would ask my-too late. Had I been better prepared as to what to expect in seminary, it is very possible this story would have a happy ending. One day I was hanging out with my lifelong friends who happened to be black and the next I was thrust into a seminary's isolated society composed of mostly well-to-do men of whom three were black.

I was naive to the point of believing that all the men in this holy place had made a commitment to serve God with all their heart, soul and might and that their lives would be a reflection of that inner sanctity.

Not long after my encounter at the lake, my spiritual adviser would listen most attentively to my account of what had happened. He seemed curious to know what I had done to entice my fellow seminarians. He concluded that "boys will be boys" and recommended that I

Dream of Being a Priest

invoke the help of the Virgin Mary through prayer and contemplation.

The sexual advances continued. They were unmistakable. At the card catalog in the library late one night I felt a hand reach under my arm from behind and caress my chest. At first I was startled, then decided to put an end to this foolishness once and for all. As the robed monk's hand began to descend, I decided to turn and hit him. Then another brother discreetly coughed and the monk behind me hurried off through the wooden

mitment of my life, not just religiously but racially and politically. Initially my parents had been unhappy with my idea of becoming a priest. But they gradually shed their objections. They would start attending the mass as I assisted at the altar, and they would hold me in high esteem for my dedication and loyalty to the faith. They sometimes talked about possibly coming to the Catholic faith themselves.

There were no black priests or nuns in my diocese in Birmingham. I would have been the first. I had no

But all this was moot, finally, when I was told I could no longer study at the seminary or represent the Birmingham diocese. Halfway through my second year as a seminarian, I was summoned to the academic dean's office and informed that I needed to fulfill a Latin requirement before going on to theology. It would be at least a year or two before the course would be offered again. The dean suggested that I return to the University of Alabama in Birmingham and enroll in the Latin course there for one

To scream racism was an impetuous move for blacks in Birmingham then. To be discriminated against was as common as breathing. So I didn't find it unusual when my parents were never contacted by the diocese, or told what I would be doing in the coming years, or invited to a banquet given in honor of the new inductees: there were eight of us, six whites, one Vietnamese and me.

At the seminary I became more and more isolated. On several occasions after finding strange objects in my food and finally having one student clear his nostrils in my unattended plate, I decided to follow the advice of the monsignor in my home parish and prepare my own food in my room. My complaints became more frequent. With each meeting one faculty member became more incensed. In our last conference he became enraged to the point of telling me to stop my "bitching, bitching, bitching," then threw me out of his office.

I asked why I should do anything that would not ultimately bring me salvation. As I watched my fellow seminarians in long white cassocks assist in the distribution of the body and blood of the Savior, I thought: "If they expect me to believe in their God, then they must act more godly; if I'm to believe in the Christ, then they must act more Christ-like."

It went on for years—I would go on to study theology at Catholic University, in hopes that all would be forgiven and forgotten on both sides and possibly my sojourn towards receiving the holy orders would resume. But it's gone now, and Catholism and the priesthood are just relics of a past that has no appreciable value for me.

There was little refuge for comfort outside the seminary grounds. In Jasper, Ind., a city of 25,000 about 18 miles from the seminary, many of the adults had never set eyes on a non-white before, I was told. Once, in the supermarket, a little kid came over to me and began licking his hand and rubbing it on my arm. He was trying to see if my black color washed off.

Nor could I find solace in the rituals. I had to harness my emotional impulses. I had long been aware that the approved atmosphere in church derived from white, not black culture. That much had been demonstrated at home by the fact that while the altar boys were all black and the 300 families in the church were all black, the priest was always white. The parishioners didn't seem to mind but elevated themselves above black Protestant churches for this reason.

On the other hand, while I wanted to be a priest, I knew I couldn't become one in the system as I saw it. I became angry that my ambitions, for all that they lingered, could not be realized. I carried my rosary, the one with which I said my "Hail Marys" and "Our Fathers" and left on the nightstand with my Bible every night, until Christmas. Then, driving along Interstate 65, I tossed the rosary out the window in a moment of frustration.

One moment I was a seminarian, and the next I was breaking stones in the brickyards of Alabama. My file would conclude that I left the seminary without cause, without provocation. In time I would abandon Catholicism and my enduring faith in God. Fallen-away Catholics have said that "many a priest has become an atheist in Rome." For me, the unraveling of a beautiful dream into an ugly reality began that day at the lake.

PARAS RAMOUTAR reports from **TORONTO**

Chilly churches keep blacks out

Express January 15 1979

Fr. Pascall

Two West Indian church leaders in Metro Toronto have charged that Black immigrants are turning away from churches because of the generally chilly reception extended by Canadians.

Rev. Winston Brown of the United Church's West Indian ministry and Rev. Ashley Smith, a former moderator of the United Church of Jamaica, feel that Canadian churches are not "sensitized" to the congregation.

Rev. Brown said that West Indians are turning off "church-going" by the attitude of white congregrations and the whole church atmosphere.

He blamed Canadian affluence and cultural differences for some of t problem. "There misunderstanding on bc sides", he said.

Rev. Smith said t West Indian feels he is p: of the Commonwealth a so expects to be accept and to participate fully h in church and other soc activities.

"Instead, he finds t often that he is treated as he comes from some remc and backward country ar is just learning to spe; English", he said.

Meanwhile, Fr. Mik Pascall, head of th Toronto-Caribbean Catholic Secretariat to me in an interview that l was not sure th: Canadians were "drivir Black people from th churches."

WARREN D. ARMSTRONG on the Black Power demonstration

EXPRESS. Sunday, March 1, 1970 Page 5 1970. TRINIDAD

WHY THEY CARRIED THEIR PROTEST WITHIN THE CHURCH'S WALLS

THE ROMAN CATHOLIC CHURCH IS W...

IS WHITE; JESUS IS WHITE; MARY IS WHI...

APOSTLES (EXCEPT PERHAPS JUDAS) WE...

ALL THE ANGELS AND SAINTS (SAVE THE...

HASTILY THE OTHER DAY) ARE WHITE

they would have been praised for being sensible, responsible young people.

But they did the unusual. They entered the Cathedral of the Immaculate Conception, draped a black cloth on St. Peter.

Just a few months ago a Trinidadian sociologist in a lecture in South had to remark on the fact that whenever you travel through the poor districts in this country, it was found that the best buildings were always the Church and the home of the priest.

Through generations of unbroken tradition, the role of the Church has never been seriously questioned until now. Its alliance with the moneyed class while counselling against "laying up treasures where moths can corrupt," and its obsession with the "sweet bye-and-bye" while its flock is catching hell right here, cannot satisfy the inquiring minds of today's youth.

So the demonstrators, turned away from all the white-owned organisations, turned their attention to the white Church which they considered to be in the same position of oppressor of the b l a c k people.

CAN ROMAN CATHOLICS BE TRULY A SUPPORT FOR THE BLACK CAUSE?

Page 10 EXPRESS Saturday, March 7, 1970

By ALDWIN PRIMUS, leader of the Black Panthers in Trinidad

ONE OF the great tragedies of Christianity is that since the death of Jesus, the world has seen no other Christian.

And when Dr. Eric Williams a few years ago said:

"The Church is the last vestige of colonialism in the West Indies," he was only laying the foundation for an eventual uprising of the masses against secular authority.

It is true that what a man sows, he shall one day reap.

The forces of history therefore responsible for the Black Power invasion of the Roman Catholic Church a few days ago are forces deep within the ruling party and the government itself.

serious politics in the statement — just as people will find out sooner or later that the Black Power Movement really holds the balance of political decision in the fourth-coming elections.

PROTEST

But: is one entitled to assume that Roman Catholic support for Black Power is knowing that the Black Power organisation is a protest organisation — an indication that the Church will like to see a new government?

If this is what the Church wants, the Black Power movement can provide the country and the church itself with a new government

achieve, and I would like to help."

We in the movement will like to tell His Grace that we understand his position.

While we are not prepared to apologise as such for what has happened, we want him to know that no intention was framed to harm his reputation as a man or his character as a human being.

But I have told His Grace more than once that his place might not be Archbishop of Port-of-Spain.

GENUINE

The reason for this is that I find in him beauty of soul and spirit and

has found himself being leader of a massive community with a terrible record of historical political involvement across the world and for whom he must daily and constantly apologise.

If it is sad for him, but that is the price of being Archbishop of Port-of-Spain.

WARNING

It is fast approaching the period when the Church will have to say clearly which government it is prepared to support — the government of the poor or the government of those who govern the poor.

It is true that those who govern, themselves do not, like to be governed. But this cannot be used as a foundation to permit the eternal subjection of the poor by the rich.

It was Oscar Wilde who said that all authority is immoral and dangerous.

MIRROR 12 FRIDAY MAY 3, 2002

14 FRIDAY MAY 3, 2002

MIRROR

In 1970 the front pews, complete with name tags, were also reserved

Whites-only seats in the Catholic Church

... Blacks were only hired as cleaners by the banks

Clive Nunez, possibly the only trade unionist in the march, (at the time he was chief organiser of the TIWU) estimates a crowd of about 200, comprising of about 150 UWI students led by Guild president Carl Blackwood, and including Geddes Granger (now Makandal Daaga), former Guild president and now leader of the National Joint Action Committee (NJAC), Dave Darbeau (now Khafra Kambon) and others.

Nunez was also public relations officer of NJAC.

By DAVID MILLETTE

THE issue today is deviant sexual behaviour, but in 1970, the most explosive contention in the Catholic Church was rank discrimination.

At the Catholic Cathedral on Independence Square, Port of Spain, strategic seats, complete with name tags, were reserved in the front pews for Whites, almost as if God had decreed those special favours.

Nunez recalls: "It was Earl Lewis, who I am sure was an agent provocateur, who, as we reached at the corner of Charlotte and George Streets, suggested 'let's go to the Catholic Church, they practise racism'.

Nunez continued: "In those days, certain pews to the front of the church were reserved with name plates for Whites and a few select Blacks.

"Daaga, Kambon, others and I went in and engaged three Whites and an East Indian priest in dialogue on racism in the Church.

"Then two of the demonstrators took off their black shirts, draped them over two of the statues and the shout went up 'we don't want any White Jesus'."

By the time the marchers were behind the bridge, Roman Catholic Archbishop Anthony Pantin would be on radio denying that the incidents of a few minutes ago were acts of desecration and admitting that his church did have a history of practising racism.

RESS

The National Newspaper of Trinidad & Tobago

FRIDAY, APRIL 19, 1974   ROMAN CATHOLIC   15 CENTS

PRIEST: RACISM IN R.C. CHURCH

...priests to "tell it like it is".

Fr. Kevin de Loughry, one of the delegates to the priests' conference now underway at Mount St. Benedict, also said yesterday that priests must face the problem and be honest about it.

Fr. de Loughry was speaking on behalf of his working group on the question entitled "Are we really ready for the exposure of this problem in depth?". Being discussed was the paper "Indigenisation — An Inescapable Challenge for Proclaiming The Gospel Of Christ".

He disclosed that one of the priests in his group felt that he (the priest) was now suffering "because he is white". Fr. de Loughry pointed out the "inevitability of the switching of roles" as far as the races were concerned and declared that the whole issue of racism in the church must be thrashed out.

"Speak about it", he urged his colleagues.

Another group pointed out that prejudice still exists to a small extent in church schools, and there were people who could cite instances to support charges of discrimination.

By RODERICK LEWIS,
SOCIAL AFFAIRS REPORTER

problem" he ever faced was his television set.

"Indigenisation — An Inescapable Challenge For ...

question of identity is not a faddish preoccupation as we are inclined to think now and then, that it is some-

Trinidad

GUARDIAN

Port-of-Spain, Trinidad and Tobago ☆ 60th. Year 18579

★ Monday, September 13, 1976   TRINIDAD & TOBAGO   25c.

Racial unity 'no polls gimmick'

By CLEVON RAPHAEL

FR. CLYDE HARVEY

GOVERNMENT has an obligation to take positive steps to promote racial harmony "among our people, not only as an election gimmick, but as an integral part of the day-to-day life of our people."

This was stressed by Fr. Clyde Harvey, a lecturer at the Roman Catholic Seminary at Mount St. Benedict, while delivering the sermon at the Fatima Devotion yesterday afternoon.

In his lengthy talk entitled "Racial Discrimination" Fr. Harvey accused "big business" of tokenism and the Church of ambiguity in this field.

The recently-ordained cleric told the gathering at Laventille.

Noting that the 1970 upheaval brought a new sense of dignity to Africans and Indians, Fr. Harvey contended that as more people achieve a higher standard of living "the black-white tensions in our society are being drained off."

Fr. Harvey said the Church's record on race questions was not altogether wholesome— in fact quite ambiguous.

"The one redeeming factor is that the Popes since 1537 have consistently condemned racism. But the members of

our society on the basis of race, especially of colour."

He declared "It left us with a society in which a dark skin was a liability and the lighter shades an asset — in which the 'frying' of one's hair was the way to beauty and in which mothers would pull up the noses of their babies to ensure that they don't grow too broad.

"Today it is generally agreed that the main reasons for this racism was economic. For the rich to remain rich they had to ensure that only a small sector of the society

Church, clergy and laity alike, have not been as Christian in the practice of the faith.

"The system of pew rent payable (now discontinued) only by those of a certain wealth, schools catering only to certain classes, the belittling of the local culture, of anything that was not European seem to us today incompatible with the Christian Gospel.

"The ambiguity is reinforced when we realise this was almost always accompanied by a dedication and zeal for Christ which was phenomenal. . . ."

The young priest said: "Some of us would like to be silent about that past and feel no good Catholic should raise its dust." But he countered:

"This we cannot do

Blackman gotta keep on jammin', Fr. Clyde

FRONT LINE

By Keith Shepherd
TT MIRROR

SUNDAY MAY 6, 2001

I HAVE known Fr. Clyde Harvey for the past 45 years or so ... give or take a year.

During the 1950s, we happened to be in the same class, several times over, during our primary school days as pupils of the old Belmont Boys' Intermediate RC School.

Clyde was always a "top five" student.

I remember that he was always there or thereabouts ... along with other "bright boys" like Clayton Hull, Kenneth Lum Shue Chan, Albert Chu Man Chew and Neil Rolingson, the PLIPDECO big shot.

I can't remember whether Lum Shue Chan, a Chaguanas boy, made it up to the Exhibition (the forerunner to the Common Entrance examination) class, or whether he and his family migrated before then.

Certainly, Clyde, Neil and Albert went on to St. Mary's College, while Hull and I opted to attend Queen's Royal College to get our secondary education.

So, when, many years later, I learnt that Clyde had entered the priesthood, I was a bit surprised.

Not because he had been a "bad bwoy" during his early days — far from it, he was always the studious, focussed type who didn't have time for frivolity or even sports, like me — but because I always imagined that he would become a doctor, attorney or professor, or even a big businessman.

Remind him about what Black Stalin says: *"Blackman gotta keep on jammin', for Blackman to get a little something."*

The bottom line is that some people would rather have a foreigner in charge, than to have someone like him (Harvey) represent them.

And, to think that I marched for national equality in 1970 and 1986 ... Sigh!

So, if you see Clyde, tell him Sheepy understands the race factor/politics in everything that has taken place, and I sympathise with him because I know that he is doing it for others, and not for himself only.

In the circumstances, I have come to regard Clyde as a true brother ... a person putting down the same kind of "wuk" as I do; but only in another sphere, another sector.

However, I always recognised that he was fighting an uphill battle in a religion that takes White supremacy seriously.

late Archbishop Anthony Pantin — who impressed me that he was his brother's keeper, and who tended to every need of the flock — then Clyde Harvey was that person.

He, too, chose to do most of his best work in areas that catered for the most dispossessed and underprivileged of residents ... in places like Laventille, Maloney and San Fernando.

And he was never afraid to get his hands dirty to identify with community and those described as unworthy, and to ruffle feathers whenever he opened his mouth to speak in their defence, or to rail about the injustices they face, daily.

Are we a cursed race? Do we have the brand of Satan (Blackness)

ally.

These people must surely feel betrayed that local stalwarts like Fr. Michel de Verteuil, Editor of the *Catholic News*, and Clive Pantin, brother of the late Archbishop, have joined with Clyde to speak out against what looks like serious recolonisation or its new handle; globalisation) in the appointment of an American, Edward J. Gilbert, as the next Archbishop of Port of Spain.

Betrayed, in the sense that both de Verteuil and Pantin may be seen as being White, and the moneyed class that thinks it controls the local church, may want to protect the late Archbishop's legacy...

After all, look how alone Martin de Porres looks in the hierarchy of the church's saints.

The only Black to get such recognition, poor Martin still has to settle for the name "Blessed Martin" before his name, while others get to parade as Saint This and Saint That.

And, although I remember somewhere that there was a Black Pope somewhere along the line, a very long time ago, it must be ions since we've had one.

on us?

And what about the Chinese, East Indians and South Americans?

They not worthy of the Papacy too?

As things stand today, a lot of alleged "good Catholics" I know would feel offended to have a man like Clyde Harvey leading the faith, nation-

FR. CLYDE HARVEY

EDWARD J. GILBERT

4 TRINIDAD GUARDIAN, Tuesday, February 11, 1975

Tracing life of an eminent Trinidadian

Trinidad Guardian February 11, 1975. P.4.

Vishnu R. Gosine reviews 'A Look at Learie Constantine,' By Udine Guiseppi (Nelson)

LORD CONSTANTINE

"POWER, prestige, fame, honour, ambition," t h e s e have corrupted our leaders and politicians. But these have failed to surface the egotistic feeling in Lord Constantine. Coming from a people who have had a traumatic experience, constantine recognised their fight with the former colonial masters.

Though schooled in the colonial era, its education did not deculturise him. He recognised his roots lay in the West Indies, and he was bent on working unceasingly to bring justice to all.

"A look At Learie Constantine," by Undine Guiseppi is merely a look at this eminent figure. To many people he was only a cricketer, and the story ends there. One has only to discover what remarkable contribution he has made to

CHURCH-GOER

Constantine was an orthodox Catholic, and a fervent church goer. In a Catholic church in New York, he was told, "Get out o' there! Niggers at the ...... This was enough. England and America are both corrupt. He had made his decision.

Constantine's awareness of racialism and colour prejudice within the society

them, and they will accept us in spite of our colour". Her words proved true.

equality of all. "In the sight of God, we are all equal", he must have said.

"A Look at Learie Constantine" also traces his early life before he rose to international fame. Life in London was lonely a n d grim, and Learie had only his wife as a source of comfort. It was his wife to whom he poured out his fears, doubts, joys and sorrows.

Very often Constantine received abusive letters, and this made him at times greatly despondent. But his ever cheerful wife was always there telling him:

"Let us turn and fight. In the end, they'll realise that basically we are just like

CARIBBEAN EMANCIPATORS

Published by Press Section, Public Relations Division,
Prime Minister Office.

1978

LEARIE CONSTANTINE
(1901-1971)

FOREWORD

The Government Broadcasting Unit series, Caribbean Emancipators, arose out of the decision of the Government of Trinidad and Tobago to organise in Trinidad a permanent gallery of Caribbean Emancipators as an inspiration to the youth of the region and for the enlightenment of the outside world.

gained him an M.B.E. in 1946.

Learie Constantine was first and foremost a great cricketer, but he was much more than that; author, lecturer, politician, diplomat and public figure in Trinidad and in Britain. He became a symbol of what the black West Indian could achieve in Britain, an inspiration to the thousands of West Indians who went to Britain during and after the war. We are fortunate to have a new biography of Constantine by Mrs. Undine Guiseppi, on which this talk is based.

Constantine's brilliance as a cricketer enabled him to become famous and admired. But as a black man living mostly in Britian, he had to encounter much vicious discrimination; He was always concerned about the position of people of his race and wrote a book about it, *Colour Bar* (1954). He tells us that he stopped attending church (he was a Catholic) because "I have suffered so much, and seen my coloured friends suffer so much, at white priests' and white Roman Catholic worshippers' hands". He often encountered discrimination in British hotels or restaurants. He could not but be deeply aware of racialism and colour prejudice.

Constantine left his job with the Ministry of Labour in 1947 and resumed studies on law; it was his long standing ambition to become a lawyer. He also continued lectures and BBC broadcasts. (Though his formal education was not extensive, he was widely read and a fluent speaker.) In 1954, he was qualified as a barrister and returned to Trinidad as Assistant Legal Adviser to Trinidad Leaseholds, an oil company.

His career entered an entirely new phase in 1956: he entered Trinidad politics and was elected Chairman of the PNM. His famous name and his prestige were of great value to the new party. In September 1956, when the PNM was swept into power, he won the difficult Tunapuna seat and became Minister of Works

COLOUR BAR

by

LEARIE CONSTANTINE, M.B.E.

With 20 Illustrations

STANLEY PAUL AND CO. LTD
London   Melbourne   Sydney   Auckland
Bombay   Cape Town   New York   Toronto

take part in religious ceremony together with white worshippers without discrimination.

Put it this way. In *your* church, would you and everyone else make no sign of difference if you found a score of coloured people *of all social classes* sprinkled about sitting in the church when you arrived? If you are a member of the Church of England, would you and all your fellow church-goers kneel in physical contact with such coloured people at the altar for Communion? Would you have your baby christened in the arms of a Negro priest or your mother buried by one? Would you permit a coloured pastor to kiss your bride, as white pastors sometimes do?

I have had some of the most painful experiences of colour segregation that I have ever suffered in churches in America, the West Indies and England. Somehow, if such things happen in cricket or in business, one is to some extent armoured against them, but when kneeling and praying, one's armour is off and the hurt seems to enter one's soul. I used to be Roman Catholic. Perhaps I could say I am one still, for my belief in God and in the perfect love of Jesus has never wavered. But I have ceased to practise my religion formally. I do not make confession or attend Mass any more, and if I felt I were dying, I do not think I should send for a priest to give me absolution; I would take my chance of God's forgiveness. This is a dreadful thing for a sincere Roman Catholic to say, but I say it because I have suffered so much, and seen my coloured friends suffer so much, at white priests' and white Roman Catholic worshippers' hands.

In the first chapter of this book, I told how a white verger interfered with me while I was kneeling at prayer in a New York Roman Catholic church, and how a friend's baby was made to wait for baptism in another church till all the white babies placed later in the list of arrangements had been christened. I could recount a hundred such instances, or a thousand, and against them, hardly even one where no prejudice was shown.

When I was working for the Ministry of Labour in Liverpool, my duties with regard to coloured people brought me a good deal into contact with Dr. David, the former Bishop of Liverpool, now dead. In all other ways a notably tolerant and kindly man, the Bishop was inflexible in regard to colour segregation. He treated me courteously, but only apparently because he was obliged to do so as a matter of business. How often, when talking to him, I remembered that tragic passage from *The Merchant of Venice*: "I will buy with you, sell with you, talk with you, walk with you, and so following; but I will not eat with you, drink with you, nor pray with you." Like so many who gain a reputation for usefulness in the colour problem, all he appeared to want from it was the ability to segregate white and coloured, and to keep the coloured people sufficiently fed and clothed and housed perhaps, but definitely "in their place".

How well I recall something which happened when I was an impressionable young man from Trinidad. A Negro man I knew was an acolyte helping to serve at the altar of a Roman Catholic church in England. One day, he was told by the priest that he need not come next Sunday to help to serve, though he would be expected as a member of the congregation; it was explained to him quite ordinarily that it had been decided to use only young persons for acolytes there in future. He went to the church on the following Sunday innocently and happily, and was astounded to see that all the other acolytes, being white-skinned, were serving in their usual places. None of the other men had been asked to leave, nor did they leave later. It was his colour, not his age, that had offended the minister of God—and only then, I suppose, when some rich members of the church, who had made their fortunes in the Colonies, prompted the priest to the action, which he was too cowardly to refuse.

I remember, too, how that coloured man quietly continued to attend his church. When I blazed out at him for doing it, he said: "One man has done me a wrong, but that is not going to separate me from God or keep me away from church." How often since have I heard that voice again, when my own anger has prompted me to take some resentful action when white people have hurt me. That man was right; I have been wrong. But how hard it is to turn the other cheek to a blow, when the cheek is dark and the hand that contemptuously strikes it is white! It would be so if the places were reversed, would it not?

In the West Indies, the coloured people's religion is in the main that of the white people who first brought them as slaves to a particular island. In Trinidad, we are mostly Roman Catholic, in Jamaica and Barbados mostly Protestant, and so on; there are also some Mohammedans and Hindus. Among the young coloured people there, as everywhere else, an increasing number profess atheism—really, I think, as an involuntary protest against the discrimination of Christian whites against them. For there is something very foreign to the Negro nature in the gaping chasm of unbelief.

In the U.S.A. most of the Negroes are Protestants, of varying denominations. In Africa, apart from many kinds of coloured Christians, there are far more coloured Mohammedans and a great number of pantheist primitives who see manifestations of gods or spirits in every stick and stone and tree. In Asia, the coloured people are mostly Hindus, Buddhists, Confucians or Mohammedans. In South America they are largely Roman Catholics or primitives, and in Australia they are primitives, too. In Europe, most coloured people above the age of thirty are Christians, and most of the younger people now profess atheism, once more because they cannot make themselves trust a Christianity whose white professors, when they come into contact with coloured Christians, deny with every action the brotherhood of God's children, and will only love their neighbours as themselves if those neighbours have completely white skins and are of the same nation and point of view. If they have dark skins, they will not under any circumstances allow them to be neighbours at all, even in a civic sense.

Man, and especially perhaps coloured man, cannot exist without a religion of some sort. That is why semi-religious organizations such as Mau Mau are springing into active and dangerous life. It is why the half-religion of Communism is being muttered under the breath from one end of the coloured world to the other. These are the perilous substitutes that frantic people accept for lack of the Gospel of Love.

If they will, a peaceful solution of the world's colour problem lies in the hands of the chief officers of the Christian religion. If the Pope and the Archbishop of Canterbury and half a dozen other such paramount religious leaders would issue a brief, categorical, uncompromising statement condemning all forms of colour discrimination in religion, not only would vast numbers of coloured people feel a new impetus towards Christian faith, but many doubting whites would do, also.

I suggest, in all humility, that such a statement might follow some such lines as these:

> "In all Christian churches, white and coloured people are to be permitted to worship together equally and without any sort of discrimination as to place or order. In all Christian churches where a considerable part of the congregation is coloured, they should be represented on all official church organizations by a proportionate number of persons of their own colour. Coloured candidates for priestly ordination will be encouraged, and appointed to churches all over the world without colour discrimination."

Perhaps that seems a crude and simple statement, and I have no doubt that it could. be bettered. But any such encyclical, worded without possibility of evasion, would open such springs of hope in the hearts of coloured millions as surpass all power of description. No one knows better than coloured people that they have much to learn, and that in general they are at a disadvantage in manners and education as against white people, but if only they could feel any sense at all of *brotherhood*, of welcome, of a spiritual plane on which they might meet the rest of mankind in love and the equality of love, the worst of "The Black Man's Burden" would be gone.

There is one other aspect, closely connected with religion, which I ought to touch on here. It has been repeated many times that the root of the white man's fear of the coloured races, and the fundamental cause of his refusal to create conditions of equality, lies in the fact that coloured races have a much higher birth-rate than white races. It is, in fact, feared by

SELWYN D. RYAN

Race and Nationalism in Trinidad and Tobago: a study of decolonization in a multiracial society

UNIVERSITY OF TORONTO PRESS   *1972*

---

150   Trinidad and Tobago

The possibility of a state-controlled curriculum alarmed the Catholic Church. To the Church the content of education in church schools was not a negotiable matter. The principles of Catholic education sprang from verities that were 'supernatural and supranational'. Nationalistic and utilitarian imperatives could not be allowed to subvert such principles. The hierarchy acknowledged that national integration was a legitimate ideal, and agreed that the Church must 'carefully avoid any action which would seem to encourage cleavages along racial lines or in any other way be divisive of the social unity of our emergent community'.[2] But the answer was not to be found in the national take-over of all schools, or in an imposed uniformity.

It was an open secret, however, that Catholic schools were prone to discriminate against children who did not have the 'proper' social or ethnic qualifications. Indians and Negroes were the ones who suffered most from these invidious selection practices. The emphasis on religious instruction to the detriment of subjects which would provide the sort of technical skills needed for a newly developing community was also lamented by the more secularly minded. In an attempt to arrive at a sort of 'concordat' with the Church, Dr Williams proposed five points as an irreducible 'recipe for national education':

It was a package which was clearly unacceptable to the Catholic Church.

It must be noted that the Catholic Church was not the only religious group to oppose state control; Hindus and Moslems were also against it. While the Catholics were accused of using the denominational school to advance whites and near-whites. Hindus and Moslems were accused of using theirs as cells for the inculcation of a creedal nationalism that was inimical to the broader interests of the society. Williams tried to rally the Hindus by noting that Gandhi had been fundamentally opposed to state support of religious instruction; but the Hindus remained unconvinced.[4] Only the Protestant churches, mainly Anglican and Presbyterian, rallied to the defence of the PNM.

2   *Ibid.*, Jan. 22, 1956.   3   *Ibid.*
4   *Ibid.*, May 18, 1955.

to teacher and pupil recruitment since the state could now use its control of the 80 per cent pupil quota to change the complexion of the schools, the churches were left relatively free to carry on as before, with only a minimum of government supervision or dictation.[36] Moreover, despite the assumption that the examination pass list would be used as the basis for the recruitment of the churches' quota, in fact it meant that the Churches were free to assign scarce school places at state expense to pupils who need not possess the achievement criteria for admission, while qualified pupils were allowed to go unplaced. With 25,000 pupils competing for 4,000 places, this was a substantial concession to make. The egalitarian purpose of the PNM was seriously compromised. Some party stalwarts were infuriated, especially since the Party had not been consulted on the issue. The author of the Report, Senator Hamilton Maurice, remained outspokenly convinced that 'in a society of competing ethnic groups, a society where religious dogma combines with racial differences, the existing educational system poses the greatest threat to national unity.' Only a unified state system could contain the strife potential of the community. 'No system that is the servant of any one particular class, race or creed can achieve this goal.'[37]

The Protestant churches were quite pleased with the settlement which the Catholic hierarchy had been able to force on the PNM, though they might very well have been chagrined by the fact that the government had bargained mainly with the Catholic Church. Between 1960 and 1965 when the issue was reopened, the Catholic Church gave open support to the PNM regime.[38] The 'opening to the right' strategy had been given additional thrust. With the Church, the Colonial Office, and the State Department neutralized, Williams could declare to the nation that the road was now cleared of all the obstacles which had inhibited the creation of the national community.

But the consolidation of the power of the PNM was a prime prerequisite for effecting this goal. The Party that had initiated the 'revolution' had to be allowed to complete it, even if this meant that some of these revolutionary goals had to be sacrificed in the short run. As Williams warned the Party, 'I for one intend to play politics. Let everybody understand that. I have been accused for four years of playing politics. Well by God, they are going to get politics now, and I hope they recognise it.'[39] The 'no deals' era had come to a close.

36 Placement in the schools, within this 80 per cent quota, was still to be determined by the parents, wherever possible.
37 *Nation*, Dec. 21, 1962.
38 The schools issue was reopened in 1965 when the PNM dramatically revoked some of the major provisions of the Concordat. Cf. p. 340.
39 Williams to the Sixth Annual Convention, January 1961.

for Castro to do a little purging and see what happens when they come back. Ladies and Gentlemen, they have it good here.[33]

The 'massas' were also accused of being opposed to the government's decision to introduce free secondary education. All the old arguments against the ascriptive bias of the old school system were again aired. In spite of the new concordat, which was not yet operative, Williams still pointed the accusing finger at the Catholic school system. 'Even if you could afford to pay, they gave preference to the Venezuelan child.' The 'massas' were up in arms against the new education system because it made it more difficult for them to bribe their way into the island's best schools. 'But they can't do that any more. Nobody is getting in unless they pass the Common Qualifying Examination.' The Honourable John O'Halloran, himself a European, also declared that whites were opposed to the new system because they knew that their sons could not compete equally with the achievement-oriented sons of lower-class parents; nor did they want to send their children to school with coloured 'rabs'.[34]

The PNM's proudest boast during the campaign was that it had now freed the educational system of the virus of influence-peddling. Education was no longer open only to the privileged aristocracy of the skin; it was free.[35] Williams warned parents that they should avoid giving their ingrained prejudices to the young: 'Set the children free. Let them show their talent and make their contribution to the building of the national community.'

He also accused French creoles of seeking to mount an economic counter-revolution: 'They are trying to get their blasted hands back at your throats after we, the PNM, have moved them. The exporters wanted to be free again to defraud the cocoa farmers, to pay them unfair prices based on quantity rather than quality. They wanted the Telephone Company handed back to the old Company. They were also planning to restrain labour, to fix wages, and return to the old practices whereby troops and scabs were used to break strikes.'[36] This was the programme that the DLP – 'the shoe-shine boys for the planters and merchants in Port of Spain' – had endorsed. 'The DLP', Williams claimed, 'was waging a last-ditch fight because they knew that if they lost in 1961 they

33   Williams at La Brea and Barataria (undated tape).
34   There was much truth in this accusation. Some white creoles, and even the brown middle-classes, were opposed to an education system in which children of black lower-class families were permitted to socialize with their offspring.
35   Education was not yet entirely free, but this was promised in the budget of 1960. The programme for 1961 was to increase secondary school scholarships from one hundred to four hundred. We have already noted that there was a loophole in the Concordat which made it possible for children to be admitted on ascriptive grounds. See chap. 15.
36   Undated tape.

Page 8, TRINIDAD GUARDIAN, Wednesday, September 28, 1994

Race in education?

Prestige Schools *Common Entrance*

INEVITABLY, the reaction to the report from the Centre for Ethnic Studies on placement patterns and practices in secondary schools has focussed on the issue of equality in the education system.

Is race a factor in who gets into which of the prestige schools? Does race carry a higher value than merit, especially in the situation where a denominational school is making up its 20 per cent quota on the basis of the Common Entrance Examination results.

The answer in the study to both questions and others in the same area appears to be a resounding "yes", and the writers of the report provide statistics to support their view.

Most at Risk

Yet it would be wrong to suggest that most of the inequities in the system are due principally to racial factors, even if one were to agree with the theory that in the special circumstances of the denominational schools, where religious affiliation is important as well, they do bear some influence.

Poverty, for example. It has long been recognised that children from low income families are most at risk in facing up to the challenge of the Common Entrance Examination.

Here the homes are less stable, supervision of school age children often does not exist, the environment does not encourage study - few books or none at all; no money to provide the special coaching which transforms so many children into machines for earning enough marks to get into a secondary school.

As the report puts it: "The evidence (also) indicated that students from upper and middle income homes stayed in school. Their proportion in the population increased relative to the lower income group. More students from lower income households left —

their proportions decreased."

So to emphasise the racial considerations in the report and give a lower priority to the issue of indigence and religious affiliation is to bypass an important factor leading to what appears as the failure of certain ethnic groups to find an equal place in the school system.

Indeed what is required, if the system is to make it possible for "all the people" to be educated according to the terms of this report as well as the one of the Task Force on education, is a revolution in the way the children of the nation are taught.

Once again we are told the Common Entrance Examination should be abolished and the system it promotes ought to be restructured.

The Task Force last year recommended that this examination be continued only until what it termed the pre-requisites for change are fully implemented in the primary schools by 1998.

Latest Study

Also, the Task Force reported that after this period placement at secondary level be on the basis of both continuous assessment and a national examination.

This view is backed in the latest study which states that the CE placement process "has legitimised inequality and inequities into the school system" and calls for abolition of the examination.

The question is if, in the search for equality in the system, a formula will be found to make it easier for children from lower income families to stand up to competition from their better off colleagues.

Continuous assessment is now the favourite means towards that end, but it is unlikely to be the end itself so long as social and other inequalities continue to exist among the races and classes in this country.

PEOPLE MAGAZINE Sunday July 13, 1986 page 7

WAYNE BROWN INTERVIEW

'If you wanted to get out you really had to claw your way out'

Valere...but in those days there'd be only about five or six girls who went on to do Higher Cert, and they would definitely not be French Creole...

Q: George Lamming once observed that in the West Indies money was not something that bought you an education but something that freed you from the need for an education...

A: Definitely. I mean, the Convent, they taught music, art, and so on, and you'd have, like, one person doing a Higher Cert. But when we went in (I think Alma Jordan went in with me) we were like the cutting edge; not because of any innate ability but perhaps because times were changing. So they (the French Creole majority) just didn't know what to do (about us). I mean, they weren't hostile. There was an admiration, there was a respect, but there was also a, "Well, you all are different." They didn't compete with you, they didn't expect to compete with you. You (ie. the coloured girls) were strange and marvellous people, and while you were there you got along okay. But

summer day outdoors at Columbia University.

me when I t everybody puldn't read ycle light ooks I read under the

been nine out. Can what, was

nition class, taught gen women, in the most was one of Street: she s, and clip papers, all at n t. Can n 11? I was And then e did there e morning re o'clock, e German up some nd, well, I went to n, Corina n.

Achong and I, we both saw The Flames! Great drama. But we were very involved in it, unlike my children, who knew about (political and military issues, like Vietnam), and...perhaps it was a defence mechanism for them, because they were always living in the thick of such things at home, but they would tend not to be very interested in that kind of thing when they were smaller. But at that age we were very...and then I went into Girl Guides, we used to knit blanket squares and roll bandages, all part of the war effort. And those were the days when, you had a radio, the whole neighbourhood came around to hear the news and so on.

Q: By the end of the war you would just about have been entering Sixth Form. What was the Convent experience like?

A: Well, what happened, eh; when we went into Convent, people like Corina and I, Convent was still predominantly French Creole. There were one or two isolated (coloured girls). Electra Harris, Merle and Joan Attal, Margery

YOUNG Patricia, after taking the Higher Certificate in '48.

it was of course very limited to within the Convent walls. Outside of Convent you just didn't inhabit the same world.

Q: Did you remain friends with any of the French Creole girls after school?

A: Well, there were a couple of them; the majority, you really couldn't see yourself...(laughing)...there really wasn't anything there, you know! But there was one girl that I often think was really ruined by her privilege, because she was the kind of girl who should have gone on to university and come out and made a name for herself. But we did everything for the first time, put out a magazine, put on plays, and she was always in the thick of it. I really think she must have been colour-blind. She impressed me a lot. And come to

think of it, she's the only one of them I ever invited home in later years.

Q: Let's leave the sociological aspect for a while. I'd like you to think back to yourself at, say, 16. What were your sort of schoolgirl dreams?

A: Definitely to go on to university. I mean, there was a big world out there I wanted to get into. Mind you, it was a world of storybooks, eh? My concept of the United States when I landed in the United States one fine early spring morning, it was such a shock to me! When I saw Harlem for the first time. Because oddly enough I wanted to go to America; I didn't have any big attraction for England. So when after school my father suggested that while waiting for results I should join the public service you cannot imagine how I rebelled at that. I thought of it as a kind of lagley; once I got into it I wouldn't get out. But I sat the civil service exam and I came very high and they sent me as a temporary clerk to the Colonial Secretary's Office. The British had just started to train an (indigenous) elite. They had started with these administrative cadets. And in those days, you would not believe the atmosphere of the upper echelon at the Red House. The only place I can think of that had the same silence would be the inner courtyard in St Joseph's Convent. I mean, they were calm, and you spoke in a hushed voice and tiptoed along—it was really an elitist thing. Dodd Alleyne was there, Eldon Warner, Wenty Thorne, Neville Perreira... You got the distinct sense of being in an elite. I was a confidential correspondence clerk, which meant that I melted red wax, dropped it on envelopes and sealed them! But the atmosphere made it tolerable.

Q: But you knew all along that you were going away?

A: Oh yes. Well, the first big disappointment was that I didn't win the Girls' Island Scholarship. Corina Achong, who's one of my oldest standing friends—from age three we went right through school together—she got it. It was the first real disappointment I'd ever had in life. Because nobody had died, I really hadn't known any kind of upset until then. But being in this Colonial Secretary's Office made up for it in a way because you felt you were, you know, special. But I spent that whole year, I think, filling out scholarship applications. Because in those days, eh, if you wanted to get out you really had to claw your way out. Now that I look back, some of my contemporaries (who didn't make it abroad) actually took to drink and thing. It was a different kind of frustration. Nowadays a lot of people, having gone away, get

Continued on page 13

CATHOLICS

"To be black and Catholic is a contradiction."

Black and white Catholic leaders officiate at prayer session, a scene the NOBC has long strived for.

VOLUME 30, No 4, 1981, U.S.A SEPIA MAGAZINE

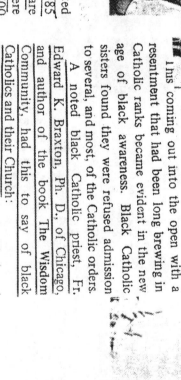

A black sister sings freedom songs in Chicago.

O f 341 Catholic Bishops in the United States only five are black. Of 58,485 Catholic priests in the U.S., only 270 are black. In 1930 there were only 10. There are 100 black Catholic brothers and 700 black Catholic sisters, 161 black deacons and 110 black deacon candidates. There are 200 black Catholic seminarians.

This coming out into the open with a resentment that had been long brewing in Catholic ranks became evident in the new age of black awareness. Black Catholic sisters found they were refused admission to several, and most, of the Catholic orders.

A noted black Catholic priest, Fr. Edward K. Braxton, Ph. D., of Chicago, and author of the book The Wisdom Community, had this to say of black Catholics and their Church:

"I have been told that to be black and Catholic is a contradiction since the Church has been, and at times still is, guilty of racial prejudice.

THE NEW YORK TIMES, THURSDAY, MAY 29, 1975

Conservative Priest Will Oppose Chicago Machine in House Race

New York Times May 29-1975

By PAUL DELANEY
Special to The New York Times

CHICAGO, May 28—A conservative Roman Catholic priest who carried the hopes of white opposition to integration during the nineteen-sixties is now carrying the hopes of Republicans attempting to upset Mayor Richard J. Daley's Democratic machine in a special Congressional election.

The Reverend Francis X. Lawlor conducted a write-in campaign to win the Republican primary, yesterday for the seat left vacant by the death in March of Representative John Kluczynski, Democrat of Illinois.

The white-haired priest defeated William G. Toms, a shipping clerk and perennial Republican candidate. Father Lawlor will face State Representative John Fary, the machine-backed candidate who easily won the Democratic primary over another write-in candidate, Frank Zabielski Jr., an unemployed salesman. Mr. Fary is the heavy favorite in the July 8 special general election.

Both Father Lawlor and Mr. Zabielski were refused places on the ballots of their respective parties because of defective petitions. The Board of Elections ruled that Father Lawlor forgot to mention in his petition that he was a Republican and wanted to run in the Republican primary and had filled out the wrong forms.

After striking the two candidates from the ballots, the board then canceled the primary election with the explanation that it was not necessary since there was only one candidate in each primary. Father Lawlor took legal action and a three-judge Federal District Court panel ordered the primary election.

United Press International

The Rev. Francis X. Lawlor

fight and challenged Mr. Fary to a series of debates. Mr. Fary said that he would be too busy in the state Legislature.

Mr. Fary said at a news conference last night, "My son was a student at St. Rita when Father Lawlor was administrator there. Now how would I look debating the good father?"

Father Lawlor has prompted controversy as a leading opponent of civil rights and the drive by the Rev. Dr. Martin Luther King Jr. against segregated housing in Chicago. At one point, the Archdiocese transferred Mr. Lawlor to Tulsa, Okla., but the fiery priest refused to remain there. Dr. King's drive had the support of the Catholic leadership.

Father Lawlor, a former teacher and administrator in Catholic schools, went on to become a city Alderman, but retired this year after one four-year term.

The Fifth Congressional District where Father Lawlor is running is 30 per cent black and 7 per cent Spanish-speaking. His major campaign issue was neighborhood stability. He said that he wanted to prevent white flight to the suburbs

DISAPPOINTED GUESTS

Essays by
AFRICAN, ASIAN, AND
WEST INDIAN STUDENTS

Edited by

HENRI TAJFEL, M.A., Ph.D.
University Lecturer in Social Psychology and
Fellow of Linacre House, Oxford

and

JOHN L. DAWSON, M.A., D. Phil.
Research Lecturer, Department of Social
Anthropology, University of Edinburgh

Issued under the Auspices of the
Institute of Race Relations, London
OXFORD UNIVERSITY PRESS
LONDON   NEW YORK
1965

2

The Colour Problem at the University: A West Indian's Changing Attitudes

KENNETH RAMCHAND

Trinidad

Kenneth Ramchand was born in Trinidad in 1939. He completed his early education there. Between 1959 and 1963 he was at the University of Edinburgh where he took his M.A. Honours in English and gained a Mackenzie Scholarship in English from the university. He is at present engaged in post-graduate work on the West Indian novel. He hopes to lecture and teach in the West Indies.

THE paperback edition of the West Indian sees him as indulging in exotic calypso colours of red and green and yellow, riotous colours that compel attention, loud colours that are taken to indicate a coarseness of visual palate, or an eye unaware of pattern and design, and unable to discriminate between variant shades of the same colour. ('You West Indians,' in despair, 'you cannot appreciate Art, you only look for the bright colours.')

If this popular image is valid, we find in the West Indian an amazing double-vision. For, in the contemplation of human groups, no society has evolved a more delicate instrument of perception. The West Indian consciousness suspends, in equipoise, considerations of racial origin and considerations of degrees of blackness. In looking at the complex construct that is colonial society, it blends elements from these categories with rare flexibility.

ROMAN CATHOLIC CHURCH see Page 114

The initial breakdown is along lines of known racial origin. Here are some children at play:

'Nigger is a nation, They stink with perspiration' (African)
'Coolie, coolie, Come for roti' (Indian)
'Chinee chinee never die, Flat nose and Chinky eye' (Chinese)
'Whitey cock-o-roach' (Not very sure)

This crude analysis is refined by a delicate perception of the variants of skin colour. At one end of the scale is 'White' (roughly = English). Next come 'West Indian Whites' (diverse European origin, many now carrying in their blood the secret of their fathers' dark connexions). After these come the 'light-skinned' or 'yellow' Chinese. Then come the black ones—Indians and Africans. Of the infinite mixtures available, all that can be said is that there is an intuitive apprehension, and a certain placing of every possible variant along the colour scale. 'Black' is complex indeed. An Indian may be black, but his highest degree of blackness is indicated in the taunt, 'Look at you, you just like a nigger.' In West Indian society, 'black' is usually reserved for 'Negro', and 'Negro' ranges from the 'tar baby' of the West Indian Reader, to the 'red nigger'. It is even possible to be blacker than black: in a book by the Trinidadian Samuel Selvon, one character is called 'Midnight' because he is the blackest in his group. A new figure comes along however, and he, impossibly, is blacker still. The delicate instrument reacts sensitively; the new man is christened 'Five-past-twelve'.

Leaving the West Indies and coming to Britain is like entering a land where the natives suffer from a curious kind of colour blindness in the contemplation of human groups. This special form of blindness manifests itself in an insensitivity to racial discriminations and variant shades within the category 'black'. It registers two crude categories, black and white.

The West Indian consciousness is outraged by the crudity of the categorization. In the rarefied atmosphere of the mother country, the delicate instrument ceases to function. All West Indians are black. Under impartial pressure, the first defensive measure is the formation of West Indian groups and

3

The Weary Road to Whiteness and the Hasty Retreat into Nationalism

ELLIOTT BASTIEN

Trinidad

Elliott Bastien graduated with a B.Sc. (Hons.) in Chemical Engineering in 1963 and then attended a post-graduate course in Petroleum Production Engineering in Birmingham.

He wrote several articles for *Mermaid* (the literary magazine of the University of Birmingham) and is now collecting material for a book on Caribbean literature.

He returned to Trinidad in October 1964 to work in the Technical Civil Service.

'THE greatest lie of our society', writes C. L. R. James, 'is that anywhere in these islands we have achieved racial harmony.' In the same vein he continues, 'In a book by a West Indian intended for West Indians I refuse to spend time disproving that racial harmony exists in the West Indies.' This may be justified, but the form of this essay does not permit the subject of racial harmony to be dismissed in quite so short a space (half of a page) as Mr. James uses. However, he does find it necessary to give a 'last word of warning' in the form of a postscript: 'Whatever the provocation, the subject demands a steady hand and a calm temper.' I shall try, along every step of the way, to keep these words before me.

To discuss racism in a West Indian context is to become hopelessly confused. One gets lost in a mass of contradictions, and vacillation seems to be the rule of the day. This is because of the peculiarly complex system of social stratification; a system under which we live, and which is accepted by us, but never examined. Never, that is, until we leave our island society and are forced to face reality. And even so, the involvement was so deep, and the brainwashing so subtle, that it is still difficult to think straight and view the whole subject objectively. (Perhaps it is not at all a good idea to be completely objective—even if this were possible—in such matters.) An amazing degree of ambivalence is shown at all levels of the society. This can have its origin in apathy, wide-eyed innocence—which is the same anyway—or just downright hypocrisy.

Here is the calypsonian, the spokesman of the masses commenting on the racial situation in two calypsoes. They are both by the Mighty Sparrow but I am not sure about the chronological order which is unimportant as the time factor is not great.

From 'Leave the Dam Doctor':

> They makin' so much confusion
> 'Bout race riot in England.
> They should kick them from Scotland Yard,
> We have the same question in Trinidad.

And then an admirably well expressed verse that has a much more than local significance.

> Well the way how things shapin' up,
> All this nigger business go' stop.
> I tell you soon in the West Indies
> Is please Mr. Nigger please.

Next comes 'Trinidad Carnival', and notice the popular national myth being flattered. He says there is 'no colour question'.

> So jump and be merry
> Don' care how you black and ugly

because

> You could jump wid black
> You could jump wid white
> Jump until is twelve tonite.

is his blue eyes, and his spit on Dauphin people is the sea.' And this is indeed brought home to the West Indian at a very early age, in the colour of the statues in the churches, in the fact that it is hard to conceive of a black pope. It is difficult for a Negro Roman Catholic to reconcile the teachings of the Church with the practice of racial discrimination by its pastors. The shock at discovering that segregation is practised in Roman Catholic churches in the southern United States is great indeed. In a Catholic college predominantly coloured, it is no accident that until recently, the Sixth Trinidad Sea Scouts (led by a priest) were all white, or that again until recently, the drama group (again led by a priest) was white to a man. To this latter statement, the aged priest-educator, a German, is reputed to have bluntly replied that Shakespeare did not write his plays for black people.

'I felt', says James Baldwin, 'that I was committing a crime in talking about the gentle Jesus, in telling them to reconcile themselves to their misery on earth in order to gain the crown of eternal life'; and the Negro position is neatly summarized. One of my African friends, himself a Christian, felt that the greatest evil to enter Africa was Christianity. The significance cannot be missed.

Religion, though, has had some effect in bringing the races together in the West Indies. But probably the greatest unifying force was, and is, the classroom, where all races mingle together. Any silly ideas of the intrinsic superiority of one race over another are destroyed by mere observation in the classroom and on the playing-fields. It is a lesson that is not forgotten in adult life, and non-white doctors and lawyers have many white people among their clientèle. From the very earliest stage, the white child comes into contact with black people, as black domestic servants are given complete control of the children of white families. Throughout his school career he meets and makes friends with coloured children, both sides realizing that after school hours they must be socially separate. The same applies to the professional relationships in later years.

It is in this way that the significant emotional experiences are

The Church at Wounded Knee

The role of Christians — and Christian churches — in the current Indian scene, and at Wounded Knee, is difficult and confusing to analyze. While many native people feel that the Christian Church has been an instrument of oppression almost from the outset, it is equally evident that there are today Christian peoples who have a sincere desire to help the churches face up to their responsibilities to peoples it has helped destroy.

The controversy and confusion is not only about how native peoples see Christians — it is also a subject of great controversy within the Church itself. In fact, there are those who blame the church for the Wounded Knee occupation.

The National Council of Churches sent a team of representatives to the occupation. "The NCC role has been to protect against loss of life and attempt to open up options in the field of negotiations," said a member of the NCC delegation, the Rev. John Adams, an official of the United Methodist Church. The NCC had helped to bring the Oglalas and the U.S. to negotiations, and had acted as observers at federal positions when a showdown appeared imminent.

Dick Wilson, chairman of the Pine Ridge tribal council, had ordered the NCC off the reservation, and sent BIA police to enforce his dictum.

The Fellowship of Reconciliation had sent a number of observers to Wounded Knee after running a large ad in the New York Times chiding the U.S. Government for over-reacting and sending in massive armament to put down the Oglalas. One observer was Sister Mary Alice Scully, a Sister of Charity nun, who tried to walk into Wounded Knee under cover of darkness on April 27. She was carrying a knapsack of food, but after becoming separated from the main party, she was picked up by a law enforcement patrol.

Sister Mary Alice said her chief reason in trying to aid was that the Indians had something to say to the nation and the world at large about spirituality. I would like to see the Indian stand up and speak out his message to a very pained and suffering world."

The parsonage occupied by the Rev. and Mrs. Orville Lansberry — who fled the night of the invasion — was burned to the foundation on the eve of the termination of the occupation. They were pastors of the Church of God there.

Rev. Paul Steinmetz, the Catholic priest at Sacred Heart Church in Pine Ridge and president of the 25-member association of missionaries who are converting and pastoring the Oglalas, said the church at Wounded Knee would probably be restored. "We intend to go back in and serve the people. We want to try to pick up the pieces in a spirit of reconciliation." Of the attacks on the church buildings, he concluded, "There's a hatred of Christianity involved here, obviously."

Some Indian groups have looked to the churches for payment of "damages". During Wounded Knee, a group of native people gathered at the padlocked gates of the Mormon Temple Square in Salt Lake City to ask the Church of Jesus Christ of Latter Day Saints for

"if any official representative of the United States comes in here except under church escort, it will be treated as an act of war and dealt with accordingly," Russell Means said at one point in the standoff.

One group which is particularly concerned about the effects of Wounded Knee on the American public are the missionaries. They depend for their livelihood on the goodwill of donors to Indian causes.

The Rev. Neal Phipps, director of the Wesleyan Indian Missions, said in his newsletter, "One priest said it has set back the Christian work among the Indians 100 years." He based his assessment on the drop in mail and income to support mission work, and he partly blamed the role of white churches in the controversy.

Phipps sided strongly with Dick Wilson and the tribal council faction in the dispute.

Only about a dozen of the occupiers are Oglalas, Phipps said. "All the rest of the troublemakers are outside agitators. . . . What is being done by the few will lower them all in the eyes of the public." Phipps says this image of lawlessness has caused the drop in contributions. Things were hard enough, he said, without Wounded Knee— only about 10 per cent of the Indians in his missions are regular churchgoers.

Phipps says the six Wesleyan missionaries on the reservation have 26 "preaching stations."

Other mission groups are using Wounded Knee as an opportunity to appeal for more funds. "To reach Indian Americans for Christ and help prevent more promised Wounded Knees" is the reason given by the Rev. R.L. Gowan, president of the American Indian Missions — with the unfortunate acronym, AIM. Gowan feels that more fundamental mission work would cool off a tense situation.

He publishes a newspaper, Indian Life & Hope, on which appears an article about Princess Pale Moon, who is active in the National Indian Cultural Exchange, which makes her a goodwill ambassador for the NICE [...]

Akwesasne Notes
Mohawk Nation
Via:
Rooseveltown N.Y. 13683

AKWESASNE NOTES

LATE SUMMER, 1973

A CATHOLIC PRIEST PONDERS THE MEANING OF WOUNDED KNEE TO HIS CHURCH

(This commentary by Father Wm. G. Muench is part of a longer article which appeared in the April 4 issue of the North Country Catholic, serving Catholic families of upstate New York.)

Church would house their much harm these Catholic missionaries did by ridiculing and destroying Indian beliefs and life style. Instead of lovingly leading them to understand, they followed the sword and imposed their ideals. The Church has always been associated with the oppressing invaders. And it seemed to want it that way.

movement. Until I realized that they were using this Church as a symbol of one of the things that they hated most.

I think of all Americans, we Catholics owe so much to these Indians. When I saw all the happenings at Wounded Knee around the Catholic Church, I was pleased. Pleased that the

We have always thought of the missionaries as the good guys and the Indians as the evil. What we do not know is how

Now we have to find our way back to these people. To weep and repent of our past sins and injustices. We have made them what they are — frustrated and unhappy. Let us begin with understanding. Read and open your minds to just who these Indians are. We cannot support the insurrection at Wounded Knee — but we can understand.

AKWESASNE NOTES

Mohawk Nation
via Rooseveltown, New York - 13683

LATE SUMMER, 1973

EXPRESS Monday, August 27, 2001 Page 5

Caribs accuse Catholic church of disrespect

Santa Rosa mass boycotted

By DEBRA
RAVELLO GREAVES

THE Carib community has accused the Catholic church of treating it with disrespect.

As a result yesterday they boycotted the traditional mass and procession to celebrate the Feast of Santa Rosa at Arima in protest over the church's alleged action.

President of the community Ricardo Bharath claimed the Caribs' role in organising the event, which marks their acceptance of Christianity, was being minimised. He accused the church of paying lip service to the preservation of indigenous people and their culture which it helped to destroy.

A lack of consultation by parish priest Fr Leo Donovan with the community over the planning of yesterday's event led to the boycott, according to Bharath who claimed Donovan did not comply with their wishes.

"The priest sat with the parish council and they decided what they were going to do," he said, insisting that it should be the other way around instead.

Bharath said Donovan decided to keep mass at the Arima Boys' RC School and while plans were not yet finalised with them, went ahead and announced that venue.

However, the Caribs refused to join Donovan for the procession and mass when he invited them over to the boys' school but instead car-

MEMBERS of the visiting Dominican Carib Community take part in the Santa Rosa Festival Parade through Arima, which was preceded by a church service at the Santa Rosa, RC Church yesterday.
Photo: STEPHENSON WESTFIELD

ried on their own procession and mass simultaneously at the Santa Rosa RC Church.

Bharath declared: "The church continues in the year 2001 to disrespect the Carib community.

"We thought that we should take a stand."

"The Santa Rosa Festival is always the responsibility of the Carib community. In the past if the priest wanted to take the procession to another route, they had to get the Caribs' permission first. They had to meet with the queen and the leaders, but now they just drop it on you," Bharath complained.

He said the community was warming to the venue but their request for a tent to cover the statue and community members was not granted.

Revealing that the community has had long-standing problems with priests, he noted, however, some of them have been very co-operative with the community.

Fr Donovan could not be contacted by the *Express* last night.

Pope John Paul II is blessed during a native American Indian ceremony in Phoenix, where he addressed a three-day conference of about 1,600 Indian.

BY RICH LIPSKI—The Washington Post

Pope Urges Indians to Forget Church's Past Mistakes

Washington Post September 15, 1987

By David Maraniss
and Loren Jenkins
Washington Post Staff Writers

PHOENIX, Sept. 14—Pope John Paul II urged Indian leaders to forget his church's past "mistakes and wrongs" and look to its current efforts for Indian rights. But a spokeswoman for Indian Roman Catholics told him in his church, and much to be done in his church, and in America.

Addressing a three-day conference of about 1,600 Indian leaders from around the United States, the pope described the initial encounter between Europeans and American natives as a "painful reality" for the natives' descendants.

"The cultural oppression, the injustices, the disruption of your life and your traditional societies must be acknowledged," he said, while specifically praising Friar Junipero Serra, the early Franciscan missionary who embodies, for Indians, all the ancient abuses of the church.

"Unfortunately, not all the members of the church lived up to their Christian responsibilities," he said. "But let us not dwell excessively on mistakes and wrongs, even as we commit ourselves to overcoming their present effects."

It was not the strong response sought by Alfretta M. Antone, of the Pima-Maricopa tribe's Salt River Reservation, in her welcoming remarks. She had asked the pope to intercede on behalf of the Indians threatened lands and culture. She also urged that the church open its doors to more Indian clerics and the greater use of Indian languages and culture in its sacramental life.

"Today, little remains of the gifts and richness which our Creator shared with us, the original peoples of these lands, Antone said. We ask you to intervene with all people

of good will to preserve our homelands for our families, our children and the generations to follow us."

The unfortunate past to which the pope referred involved the memory of many Roman Catholic priests who accompanied the Spanish conquistadors colonizing the West in the 17th and 18th centuries, proselytizing among the Indians they encountered and, often killing those who would not convert.

"The church still has much to answer for to us," said Sacheen Little Feather, an Apache delegate to the Indian conference here. "It is a matter of the church's cultural genocide against the Indians that must still be addressed by the missions."

To the Indians, the chief representative of that dark era of Spanish-Catholic colonization is Serra, a Spaniard who helped found the Catholic missions of California. Catholic history records him as a staunch defender of the Indians, whom he worked zealously to convert. Indian history remembers him for the deaths of Indians who resisted his efforts.

Pope John Paul II had been expected to honor Friar Serra's missionary labors in the 18th century by beatifying him, a church step toward proclaiming him a saint. But the protests of native Americans forced the pope to reconsider.

Nonetheless, in his address today, the pope praised Serra, a church martyr known as the "Apostle of the Californias" for his evangelizing mission.

Jeannette Henry Costo of the Eastern Cherokee Tribe and spokeswoman for the Indian Conference said: "I'm sorry. I'm terribly sorry he said that. I think it's discussing. We have presented evidence here that Serra committed atrocities at his California missions

against Indian peoples. The pope talked about perpetuating our language, but praised a man who tried to destroy it."

The conference here was named for Kateri Tekakwitha, a young 17th-century Mohawk woman who was beatified in 1980. Native Americans had hoped the pope might canonize her during this visit, but the Vatican has said the review is not complete.

Tekakwitha was baptized in 1676, and her vow to remain a virgin inspired so much contempt among her tribe that she fled, preaching among other tribes. She died of smallpox at the age of 24, and legend has it that her scars vanished the moment she died.

The pope's visit to Phoenix marked the midpoint of his 10-day U.S. tour, which will include Los Angeles, Monterey, Calif., San Francisco and Detroit before he travels to Canada. In this city that has grown tenfold in the last 40 years, to 900,000 residents, the pope advanced one of his favorite themes: the need to balance progress and development with what he called "a transcendent humanism."

His view of the United States, revealed at every stop on his second American visit, is that residents tend to be self-centered and materialistic. Phoenix's "amazing growth," he said in a speech at Saint Mary's Basilica, brings with it obligations.

Before reaching Phoenix, the pontiff spoke to the Catholics of New Mexico from on high—about 30,000 feet high. Through an unusual radio hookup, he addressed them in a radio broadcast as he flew over the state, making special mention of the Indians by saying that New Mexico's "ancient Indian dwellings . . . speak eloquently of the richness of your unique heritage."

But this day also had a decidedly Hispanic flavor. The pope's alarm clock at 5 a.m. in San Antonio was a mariachi band playing outside his window. Before noon in Phoenix, he had heard most of the classic Mexican songs, including the popular new version of "La Bamba," and some beautiful chants. And the crowds along his parade route, from the St. Joseph's Hospital where he visited gravely ill children to St. Mary's Basilica where he spoke to the city, were largely Hispanic.

In the early evening, between student cheers of "John Paul II, we love you," the pope celebrated communion with more than 70,000 people in the Sun Devils Stadium at Arizona State University.

It was the most colorful of events so far, played out under a gorgeous desert sunset amid multicolored banners, bird-of-paradise flowers and young Hispanic dancers.

It was also a ceremony of contrasts. Humorist Erma Bombeck provided a light start with a jibe at the ASU football team: "During football season, this stadium is known as Our Lady of Perpetual Anxiety." Later, John Paul II preached an intensely theological homily on the crucifixion.

Near the end of the mass, the pontiff anointed 25 injured or dying Arizonans with oil, a tradition dating to the early Christian Church. Making a distinction between what he was doing and the faith healing practiced by some Protestant evangelists, John Paul II explained that "this holy anointing does not prevent physical death, nor does it promise a miraculous healing of the body. But it does bring special grace and consolation."

Staff writer Laura Sessions Stepp contributed to this report from Tempe, Ariz.

Pope begs pardon

Newsday March 13·2000

VATICAN CITY: Pope John Paul II yesterday asked for forgiveness for many of his church's past sins, **including its treatment of Jews, heretics, women and native peoples.**

It was believed to be the first time in the history of the Catholic Church that one of its leaders sought such a sweeping pardon.

Dressed in the purple vestments of Lenten mourning, the 79-year-old pope addressed an audience at St Peter's Basilica on the Catholic Church's "Day of Forgiveness" for the 2000 Holy Year. He and his top cardinals grouped the past sins of their church into seven categories.

"We forgive and we ask for forgiveness," the pope said in a clear voice. The pope's homily did not name groups or historical events, but prayers during the Mass were more specific. On behalf of the church, five Vatican cardinals and two bishops made a confession of sin, with a response from the pope.

Vatican spokesman Joaquin Navarro-Valls had said last week that the pope would ask "pardon from God," not from individual groups who have been wronged. Jewish groups had voiced hope that the pope would use the Day of Forgiveness to expand on the church's condemnations of Catholic treatment of Jews — particularly during the Holocaust, in

which the Nazis killed 6 million Jews.

But no speaker mentioned the Holocaust. Cardinal Edward Cassidy read the prayer for forgiveness for sins against Jews, saying: "Christians will acknowledge the sins committed by not a few of their number against the people of the covenant."

"We are deeply saddened by the behaviour of those who in the course of history have caused these children of yours to suffer, and asking your forgiveness we wish to commit ourselves to genuine brotherhood," the pope responded.

Rabbi David Rosen, head of the Jerusalem office of the Anti-Defamation League of B'nai B'rith, told Reuters the inclusion of a request for forgiveness from Jews in a Roman Catholic liturgy in St Peter's was "a significant step".

In 1998, the Vatican apologised for Catholics who had failed to help save Jews from Nazi persecution and acknowledged centuries of preaching contempt for Jews.

The pope specifically asked for forgiveness for sins against Israel. He is preparing for a trip to Jerusalem later this month. The pope, bishops and cardinals spoke of seven categories of forgiveness: general sins; sins in the service of truth; against Christian unity; against the Jews; against respect for love, peace and cultures; against the dignity of

women and minorities, and against human rights.

"We ask forgiveness for the divisions among Christians, for the use of violence that some Christians used in the service of the truth, and for the behaviour of diffidence and hostility sometimes used toward followers of other religions," the pope said in his homily before the prayers.

POPE JOHN PAUL, dressed in full Lenten mourning wear, embraces a wooden crucifix during his sermon in which he asked for forgiveness for the sins of the Catholic church.

of truth" is an often-used reference to the treatment of heretics during the Inquisition, the Crusades and the forced conversions of native peoples.

"For the role that each one of us has had, with this behaviour, in these evils, contributing to a disfigurement of the face of the church, we humbly ask forgiveness," he said.

No reference was made to homosexuals, who had asked to be included on the list. The prayer for forgiveness from women and minorities said Christians had been "guilty of attitudes of rejection and exclusion, consenting to acts of discrimination on the basis of racial and ethnic differences."

Catholic Church establish forgiveness framework

Page 56 NEWSDAY Thursday March 2, 2000

PARIS: The Catholic Church, seeking to cleanse its conscience at the start of a new millennium, yesterday outlined a framework for seeking forgiveness for past errors without necessarily admitting responsibility for them.

The long awaited Vatican document, "Memory and Reconciliation," cited just a handful of areas where Pope John Paul II believed the church had erred, including its treatment of Jews, the Inquisition and enforced conversions.

"We have mentioned a few errors, but we could have had a very long list, too long a list. I fear the list will never be finished," said Father Jean-Louis Bruges, one of the experts who advised the papal commission that drew up the report.

The report, which was written in Italian, is to be officially presented next week.

The French language version came out ahead of time because of last-minute delays from the Vatican. Catholics around the world are due to mark a day of "Request for Forgiveness" on March 12 — one of dozens of theme days the Church has chosen for millennium celebrations.

"Memory and Reconciliation", prepared under the auspices of Cardinal Joseph Ratzinger, lays the ground work for that event, establishing for the first time a theological foundation for church leaders to repent of the sins of their predecessors.

"The Christians of today are not responsible for the errors of the 19th or 16th century. We are not responsible for errors we did not

commit," Bruges told a news conference.

"We have had to find a way to liberate and purify memory without talking about responsibility," he added.

The document, which was laden with quotations from past papal pronouncements, defines three types of forgiveness and makes clear that asking pardon does not necessarily imply guilt.

Bruges said Catholics from outside Europe and the United States expressed discomfort at the notion of atoning for the sins of the dead, making new definitions of forgiveness vital.

"There was also concern, especially in areas where Christians are in a minority, that seeking forgiveness might be seen as a sign of weakness," Bruges said. Pope John Paul has said in the past that although the Church's history contained many examples of holiness, it had to acknowledge there were also events which constituted a counter-testimony to Christianity.

He has made it clear that the church would use the new millennium to confront its past and start a fresh

phase. Detailing previous "errors", "Memory and Reconciliation" lamented relations with the Jews.

"The hostility and wariness of numerous Christians towards Jews over the course of time is a painful historic fact," the document said, adding that while some Christians had helped Jews during the World War Two Holocaust, others had not done enough.

In a major 1998 document, the Vatican apologised for Catholics who failed to help Jews against Nazi persecution and acknowledged centuries of preaching of contempt for Jews.

"Memory and Reconciliation" said Catholics might also bear some responsibility for the recent decline in church goers and criticised the use of violence in the past to try to keep people within the Catholic fold.

Bruges said this was "a reference [...] the Inquisition, which was marked by the torture and killing of people branded as heretics, and the enforced conversion of non-believers.

(REUTERS)

POPE JOHN PAUL II greets an Italian group from Pisa [...]

WORLD HISTORY
MADE SIMPLE

REVISED EDITION

BY

JACK C. ESTRIN, M.A.

Chairman, Social Studies,
Richmond Hill High School, N.Y.C.

1968

MADE SIMPLE BOOKS
DOUBLEDAY & COMPANY, INC.
GARDEN CITY, NEW YORK

this practice of preaching without permission of the bishop, Waldo ignored the order and began to attack the Church itself *as unnecessary for salvation.* Waldo taught that any Christian could find salvation by learning from the New Testament what Christ commanded and by living accordingly; the sacraments, he taught, were useless. In 1181 he and his followers were condemned as heretics.

Albigensians believed in a revived form of Manicheanism; that not one, but two deities ruled the Universe—God and Satan, good and evil. Things spiritual were God's; things material, Satan's. To eliminate as much as possible of the Satanic from life, Albigensian priests practiced absolute celibacy, ate no animal food, owned no property, etc.

Because they despised things material, the Albigenses taught that material creation came from evil forces, that the God of the Old Testament was evil, that Christ could not have adopted the human form, that the Eucharist was a false sacrament because Christ could not appear in the materials of bread and wine, that marriage is an evil, that the Pope was the successor, not of Peter, but of Constantine since he was associated with the temporal universe, etc. Eternal damnation was rejected and a doctrine of reincarnation substituted. Suicide was advocated as a means of freeing the soul from its material prison.

Church Discipline. How to cope with a rising heresy was a major problem for the Church. Reform of abuses was undertaken vigorously. Argument and persuasion were tried. These having failed, more forceful means were available. The canon law provided for **excommunication, anathema and interdict.** Excommunication could remove the heretic from all legal and spiritual association with the Christian community. Anathema, usually added to an excommunication, was a remarkably detailed curse placed upon the heretic and upon all his acts. The interdict was a suspension of all or most religious services for all the people in an area (both the guilty and the innocent) in the hope that the innocent would compel action against the heretics. If the heresy persisted, then the Church could apprehend the heretics, jail them and submit them to a Holy Inquisition.

The Albigensian heresy was exterminated by the Inquisition. During the course of the heresy, the Pope and the Emperor Frederick Barbarossa had ordered the clergy to proceed to the infected areas and to conduct inquests. If they found any who would not be "instructed" by them, they were to turn them over to the secular authorities for punish-

ment. The penalty was to be banishment and confiscation of property. This was a relatively humane punishment since the common people were putting heretics to the torch.

Frederick II ordered in 1224 that heretics were to be punished by fire and mutilation; this barbarous practice was then endorsed by Pope Gregory IX. Pope Innocent IV then legalized the use of torture to secure recantations. In the thirteenth century the Inquisition was turned over to two new organizations, the Franciscan and Dominican Friars. They gave to it an orderly procedure. The primary object of the Inquisition was to save the soul of the heretic. For this purpose he was confronted with the accusation (not the accuser), asked to confess and to do penance. If the heretic recanted, he was punished by temporary imprisonment, banishment, property loss, or he was forced to go on a pilgrimage. If he was stubborn, he was then subjected to torture of the cruelest kind to force a confession from him. This failing, he was turned over to the secular arm for burning or mutilation.

It would be wrong to view the Inquisition with the eyes of the more tolerant Twentieth Century. The Inquisition was a product of its own times, times that did not understand the meaning of tolerance in matters of religious belief. Certainly it had the approval of the majority of the people. It was aimed at what was considered the most horrifying of crimes, heresy. It did seek to reform before it punished. But, these qualifications having been noted, it is still an historical fact that the Inquisition was a monstrous evil. It has overcast so much that was wonderful in the Middle Ages and discouraged thousands from reading the history of this period with an objective eye. It created a pattern of inhumanity to man—accusation without accuser, torture to enforce conformity, death for freethinking. *It did not abolish heresy for long* and so failed in its primary purpose.

Widespread heresy could be met by the ultimate weapon only—the crusade. When Innocent III took papal office, the Albigensian and Waldensian heresies were rife in Toulouse, in the southern part of France. He tried persuasion through dispatch of preachers into the region, but to no avail. Raymond VI, count of Toulouse, was tolerant of these heretics (while formally a Catholic) and refused to use force against them. He was therefore excommunicated. Raymond ignored the excommunication. Innocent had no choice but to preach a crusade against Toulouse. He did so and in 1209 Philip Augustus of Paris (who was more interested

Role of the Pope — the question of jurisdiction

UDTAH, January 20, 1985

Guardian

By REV. P.J. TIERNAN, O.P.,
of Holy Cross, Arima

POPE JOHN PAUL II
...Bishop of Rome

Three particular texts play a most prominent part in the Catholic understanding of the Petrine Office. Matthew 16 shows Jesus calling Simon, his original name, a "rock" or "petros," and saying that it is on this "rock" he would build his church. He then gives the power of the keys, or authority over the church, to Peter. In Luke 22, Jesus promises to pray for Peter so that he will strengthen the others when needed. In John 21 after the resurrection, Jesus instructs Peter to feed the sheep and lambs.

Catholics concluded from these biblical foundations that Peter was specially chosen by Jesus to hold a role of leadership and guidance in the church. We admit that Peter is not called "Pope" in sacred scripture but, for that matter, he is not given this title nor are his successors, in the Code of ... "Pope" is a term of endearment for Catholics. The title is not important; the office is essential.

The Petrine Office or papacy was established at the commissioning of Peter by Jesus, which gives it a divine origin. It is not a human institution that grew up over the years after the death of ... in the person of the Bishop of Rome.

This, of course, is a highly disputed point. For Catholics it is a fact that there is an unbroken line of succession from Peter to John Paul II. They enumerate the holders of the office. This fact is not chance but the fulfilment of the promise made to Peter when he was called a "rock" or permanent foundation. The papacy must endure, because of the divine promise; in fact it has endured — such is the Catholic teaching.

But why is the Bishop of Rome always the Pope? This is a long-standing tradition that goes back to the second century. There are no absolutely conclusive proofs that Peter was ever in Rome or that he was its bishop. There are weighty arguments and circumstantial evidence which assert that he lived and died there and that he was the first of its bishops. These argu...

The Second Vatican Council, following on previous councils, sums up the papal authority in four adjectives: supreme, full, immediate and universal. These mean that there is no higher authority than the Pope, that he is not dependent on or accountable to a church ecumenical council or to the college or body of bishops for his decisions. He has authority over everything pertaining to the church and over all persons in the church, including other bishops. He is not merely "the first among equals." Nor is there any intermediary between him and individuals or "local" churches.

This authority is limited to matters of faith and morals about which he teaches, and to the discipline and government of the church for which he can make and enforce laws.

TRINIDAD GUARDIAN
January 20, 1985

Roytrin Unit
Income & Growth Fu

19.30 %
Annualised Rate of Return

The National Newspaper of Trinidad & Tobago

© COPYRIGHT TRINIDAD EXPRESS NEWSPAPERS

$1

•11,773   96 PAGES   MONDAY, SEPTEMBER 11, 2000

Vatican: Hindus inferior

—Page 7

Are Catholics closer to God?

Vatican says yes

Express September 11, 2000

EXPRESS "Monday," September 11, 2000 "Page 7."

By NATASHA COKER
Religion Reporter

A NEW Vatican declaration describing all religions outside of the Roman Catholic Church as having defects that render them inferior has upset religious leaders worldwide.

From Hindu leader Sat Maharaj to the Archbishop of Canterbury in Great Britain, priests, imams and clerics say the Pope has taken a backward step.

Released last Tuesday at a news conference, the declaration, entitled "Dominus Jesus on the Unicity and Salvific Universality of Jesus Christ and the Church", was presented by Cardinal Joseph Ratzinger, prefect of the Congregation for the Doctrine of the Faith.

Through it, the Vatican attempts to clarify certain aspects of its faith, including: the fullness of the revelation of Jesus Christ; the Holy Spirit in the work of salvation; the unity of the Church; and the Church and other religions in relation to salvation.

The declaration rejects the argument that all religions are different paths to God and seeks to combat the "so-called theology of pluralism".

Still, the Vatican says, although these "separated churches" suffer reserve comment until he had studied the document further.

He did agree that, on the surface, the document seemed to assert that the Catholic Church was superior to all other religions. "Which I don't think will be faithful to the document of Vatican II and faithful to the position of the Holy Father."

The Rev Clifford Payne, acting senior programme officer of the Caribbean Conference of Churches, said, "As one who came to theological adulthood around the time of Vatican II (1962-65), I must express my profound sadness on reading the Declaration Dominus Jesus."

He added that the document, like no other official Roman Catholic publication of recent time, "exudes the harsh, combative spirit of pre-Vatican II Catholicism which I knew as a boy".

"Religious leaders say the document undermines the groundwork for ecumenical discussions with non-Catholics. In March, for example, the Pope visited the Middle East and called for a more mature understanding among Christians, Jews and Muslims.

Payne said: "It is hard to understand why Pope John Paul

THE NATION

Jamaica

Vatican says no religion equals Roman Catholicism

VATICAN CITY, (Reuters) — The Vatican yesterday rejected the concept that other religions could be equal to Roman Catholicism and ordered its theologians not to manipulate what it called the truth of the faith.

The Vatican's restatement of its position was outlined in a complex theological document, the English title of which was "Declaration. The Unicity and Salvific Universality of Jesus Christ and the Church".

The document repeated Church teachings that non-Christians were in a "gravely deficient situation" regarding salvation and that other Christian churches had "defects", partly because they did not recognise the primacy of the Pope.

The 36-page document, which was bound to spark fresh debate, was prepared by the Vatican's Congregation of the Doctrine of the Faith and approved by Pope John Paul.

It said the clarification and restatement of the official Catholic position was necessary to contest "relativistic theories which seek to justify religious pluralism" as a principle rather than a de facto practice.

It said only the revelation of Jesus Christ was "definitive and complete". Asserting that Christian revelation could be complementary to that found in other religions was "contrary to the Church's faith".

The document was addressed primarily to Catholic theologians but it appeared destined to spark dialogue on all levels with other Christian

Churches and with non-Christians.

At a news conference to present the document, Cardinal Joseph Ratzinger, the Vatican's doctrinal head, said some theologians were "manipulating and going beyond the limits" of tolerance when they put all religions on the same plane.

Ratzinger said this did not reflect what he called "an objective and universal truth".

Walking a theological tightrope, the document said the "Church of Christ" was present and operative in other Christian Churches today.

But, in the Vatican's view, it subsists fully in the Roman Catholic Church because the Pope is the successor to St Peter, whom Christ named as his first Vicar on Earth. Papal primacy was divinely willed, it said.

"Therefore, there exists a single Church of Christ, which subsists in the Catholic Church, governed by the Successor of Peter and by the bishops in communion with him," it said.

Some other Christian churches, while not in "perfect union", remained united to Catholics by close bonds, it said.

"The Church of Christ is present and operative also in these Churches, even though they lack full communion with the Catholic Church since they do not accept the Catholic doctrine of the primacy; which, according to the will of God, (the Pope) objectively has and exercises power over the entire Church," it said.

While other Christian churches "suffer from defects", the document said they had not been deprived of what is called "significance and

POPE JOHN PAUL II... other churches have defects because they don't recognise his primacy.

PÒPE JOHN PAUL II says document

importance in the mystery of salvation".

But it was the Catholic Church which possessed and had been entrusted with "the fullness of grace and truth".

It said because Christ was the Son of God, non-Christians were at a disadvantage regarding salvation.

"The truth of faith does not lessen the sincere respect which the Church has for the religions

of the world, but at the same time, it rules out, a religious relativism which leads to the belief that one religion is as good as another," it said.

"If it is true that followers of other religions can receive divine grace, it is also certain that objectively speaking they are in a gravely deficient situation in comparison with those who, in the Church, have the fullness of the means of salvation."

ROMAN CATHOLIC CHURCH

RELIGION

To serve, the church must heal its own racism

By BILL MAXWELL

Newsday February 11, 2001

AS MIDDLE-CLASS white Catholics abandon the church's 19 inner-city parochial schools for those in suburban parishes, Cardinal Keeler is determined to keep the schools open.

In his 1926 book, *Healing Ourselves: The First Task of the Church in America*, ...

Baltimore...

In this light, I applaud the recent action of Cardinal William H Keeler, head of the 500,000 Catholics in the statewide Archdiocese of... Catholic school because of...

manners and benign acts, racism and perceptions of racism are like dormant volcanoes that erupt in our faces when we least expect it.

Given today's anti-black chic, the growing popularity of denying the existence of racism and the ever-growing concentration of wealth in fewer hands, dispossessed groups need their rights espoused and protected more than ever.

poverty is in the rest of the nation's urban centres, is tied to race. And instead of using the sermon as mere penance, Keeler committed the church to action.

"We will not abandon our city," he said, as reported by the *Times*. "We will keep our schools open. We will serve the poor and the children of the poor."

Many black parishioners who heard the sermon and who know Keeler praised the cardinal's efforts. During a telephone interview, Nancy Linzy, 42, said that she wants her two children to attend

moved to the suburbs, will not try to derail his efforts prematurely.

Whatever the outcome, Keeler, like Elmer T Clark did so many years ago, knows that the church can serve others only after it

heals itself — by confronting its own race problems and acting decisively.

Bill Maxwell is a columnist with the *St Petersburg Times*, Tampa, Florida

NEWSDAY Sunday February 11, 2001 Page 33

144

other peoples around the world about bigotry until they first rid themselves of racism. Bigoted Christians, moreover, had no moral standing to save the heathen soul in faraway lands, Clark wrote.

The chapter titled "Helping the Negro Uphill" is striking for its candour about the plight of the "Negro" and the direct role the church played in bringing misery to an entire group of people.

"In thinking of the Negro, let us remember that he did not come to us of his own free will and accord," writes Clark, then publicity secretary of the Centenary Commission of the Methodist Episcopal Church-South. "If there is a problem with unpleasant features, no iota of the blame for it can be laid at his door. He did not seek us. On the contrary, we sought him. And all the distress he has caused us is not comparable to the manifold miseries we have laid upon him. For what people has suffered as the American Negro has suffered?"

Even though a deceptive brand of new right-wing politics and naive libertarianism has changed Americans' opinion about the enduring effect of racism on its victims, the reality of this evil is another matter altogether.

Beneath today's subtle racism is a thing of the past and acknowledged the pervasive ugliness of racism in American culture and institutions. As he began his sermon at Baltimore's mostly white Basilica of the Assumption of the Blessed Virgin Mary, Keeler pointed to the rear balconies in the ornate sanctuary. There, he said, black Catholics had been segregated from white Catholics for decades.

"We gather this evening mindful of an evil," the cardinal said, urging worshippers to remember that racism is "a spiritual malady that has gnawed at the moral fibre of our nation, our community and our church from the early days of colonial America."

Keeler's words have come at a critical time for Baltimore, when middle-class white Catholics are abandoning the church's 19 inner-city parochial schools for those in suburban parishes. The result is that these inner-city schools have been populated by 4,000 poor, minority children who are not Catholic.

Knowing that race is influencing much of the white flight, Keeler is using the crisis as an opportunity to confront the race issue directly. He apparently knows that the poverty in inner-city Baltimore, as part of the school community," Linzy said. "I don't mean to put down the public school my children used to attend, but I feel that my children are treated more like people in the Catholic school. We're not even Catholic, but the teachers treat my children warmly. And they are learning. Cardinal Keeler is a saviour for keeping the schools open for our kids."

Baltimore's black leaders laud Keeler's decision because it comes when other church officials have recommended shutting down the schools.

"The Catholics moved out, but we're serving whole neighbourhoods now," Keeler told the *Times*. "We have an obligation to help these kids get out of the prisons they're in — intellectual prisons."

True to his word, Keeler has started soliciting $1.5-million a year from businesses. The money is being used to pay a third of each student's $2,900 annual tuition. According to the *New York Times*, families pledge to pay the balance.

Although some black parishioners remain sceptical of Keeler's commitment to serve Baltimore's minority schoolchildren, they say that they will keep an open mind and pray that his many white Catholic detractors, who

Caribbean Certificate History

Arawaks to Africans

Book 1

R. Greenwood
S. Hamber

MACMILLAN
CARIBBEAN

Cosmic Book
Services Ltd.
Upper Level, West Mall Westmoorings

TRINI IN UK CHURCH WAR

THE BOMB FRIDAY, JULY 9, 1976 PAGE 15

A Trinidad-born primary schoolmaster in England is playing a leading role in shaking up a church with world-wide membership.

A colour problem is hitting the Seventh Day Adventists Church in Britain as black members are demanding a greater share of the power.

For the first time in the history of any church in Britain, there is now a black majority among the rank and file, all because of emigration from the West Indies.

The pastors and administrators of the church in Britain are predominantly white. But the black majority are making a bid for equal say at the conference of the church, due to be held shortly in Manchester.

Prominent among the dissidents is Trinidadian Mike Kellawan, a teacher who went to Britain several years ago.

He says that when there is reform in the British church to give blacks an equal voice in the administration of its affairs, he will hand over the money.

If not, he is going to send the money to the Seventh Day Adventists in Trinidad. So far, Kellawan's tithe has accumulated to $3,000.

Kellawan says:

"The situation is almost explosive. Of the 13 members of the South England Committee, only three are black. White pastors just do not understand the problems of black folk.

"Pastor Foster has warned me not to wash dirty linen in public. Well, we've been washing it in private and for years there's been no effect."

Pastor Foster is President of the British Seventh Day Adventists Union. He says however;

"Many black congregations regard it as almost a status symbol to have a white pastor.

The particular black-white problem in Britain is said to have been growing for years but has only now come out into the open.

Most of the 23 churches in London have more black than white members. And there is resentment that their sacrificial tithe payments fall into hands that are mostly white.

The Seventh Day Adventists Church originated in America in the 1860s and regards the American Ellen G. White, who died in 1915, as its "special messenger from God."

It has a world-wide membership of 2,500,000 and its headquarters are in Washington, DC.

In Britain there are 124 Seventh Day churches with full membership of 13,000.

Holy UK! Apartheid in Christianity?

Gleaner May 12, 1996

THE SUNDAY GLEANER • MAY 12 1996 • 5D *JAMAICA*

> "Racism and segregation is not only a SDA problem..."
>
> – Pastor Lovell Bent
> (London S.E.)

CARL B. MOXIE
CONTRIBUTOR

WHITE CHURCHGOERS IN the United Kingdom will soon find out whether or not the British Union Conference (BUC) will rule favourable in their request for a "White only" church branch. This conference is scheduled for sometime in July.

According to a report in a March issue of "The Voice – Britain's Best Black Newspaper", Potential Christians are being scared off by Black churchgoers, said a spokesperson for the Seventh Day Adventist (SDA) church. Now, they (SDA) may opt for "White only" churches.

A recent trip to the U.K. caught me off-guard, as an escalated racial feud is in the making among churchgoers. SDA church members are "pushing" SDA church executives to set up a White only "Branch".

It is also reported that there is a suggested merger of Wales, Scotland and Ireland into one conference which is to be known as the Celtic conference, and England, with its inner city Black congregation, as another.

Jamaican-born, Pastor Don McFarlane, 44, president of the SDA south England, told news reporters that: "It is the responsibility of the church to meet the needs of all its members, whatever they are." He said the issues that will be discussed at the conference includes creating a department at a national level to look after "White only" affairs.

According to the Voice, an estimated 18,000 SDA members in Britain are currently divided into regional conferences. Since Blacks started migrating to the U.K. in the 1940s, White church members have fallen drastically. It is now estimated that there are only 4,000 White SDA members in Britain today.

He added: "In the 1950s and 1960s when we (Afro-Caribbean) started to attend U.K. churches – at the end of the sermons they (Whites) would tell us, thank you for coming, but we will not have you come again because we will lose our white congregation.'"

This, however, prompted Blacks to form their own churches in their homes and gave them new names.

...So racism and segregation still exist in the churches, always have," he explained.

"Racism and segregation is not only SDA Church problem," said Jamaican-born Pastor Lovell Bent, who presides at five New Life Assembly

Caribbean Union **Gleanings**

OFFICIAL ORGAN OF THE CARIBBEAN UNION OF SEVENTH-DAY ADVENTISTS

VOLUME 53   SECOND QUARTER, 1980

ADVENTISTS ELECT BLACK TO SECOND HIGHEST POST

Caribbean Union Gleanings, Offi
Seventh Day Adventists Church

RELIGIOUS NEWS SERVICE

Volume 53 (April 22, 1980) Second

Pastor G. Ralph Thompson,
Secretary, General Conference.

DALLAS (RNS) - - G. Ralph Thompson, a vice-president to the General Conference of Seventh-day Adventists since 1975, became the first black man to be elevated to the church's number two spot when he was elected secretary for the 3.3-million-member denomination.

The 53rd Adventist World Conference in the Dallas Convention Center here, also elected Neal C. Wilson by a unanimous vote to the church presidency. Mr. Wilson has held that post in the interim since January 1979, when his predecessor, Robert H. Pierson, retired.

Mr. Thompson is a native of Barbados who has held numerous church positions in Trinidad. He began as a professor at the Caribbean Union College in 1953 and later became pastor of the college church and chairman of the theology department from 1959 to 1964. He replaces Clyde O. Franz who is retiring after 10 years as secretary.

Women must have a voice
says head of Adventists

TRINIDAD GUARDIAN, Monday, July 28, 1997, Page 3

BY VERNE BURNETT

THE VISITING President of the World of Christ lived Christ Church of Seventh-day Adventists, Dr Robert S Folkenberg last Saturday affirmed the role of women in the Church.

Stressing that "this Church is a modern, up-driven Church," he said, "it is time to make sure that the women have a voice that will represent their commitment" to the gospel and the work of the Church.

Dr Folkenberg's comments came during a Roundtable Discussion titled "Social and Religious Issues Facing the Seventh-day Adventist Church in the 21st Century." The discussion took place at the Queen's Park Oval where more than 16,000 Seventh-day Adventists had gathered for a National Convention.

He is on a three-day visit to participate in activities marking the 170th Anniversary of the Caribbean Union College at Maracas, St Joseph.

will." He said it would take courage but if everyone who claimed the Life of Christ lived Christ "that will be an argument, no one could deny.

Speaking on women's ministry in the Church, Dr Folkenberg urged members in Trinidad and Tobago to "send plenty women" as delegates to General Conference sessions (the Church's highest legislative body).

Israel Leito, President of the Church's Inter-American Division, said his division insisted on having women on all decision-making committees and urged the local congregations to do the same.

Leito added that the American Conference session had already approved the election of women elders and their ordination if they proved themselves in service.

On the ecumenical movement, Dr Folkenberg said the Seventh-day Adventist Church has observer status on the World Council of Churches (WCC) but is not a member and is not considering becoming a member.

beliefs they cherish but which Adventists disagree with," and is not willing to agree to enter on the agenda for another organisation asking us to downplay a belief we hold dear."

He added that the Seventh-day Adventist Church does engage in discourse with other denominations and is now concluding the third in a series of dialogues with the Lutheran World Federation. However, he emphasised that this dialogue is "with a view to understanding, not to compromise."

Dr Folkenberg also restated the Church's opposition to homosexuality based on the Bible's clear condemnation of the practice.

"He stated that racism is never justified. Never, It is a contradiction of a basic Christian value. It has no place in the Church. It has no place in society."

"Commenting on the existence of separate white and black conferences in two divisions of the Church in North America, Dr Folkenberg said he was saddened and "embarrassed" by

the situation and noted that no one has been willing to place the matter on the agenda for discussion.

— He said white officials of the Church were reluctant to raise the matter for fear of being accused of being racist and of trying to take control of black racially divided organisations.

churches. According to Dr Folkenberg, black Adventists had also not raised the issue.

He told the convention that in South Africa, the Church is moving rapidly to merge racially separate conferences because the law in that country forbids racially divided organisations.

Dr Folkenberg wound up the second day of his stay in Trinidad with a banquet at the Trinidad Hilton at which House Speaker Hector McLeon delivered the keynote address. He ended his visit yesterday with his return to the United States.

[handwritten annotations: "Racism", "Racism"]

C2 MONDAY, OCTOBER 14, 1985 THE WASHINGTON POST

Church Official Offers Apology on Race Memo

By Victoria Churchville
Washington Post Staff Writer

A top official of the Seventh-day Adventist Church, acceding to a demand first made by black church leaders six years ago, publicly apologized yesterday for a remark he made in a 1979 internal memorandum that the leaders said was offensive to black members. Nearly a fourth of the church's North American members are black.

Ken Mittleider, who is white and one of five vice presidents of the church, told about 200 church leaders from around the world gathered for an annual conference at the Seventh-day Adventist Church in Takoma Park that his remarks arguing against hiring a white woman he described as "a crusader" for black causes was not meant as a racial slur.

"I ask forgiveness of anyone who came to that conclusion. From the depths of my heart I ask that you please forgive me," a church spokesman quoted Mittleider as saying during an unscheduled, 15-minute speech detailing his motives in writing the memo Oct. 30, 1979.

In it, Mittleider urged that Carol Rayburn, a former officer of the Black Forum, a student group at Andrews Seminary in Michigan, be denied an internship at the Potomac Conference and a pastoral associate post at Sligo Church in Takoma Park. Rayburn filed a complaint with the Equal Employment Opportunity Commission alleging that the church refused to hire her because of her ties with blacks and black-oriented church groups. The case later went to court.

A federal appeals court, citing the constitutional separation of church and state, ruled last month that antidiscrimination laws did not apply in Rayburn's case.

In the 1979 memo, Mittleider wrote of Rayburn, "She is a crusader. You will notice one of the activities she joined in at Andrews is the Black Forum. She will constantly be working [for] the 'underprivileged,' trying to better their situation from a material standpoint."

Warren Banfield, director of the Seventh-day Adventist Office of Human Relations and general conference field secretary, said, "The statement when it first came out shocked a lot of people. It haunted us all the way down to now."

"We took this statement as an offense to black people," said Donald George Morgan, president of the International Layman's Action Committee for Concerned Adventists, a 300-member group of black and minority church members. Members of the group picketed the church meeting last week.

"At least for a while it [the apology] heals this wound, but in terms of healing the racism it doesn't, because racism is a cancerous thing in the church," Morgan said yesterday. "It's there, and it will come out again in different form."

In a telephone interview yesterday, Mittleider said, "Morgan championed this thing on his own. If an individual wants to picket that's fine—that's one of the great things about our society, freedom of speech."

Banfield said yesterday, "Churches are going to have to learn to live with this openness: There's nothing private anymore, and we're going to have to give an accounting of ourselves publicly—and that's not all bad."

THE NEW YORK TIMES, SUNDAY, OCTOBER 11, 1981

Seventh-day Adventists Accused of Sex Bias

WASHINGTON, Oct. 10 (UPI) — The Seventh-day Adventist Church, already embroiled in internal and external controversy, has a new problem: a discrimination suit filed by a magna cum laude graduate of its top school.

The suit by Carole Rayburn, a clinical psychologist with a master's degree from Adventist Andrews University and a doctorate from Catholic University, contends the church denied her employment because she is a woman.

The case, filed in federal court in Baltimore, names the denomination's top officers as well as the Potomac Conference, its regional group. The denomination is based in Takoma Park, Md., a

suburb of Washington.

The suit raises delicate church-state questions and could test just how far anti-discrimination provisions of the law can be applied to religious institutions without constituting excessive government entanglement in religious affairs.

The denomination, with 3.5 million members worldwide, has recently been involved in a dispute over the writings of its founder, Ellen G. White. A Seventh-day Adventist minister in California has asserted, that Mrs. White committed wholesale plagiarism in her 70 books. The minister has since been thrown out of the church.

At the same time, the church is in-

volved in an internal audit to determine how much money its various regions and agencies have lent a prominent member who has filed for bankruptcy since his real estate dealings collapsed.

The discrimination suit asserts that Miss Rayburn was denied employment as an associate pastor of the Sligo Seventh-day Adventist Church in Takoma Park and as an associate in the pastoral care internship program with the Potomac Conference because of her sex and her race. "In that she was a white person who had associated with black persons."

Although the church does not ordain women, neither post is closed to women.

Miss Rayburn made public an internal memorandum from a top Potomac Conference official in which she was described as "a crusader."

"You will notice one of the activities she joined in at Andrews is the Black Forum," the memorandum said. "She will constantly be working for 'the underprivileged,' trying to better their situation from a material standpoint."

SEVENTH-DAY ADVENTIST
in
JAMAICA
WELCOME

DR. RS. FOLKENBERG

World-President of the General Conference

of

Seventh-day Adventists

&

His Wife

November 4,5, 1994

PETER, JOSEPH SUE CHURCH

A LAWSUIT claiming some $24,000 has been levelled against a Church.

The organisation, the Worldwide Church of God, was sued by Joseph Marfan and Peter Johnson, two former members who are alleging that the Church obtained their money under false pretences.

They claim that they were ordered to pay one-tenth of their salaries to the Worldwide Church, based in Mucurapo, after joining the religious organisation eight years ago.

And while they gave the Church to carry out it's work throughout the world, both Joseph and Peter are claiming that the Worldwide Church used the money to support projects and beliefs that were against its initial teachings.

The men told the Mirror that the Worldwide Church was a strong supporter of the apartheid regime in South Africa and practiced racial segregation among it's United States followers.

"Blacks cannot marry Whites in this Church," said Joseph.

"Even in any of its social gatherings, the Church discourages any socialising between the races.

"On top of that, the body which runs the Church calls themselves the Government of God, and its leader, Herbert W. Armstrong, must be accepted by followers orders of this organisation.

"And if any one stands up to argue, he is told that he must obey, and if Armstrong is wrong then God will correct him.

Herbert Armstrong, otherwise we will be disobeying the word of God.

* * * *

"in other words, if Armstrong says the sky is green, then everyone in the Church must agree to that."

TnT Mirror FRIDAY SEPTEMBER 13, 1985

suit against the organisation.

Joseph explained:

"In 1983, the Pastor of the local branch of the Church demanded a mandatory second tithe...which is a second payment of one-tenth of members salaries...from the Church's congregation.

"This second tithe was to go to pay for members' participation in a celebration we call the Feast of Tabernacles, which is normally held in Tobago.

* * * *

even get past the door.

"We eventually questioned the Pastor, who told us that we had broken God's law.

"We said that it wasn't God's law, but Herbert Armstrong's, and he stated that Armstrong's law was God's law, as he was the only servant of God.

"We understand that photos of us had been circulated to the Barbados branch, too, as the Church's management thought we would go there.

"In St. Lucia, we were treated like real criminals, with the Pastor there telling us we were sponging off other members.

"We couldn't

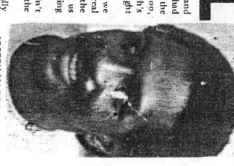

JOSEPH MARFAN

Port-of-Spain lawyer Jawara Mobota is handling the lawsuit together with solicitors D; De Peiza and Company.

Both Joseph and Peter added that they were surprised to discover that the Worldwide Church was not registered as a religious organisation, but as a limited liability company, which they claim is "strange."

NEWS FLASH: Armstrongites 'born again'?

Sunday Gleaner, May 5, 1991

By Ian Boyne

IF, despite Herbert Armstrong's contrary view during his lifetime, man does really have an immortal soul, then Herbert Armstrong's soul must be enduring one helluva torment.

After fighting furiously for over 52 years to maintain the purity of his "one true Church" which he founded in 1934 in America and after condemning all other churches as teaching a false gospel, his Worldwide Church of God (WCG) under more liberal leadership, has been steadily overturning his cherished teachings.

For old timers and long-time Armstrongologists, as well as informed religion reporters, the changes which have taken place in the WCG since Herbert Armstrong died in January, 1986 are amazing. You can now throw out all the anti-cult books that you have on the Worldwide Church of God and you pastors and evangelical activists had better stop reciting information in pre-1986 WCG literature:

the word is now officially out that all the church's literature is under review and so are the church's doctrines. Evangelicals were pleasantly surprised recently when the WCG's new leader, Joseph Tkach (of Russian descent), came out with the bombshell announcement that Herbert Armstrong was wrong and that "Christians are really 'born again'" now, after all. For many years Armstrong had drawn away from the evangelicals with the teaching that Christians will be born again only at the resurrection when they would be changed into spirit beings. The evangelicals, who are called "born-again Christians", have always insisted that one is born again at conversion.

But according to Armstrong, the text which says "whosoever is born of God cannot sin" totally disproves the view that one is born again now.

Born again

For many years Herbert Armstrong's booklet "Just what do you mean born again?" was one of the most requested and most believed. It seemed to have stumped evangelicalism right at its roots. Now, the present leadership of the WCG has admitted that the evangelicals were right, after all, though the WCG still teaches that Christians will be composed of spirit at the resurrection. Tkach has reportedly stressed that the church's teaching has not really been changed in essence and but only that additional information about the Greek text in John reveals that Armstrong did not understand everything clearly in the early days.

But, no matter how Tkach dresses it up, observers know that a major plank in the church's foundation has been torn down. But this is merely the latest of a number of changes which have made the WCG into a more respectable middle-of-the road organization, which some say will soon be indistinguishable from an ordinary evangelical church, possibly with the exception of its Sabbath and holy day observances.

Many of the changes which have been made would strike the average reader as so elementary that he might wonder what the fuss is about. But when one understands how the formerly intensely conservative, cultic organization stressed these "truths" and how those doctrines wrecked lives and broke up families and friends, then a different picture emerges.

Before reformer Tkach came on the scene there was another more celebrated reformer who held sway but whose reign was brought to an inglorious end when he was excommunicated after the conservatives convinced Herbert Armstrong to bring back the church "on track". That man was Armstrong's son, Garner Ted, in 1974 there was a major rebellion and split in the church and thirty-five leading ministers walked out on the Armstrongs. It made headlines in big papers and Time magazine came out with an article, "Trouble in the Empire".

After pointing out that the church's divorce, tithing and money-spending policies were at the root of the controversy. Time magazine says of the Armstrongs had two choices: either to step down or to

have Garner Ted "initiate his own aggressive programme of reform." Ted Armstrong chose the latter. While Herbert Armstrong was busily wining and dining with kings and presidents all over the world, ostensibly preaching his one true Gospel of the Kingdom of God, Ted was at headquarters promoting intellectuals and scholars and radically overhauling church doctrines. The first was the divorce doctrine. The church had before 1974 taught that persons who were divorced for whatever reasons could not remarry as long as the marriage partners were alive.

This meant that if two persons had been happily married for 15 years, with four kids and a stable home and were interested in becoming members of the church, they would have to break up if either had a former mate still alive.

Ted's urging

The doctrine caused incalculable suffering and after one man committed suicide some ministers began to pressure the Armstrongs to change. They did, under Ted's urging.

Healing was another sore point. The church formerly taught against medicine, saying it was idolatry to go to doctors rather than rely on God. Ted Armstrong changed it.

Celebrating birthdays was sinful and inter-racial marriage was a stench in God's eyes and a sin Ted Armstrong changed all that. Wearing make-up was also considered sin by Herbert Armstrong but the younger Armstrong declared it a non-issue, saying the Bible did not condemn it.

LOOKING BACK

By Io Smith

■ Rev Io Smith is the Pastor of the New Testament Assembly in East London. She also serves as the co-chairman for the Conference of Christian partnership and is on the staff of Zebra Project.

Approximately thirty years ago, black immigrants began to arrive on the shores of Great Britain. Included in these numbers were those with a deep spiritual awareness and steadfastness in their christian faith and beliefs. Soon after their arrival it became obvious that they were to experience great problems. These problems were at first underlying but when these immigrants began to settle within the community, the problem surfaced and indeed worsened.

Even the christians were faced with great obstacles, the gravest of which was acceptance into the white-led established churches. The black christians were particularly discouraged by the attitudes and insulting mannerisms of the white ministers. This behaviour resulted in many of the black christians ceasing to attend church of any kind, and more seriously depart from the faith altogether. But for others however, it was a great challenge.

Within the first ten years of the black churches history in the United Kingdom, things began to look brighter. Many areas were now being reached, and, where one would have had to travel from east to west to find a black church, churches began to spring up all around the London area. Within a few years, areas such as Brixton, Willesden, Hackney, Dalston, Tottenham, Lewisham, Balham and Tooting had their own established churches, and resolutely the black church began to spread its wings.

THE WORK GOES ON

Today in multi-racial multi-cultural Britain, many black churches are committed to fight racism, this is no easy task because of many complications. The interpretation of racism that I have, is that it is an attitude of prejudice that generates from the heart.

White christians do not always respond positively to racism awareness. In general, they are defensive, prevaricative, and cold. These negative attitudes flow from guilt. Those of us who are involved with racial issues, need courage, faith, confidence and co-operation for survival and to establish a just society, with peace between all inhabitants of Britain, regardless of colour, creed or race. This programme is neither a short nor an easy one. It is long and hard and sometimes painful, but there are some of us who are not prepared to let up. The question of peace and justice among races is an important one and the fight must continue.

WEST INDIAN WORLD :: The Paper for West Indians

JUNE 1986

ROLE OF BLACK LED CHURCHES IN BRITAIN

In attempting to define the role of Black-led Churches in Britain, we do ourselves and other a great disservice if we do not try to put the role into some kind of context. "It has been suggested that the emergence of Black-led Churches was connected in some way with a cool reception from mainstream churches. Similarly, the reason has been attributed to the form and nature of christianity in Britain". Also, "the growth of these movements is in large part due to disappointment with the Christianity of the 'motherland' and the hidden paternalistic and racist attitudes of British Christians." (from *Living Together* by Roswith Gerloff) To these may be added the fact that some Black churchgoers were asked to sit to the back of the church during worship, some were advised to go to other churches, and some were asked not to come back because their presence offended parishioners. Clearly a number felt that they could no longer endure such indignities from so-called "Christians". Though there are other important factors, it is surely racism and the rejection of Black people in Britain that has done

REV. D.V. PEMBERTON

more than anything to create Black-led churches.

Black-led churches are of course not unique to Britain, nor are they something new as some would have us believe. for instance, in article written for the Handbook of AWUCOC, 1984 Edition, Rev. Dr. Ashton Gibson points to the work of the Black-led church in the USA in the days of slavery:

"Before the black slaves of America had any formal organisations to protest against the evils of slavery, the church kept alive the flame of freedom in the hearts of the slaves. In spite of the dehumanising effect of slavery, though slaves should have lost hope, the Black Church Movement

taught them to know they were God's children, that he loved them and that they should not despair."

He goes on to identify the Black Churches as the only group of people who attempted to meet the needs of West Indian immigrants in the 1950's

"From its earliest beginnings the Black-led Church movement was able to accommodate and relate to the first post-war waves of Westindians in their own cultural register. Its most valuable contribution is its ability to nature the more positive virtues of Westindian cultural life."

Rev. Dr. Gibson (and others, I believe) has done the Black Community a great service in his clear, direct and honest analysis of our contribution.

In an attempt to explain why so many African Christians are abandoning the "Mission Churches" in favour of the independent Black-led Churches, Professor J S Mbiti, in his book *African Religions and Philosophy*, says :

"African Christians often feel complete foreigners in Mission Churches. Beneath the umbrella of independent churches African Christians can freely shed their tears, voice their sorrows, present their spiritual and physical needs, respond to the world in which they live and empty themselves before God."

UK, Irish churches admit gypsy prejudice

Newsday July 14 1998 - page 24

LONDON: British and Irish churches have admitted to substantial racial prejudice against gypsies by clergy and congregations and pledged to stamp it out.

A report by the Churches Commission of Racial Justice (CCRJ) said prejudice ranged from open personal hostility to ejection from churches and campaigns against stopping sites.

"Even among Christians clearly committed to racial justice, there can be negative stereotypes of gypsies," the report said.

Commission chairman Reverend Theo Samuel said the report was in response to complaints made by gypsies.

He said the onus was now on the churches to provide better education for clergy and congregations.

"We want the local churches to know that what they are doing to these people sometimes wittingly but in the most part unwittingly is not acceptable and that there is no place for racism in the church at all," Rev Samuel said.

Terry Hurst, a gypsy preacher, said many Christians were being excluded from mainstream churches and communities.

"Spiritual acceptance is the first thing but the second is that the churches could use their weight to help these people," he said. (REUTERS)

Critics slam racist 'church

July 6, 1999 Toronto STAR

'Religion for and by sociopaths,' observer says

BY CHRISTOPHER THORNE
ASSOCIATED PRESS

EAST PEORIA, Ill. — It styles itself as a religion, but the World Church of the Creator — to which alleged racist killer Benjamin Nathaniel Smith once belonged — has no altar and no place of worship.

The group dates back to 1973, when it was formed by Ben Klassen, a Florida real estate man and politician who became wealthy after inventing an electric can opener.

Before he committed suicide in 1993, Klassen wrote tracts of explosive racism, urging whites to push blacks, Jews and other "mud races" off the face of the planet.

Potok and others believe the World Church of the Creator is responsible for encouraging violence like the two-state shooting spree that left two dead and at least eight wounded, and ended in Smith's suicide late Sunday in Salem, Ill.

While the church's Web site included a note saying it does not condone violence, it also called for a racial holy war and extermination of non-whites. Members have been convicted of murder, beatings and conspiracies to bomb NAACP offices and black churches.

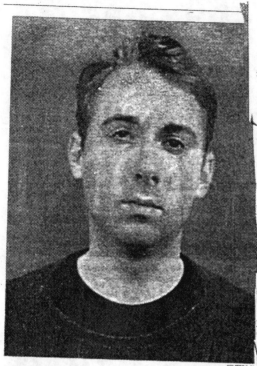

REUTERS PH

MURDER SUSPECT: Benjamin Nathaniel Smith, 21, shot and killed himself Sunday while being chased by police after a shooting spree.

Barbados Advocate March 22, 1991

Barbados Advocate 22 March 1991
1991

Blacks likened to 'wild animals'

DURBAN, South Africa, Thursday, (Reuter) - A member of a white religious sect told a South African murder trial yesterday blacks were wild animals and did not have souls worth saving.

Karel Liebenberg of the Israel Vision Church was giving evidence in mitigation of sentence in the case of Eugene Marais, one of three men who ambushed a bus and killed seven blacks.

The church has no links with Israel or Judaism.

Marais and his colleagues in the neo-Nazi Afrikaner Resistance Movement, David Petrus Botha and Adrian Smuts, have pleaded guilty to murder. Marais has been convicted; the others are awaiting judgment.

Liebenberg told the Durban Supreme Court, Marais was a pleasant person who had become too involved in politics.

He said that out of concern for Marais' soul he had taught him that white people had been created in God's image and that this raised questions about blacks.

"I said they (blacks) were the wild animals of the field and that they do not have a redeemable soul because they are not chosen by God and therefore cannot go to paradise," he said.

Liebenberg, assistant town clerk at the port of Richards Bay, said he was a senior member of the sect and Marais, while not a member, had become involved with its activities.

The attack happened a few hours after a group of blacks led by a man with a history of mental illness went on a stabbing spree on the Durban beachfront on October 9, wounding eight whites. One of the whites later died.

The three whites said outrage at this attack motivated their ambush of the bus on the outskirts of Durban.

Eighteen blacks were wounded in the ambush and many of them, some frail, others on crutches, have been called as witnesses.

2A SUNday News |||||||||||||||||||||||||||

Barbados

Bajan cops face hardships in Namibia

In a letter home, Inspector David Callender,

"Sad to say, in Gobabis there are churches for all Whites, a hospital for all Whites and even a cemetery for Whites only. Those considered the Coloureds and the Blacks have separate resting places so that, even after death, there is no possibility of uniting," wrote Callender of the race troubles under apartheid.

Such is life for the Barbadian contingent of policemen now in Namibia, south-west Africa.

BARBADOS' FINEST in Nigeria are (top row, left to right) David Franklyn Gibbs, Jeffrey Watson, Kenneth Carrington, Anderson Bishop, David Husbands, Glenroy Boyce and Joseph Edey. (bottom row) Sgt. Lloyd Joh Luther Moore, Sgt. Hartley Reid, Sgt. Glenroy Walker and Anthony Dott

TRINIDAD AND TOBAGO

Senate Paper No. 7 of 1969

Laid before the Senate on the 19*th August,* 1969

GOVERNMENT PRINTERY, TRINIDAD, TRINIDAD AND TOBAGO—1969

Report of a Cabinet appointed enquiry into discrimination against nationals of Trinidad and Tobago in the United Kingdom, Canada and the United States of America, by Clive Spencer, President, Trinidad and Tobago Labour Con-

127. Discussions with the probation authorities brought out some very important areas of concern. For instance the Probation Department was desirous in seeing some method of discouraging parents from coming to the United Kingdom and leaving their children behind, because this had the problem on reunion of re-orientation of the children, moreso with those who had grown into juveniles. The question of the care of babies came up, and the extent to which infants were uncared for and the effect this had on their development. The gross misunderstanding that immigrants had in trying to re-orient themselves in communities different to those from which they came.

128. My discussions with the police of New Scotland Yard revealed that where police brutality was concerned, that all complaints made to the police were investigated by a civilian section of New Scotland Yard and that in two cases such investigations led to dismissals and in others to lesser forms of punishment whenever this was proven. It was pointed out, however, that there were difficulties, more often than not, in getting conclusive evidence to enable discipline to be taken because it is not unusual to find that such incidents had occurred with only the defendant and the complainant present. Moreover, police brutality was a generalisation that was frequently made despite the efforts of the police to reduce the friction between police and civilian, these generalities are still referred to.

129. My discussions with the Trade Union Movement in the three countries was as shocking as when I was told that there was discrimination in the Churches. As a Trade Unionist and because the brotherhood of the fraternity of Trade Union is unity and equality, I never realised that this was so. However, the statements on the part of the movements of these three countries are that whilst their respective Congresses were opposed to racial discrimination, in fact there were unions that did practice racial discrimination to the extent of having certain conditions written into their individual constitutions. However, by persistently getting after them they have succeeded in having some of these clauses removed, but this did not in fact mean that they had ceased the practice in all cases.

**OFFICE OF THE PRIME MINISTER
TRINIDAD AND TOBAGO
PUBLIC RELATIONS DIVISION
PRESS RELEASE**

ADDRESS BY DR. ERIC WILLIAMS, PRIME MINISTER OF
TRINIDAD AND TOBAGO, TO THE INDEPENDENT BAPTIST
MISSION CHURCHES OF TRINIDAD AND TOBAGO, AT
TICFA HOUSE, SUTTON STREET, SAN FERNANDO ON SUN-
DAY 28 AUGUST 1977.
THEME: "THE MARCH TO LIBERTY THROUGH JESUS CHRIST"

With the European church uppermost, until the conditions were
such that you get, principally in the United States, a separate
church movement, Methodist, Baptist, etc., non-white, because
of the conditions, not only in the United States, everybody
knows the United States it is good for you to look at something
outside, the so-called Latins who were so tolerant of blacks etc.
You had in the cathedral city of Cuzco three priests - two to deal
with the Spaniards and the other one to deal with the slaves and
the Amerindians. You had separate churches in one place so that
the whites went to the cathedral, Amerindians went to another church,
and blacks to a third church. All Americans and people who know
about America know about segregation in terms of pews, putting
black people nearer up to heaven in the balcony etc. Then you
had one of the basic developments in the field of Christianity
since the discovery of America, the emergence of a Christian
church totally separate from the white hierarchy. Much of
American black history and civil rights campaigns related to that
development, special reference being made to the role of Baptists
and Methodists in the slavery period in particular in places like
Jamaica and Trinidad.
What about the Asians, the coolies, what about them, the whole
attitude, the m arch for liberty through Christ Jesus. These were
the "savages", Hindus and Muslims, who were to be "civilised".
The established churches in Trinidad, Catholic, Anglican wished
to have nothing to do with that. So you have the Presbyterian
Mission to the Indians developing among the Canadians to come
here to civilize (these are the reports of Governor after Governor),
to civilize these Asian "savages" as the official reports called
them.

SOME HISTORICAL REFLECTIONS

ON THE CHURCH

IN THE CARIBBEAN

An Address by Dr. the Rt. Hon. Eric Williams, Prime Minister of Trinidad and Tobago, to the Synod of the South Caribbean District of Methodist Church at the Tranquillity Church, Port-of-Spain, on 24 January, 1973.

I am very grateful indeed to the Rev. Mr. Lyder for giving me this opportunity of speaking on the occasion of the Methodist Synod here in Port-of-Spain, not only because, as he said, my principal concern for most of my adult life has been the history of our area, but also because (if I may say this to modify any suggestions that have been made about the time taken in this and other commitments etc.) I was actually at this moment engaged in some further work on the West Indies which revolved around this subject of the Church. So this is a wonderful opportunity for me to clarify my ideas, bring them together, especially before such an appropriate audience. I would merely like to say, if it is not already clear from what the Chairman has said, that I come here as a student of history, and as far as I am concerned there is no Prime Minister present.

I would like to begin, as it is going to become more and more important for more and more of us to be paying attention to the historical past that has us by the throat whatever we try to do in the present, I shall begin by indicating to you what was the position as far as what we call the Church collectively was concerned on the discovery of the West Indies.

There was generally speaking only one Church, the Roman Catholic Church, at the time which governed directly or indirectly a large part of Europe. It was not only a Church, it was also a most powerful state.

Shortly before the discovery of America, the Spanish authorities who were connected with the discovery of America were able to get rid of the last remnants of Islamic influence and power in Spain itself. But as the Church came to the West Indies, the stage was already set in Europe for the Protestant Reformation. So that shortly after the discovery, 50 years, 40 years or so, there was the emergence of a number of Protestant sects and powers, particularly England and Holland, who, looking at their Catholic rivals with all their wealth from the New World, thought that whilst they could get a share of that wealth themselves they could also, in what was then pre-eminently an age of religion, have some say, this time a Protestant say, in the salvation of souls.

So apart from the mundane interest of Queen Elizabeth of England in British prosecution of the slave trade or piracy against Spanish vessels, there was a powerful Protestant motif which was there with the Dutch also and which was there with the Puritan military dictator in England, Cromwell, who worked out what he called a western design for challenging Spain in the New World out of which came the British conquest of Jamaica. That was the position within a century and a half of the discovery by the Spaniards.

The Church came to the West Indies with enormous powers naturally derived from its pre-eminent position in Europe. It had the Inquisition for rooting out

Some Reflections on the Church in the Caribbean

aries (otherwise known as agents to the villainous African Society [that was the society for the abolition of slavery]), a party of respectable gentlemen formed the resolution of closing the Methodist concern altogether; with this view they commenced their labours on Sunday evening, and they have the greatest satisfaction in announcing that by 12 o'clock last night they effected the Total Destruction of That Chapel".

The missionary fled to St. Vincent, they went on, "thereby avoiding that expression of the public feeling towards him, personally, which he had so richly deserved." They expressed the hope "that all persons in other colonies who consider themselves true lovers of religion will follow the laudable example of the Barbadians, in putting an end to Methodism and Methodist chapels throughout the West Indies." A combination of State, Established Church, and landed aristocracy to prevent religious toleration and to prevent the operation of a particular mission in Barbados *

The second area is Jamaica with the Baptists. I think perhaps that it would be a little more satisfactory if I were to tell you what the Baptists themselves said. I don't think you know much in Trinidad about the history of Jamaica anyhow, and the Baptists were more important in Jamaica than they were in Trinidad. One

of the most powerful missionary fighters against slavery in the West Indian colonies was a Baptist minister in Jamaica, Rev. William Knibb. I want to give you an idea of the quality of the attack of the man and the depth and comprehensiveness of the mission in a brief extract (I would like to give it all to you but it is too long) from a speech that he made to the Annual Meeting of the Baptist Missionary Society in London, on the 21st June, 1832, within a year of the abolition of slavery.

He was talking to them saying he appeared as "the feeble and unworthy advocate of 20,000 Baptists in Jamaica," etc.

"Among this deeply injured race I have spent the happiest part of my life. I plead on behalf of my own Church where I had 980 members and 2,500 candidates for baptism, surrounded by a population of 27,000. Their prayers are put up for you; put up yours for them. By prayer we have, by prayer we must, by prayer we will, prevail. God is the avenger of the oppressed, and the African shall not always be forgotten. I plead on behalf of the widows and orphans of those whose innocent blood has been shed. I plead that the constancy of the Negro may be rewarded. I plead on behalf of my brethren in Jamaica, whose hopes are fixed on this meeting. (It is within a year of the abolition of slavery.) I plead on behalf of their wives and their

* The Methodists in the United States were most vehement in their opposition to slavery. A conference of Methodists in Virginia in 1784 resolved as follows:

"We view it as contrary to the Golden Law of God on which hang all the Law and the Prophets, and the unalienable Rights of Mankind, as well as every Principle of the Revolution, to hold in the deepest Debasement, in a more abject slavery than is perhaps to be found in any Part of the World except America, so many souls that are capable of the Image of God."

The early custom was for blacks to attend the same churches as the whites. But the Quakers, militant as they were in their conversion policy, showed the greatest distaste and reluctance for making Blacks Friends—that is to say, Quakers; and encouraged the blacks they had converted to go to other churches. One Episcopal Church in Virginia painted certain benches black and reserved these only for Blacks. By 1790 of the Methodists in Virginia, one in five was black; the proportion among Baptists was probably even higher. The result was that, with the active connivance and support of whites and many of the churches, the African Methodist Episcopal Church was born in Philadelphia, opening its doors in July 1794. The one institution which had been prepared to accept black equality, the Church, now moved in the direction of separatism and segregation. (E.W.)

Some Reflections on the Church in the Caribbean

aries (otherwise known as agents to the villainous African Society [that was the society for the abolition of slavery]), a party of respectable gentlemen formed the resolution of closing the Methodist concern altogether; with this view they commenced their labours on Sunday evening, and they have the greatest satisfaction in announcing that by 12 o'clock last night they effected the Total Destruction of That Chapel".

The missionary fled to St. Vincent, they went on, "thereby avoiding that expression of the public feeling towards him, personally, which he had so richly deserved." They expressed the hope "that all persons in other colonies who consider themselves true lovers of religion will follow the laudable example of the Barbadians, in putting an end to Methodism and Methodist chapels throughout the West Indies." A combination of State, Established Church, and landed aristocracy to prevent religious toleration and to prevent the operation of a particular mission in Barbados *

The second area is Jamaica with the Baptists. I think perhaps that it would be a little more satisfactory if I were to tell you what the Baptists themselves said. I don't think you know much in Trinidad about the history of Jamaica anyhow, and the Baptists were more important in Jamaica than they were in Trinidad. One of the most powerful missionary fighters against slavery in the West Indian colonies was a Baptist minister in Jamaica, Rev William Knibb. I want to give you an idea of the quality of the attack of the man and the depth and comprehensiveness of the mission in a brief extract (I would like to give it all to you but it is too long) from a speech that he made to the Annual Meeting of the Baptist Missionary Society in London, on the 21st June, 1832, within a year of the abolition of slavery.

He was talking to them saying he appeared as "the feeble and unworthy advocate of 20,000 Baptists in Jamaica," etc.

"Among this deeply injured race I have spent the happiest part of my life. I plead on behalf of my own Church where I had 980 members and 2,500 candidates for baptism, surrounded by a population of 27,000. Their prayers are put up for you; put up yours for them. By prayer we have, by prayer we must, by prayer we will, prevail. God is the avenger of the oppressed, and the African shall not always be forgotten. I plead on behalf of the widows and orphans of those whose innocent blood has been shed. I plead that the constancy of the Negro may be rewarded. I plead on behalf of my brethren in Jamaica, whose hopes are fixed on this meeting. (It is within a year of the abolition of slavery.) I plead on behalf of their wives and their

---

* The Methodists in the United States were most vehement in their opposition to slavery. A conference of Methodists in Virginia in 1784 resolved as follows:

"We view it as contrary to the Golden Law of God on which hang all the Law and the Prophets, and the unalienable Rights of Mankind, as well as every Principle of the Revolution, to hold in the deepest Debasement, in a more abject slavery than is perhaps to be found in any Part of the World except America, so many souls that are capable of the Image of God."

The early custom was for blacks to attend the same churches as the whites. But the Quakers, militant as they were in their conversion policy, showed the greatest distaste and reluctance for making Blacks Friends—that is to say, Quakers; and encouraged the blacks they had converted to go to other churches. One Episcopal Church in Virginia painted certain benches black and reserved these only for Blacks. By 1790 of the Methodists in Virginia, one in five was black; the proportion among Baptists was probably even higher. The result was that, with the active connivance and support of whites and many of the churches, the African Methodist Episcopal Church was born in Philadelphia, opening its doors in July 1794. The one institution which had been prepared to accept black equality, the Church, now moved in the direction of separatism and segregation. (E.W.)

EDUCATION AND DECOLONISATION

Address by Dr. Eric Williams,
Prime Minister of Trinidad & Tobago
to the Caribbean Union
Conference, Maracas
on 29th August, 1974

It was the same with British rule in India, where Lord Macaulay, in demanding university education in India on the British pattern, arrogantly dismissed the whole native literature of India and Arabia as inferior to a single shelf of a good European library. It was the same in Haiti with the United States military occupation in 1916, when every effort was made to replace the French bias inherited from the colonial period, however absurd and inadequate it was, by the American system, however superior it was in its relevance to Haiti's basic needs.

(2) The handmaiden of the imperialist power was the Church, the guardian of morality and with its monopoly of education in the Europe of that time. Sword and cross went hand in hand. The Church was enjoined by royal decree, to instruct Amerindian boys in reading, writing and matters of the faith in the settlements to which the Amerindians were to be compulsorily removed to be closer to the areas where the Spaniards required their labour. In the field of morality the Church was particularly concerned with the enforcement of monogamy and opposed nudity, fornication, adultery, and above all, against the background of the Europe of the day, sodomy.

(3) From top to bottom the metropolitan system was racist, dominated by white racism. The so-called inferior races were debarred from prescribed professions, the list at various times including particularly the priesthood, medicine, law and university education in general. The Spaniards stressed racial purity as a prerequisite to those professions; a French decree stated that it was indecent to see blacks studying to be lawyers. Similarly, blacks, whatever their shade of colour, were banned from trades and occupations reserved for whites, as happened in the Southern States of America under slavery and as happens today in South Africa under apartheid. Non whites were discriminated against by the guilds of that time as they are discriminated against today by the contemporary trade unions.

The Independence of Trinidad and Tobago, in the critical decades of the sixties, was a part of the world movement against colonialism, clericalism, racism and all their works, including cultural imperialism. Decolonisation ran riot particularly after the independence of Algeria where the nationalist movement had pledged to substitute the native Arabic for the imposed French of colonialism.

The established Christian churches came under heavy fire—the legalisation of abortion (as of today in 28 countries with 60% of the world's population); the use of the pill; the spread of divorce (most recently to Italy of all countries); the obsession with sex; the popularity of pornography; the spread of nudity (we now have even nude marriages and our own Frederick Street has its daytime fashion show emphasising the string look); the aggressiveness of homosexuality which, in our world, can no longer be defined as love that dare not speak its name or a group of queers who neither marry nor are given in marriage; the revolt against the celibacy of the clergy; above all, the emptiness of the churches.

The decline of the churches has not yet spread to Islam and does not include Christian sects traditionally closer to the grass roots (your own Seventh Day Adventists would be an outstanding example), or the Black Church in America, while African revivals — always present in Hailti and parts of Brazil — are gaining ground. The decline of the influence of the Christian Church is particularly evident among blacks, who have for so long associated the Church with white racism, where the discrimination involved the blacks sitting in a segregated gallery, or a ban on their kneeling on cushions, or where the price for a black funeral was fixed at less than a white funeral because the church bells did not toll so long — all part of the conscious policy, as the French put it so well, to do nothing "to weaken the humiliation attached to the species" and to demonstrate that "colour was wedded to slavery" and that "nothing could render the black man the equal of his white master."

This was the world climate in which Trinidad and Tobago prepared its 15 year education development plan of 1967. The key was the secondary school, which by 1967 was enrolling almost 30,000 students, double the number for 1961, of whom nearly 6,000, or double the number of 1961, came in on the merit system irrespective of class and colour through the common entrance examination.

The principal objectives of the 1967 Education Plan were as follows:

(1) Elimination of the Common Entrance Examination in 15 years.

(2) The introduction of a new school, the Junior Secondary School, with a three-year course in general training principally as a substitute for the colonial anachronism of the all-age primary school with its pupils over 12.

(3) To cope with the problem of numbers, in the context of a high capital cost (a million dollars for a school), the introduction of the double shift system in the Junior Secondary School.

(4) The conversion of the existing secondary schools, Government or denominational, either by lopping off the lower forms and converting them into senior secondary schools, or by removing the higher forms and converting them into junior secondary schools.

(5) The target at the end of the 15-year period of the absorption of 90% of the eligible primary school children into Junior Secondary Schools and 37% of the eligible Junior Secondary School children into Senior Secondary schools.

(6) The organisation of a national system of planned teacher training, in-

Eric Williams remembered

The man, the myth

'...he is, unquestionably, the greatest Trinidadian of the 20th Century—the person who has had the greatest influence on the affairs of the country...'

By JEFF HACKETT

IN THE 1950s and 1960s, word

and built the PNM into an impregnable political force. He

Moyou and his secret wedding to Frederick Street dentist Mayleen Meek Saw in 1958 did not last as

Barbadian leader Errol Barrow and Kamaluddin Mohammed, as Minister of West Indian Affairs

EXPRESS Thursday, March 26, 1998 Page 23

THE NEW YORK TIMES, SUNDAY, AUGUST 12, 1979

Scholars Search in Ethiopia In Study of Early Christians

By KENNETH A. BRIGGS
Special to The New York Times

COLLEGEVILLE, Minn., Aug. 8 — The mountainous regions of northern Ethiopia are dotted with hundreds of monasteries, many of them chiseled from solid rock centuries ago. If experts here are right, the monasteries are a storehouse of ancient manuscripts that could greatly alter prevailing views of early Christianity.

The Coptic church of Ethiopia was founded about A.D. 400 by missionaries from Syria who made their way through Egypt. The Rev. Godfrey Diekmann, a Benedictine monk and a professor of early church history at St. John's University here, believes that invaluable texts of Ethiopian Christianity have been preserved because of several factors.

These include a penchant of Ethiopian monks for insuring the longevity of texts by using nonperishable materials; the extreme care generally given to sacred documents throughout the Ethiopian church; the dryness of the climate, which would offer another form of protection, and the uninterrupted development of the country.

With that belief, Father Diekmann and his colleagues at St. John's are seeking access to the remote monasteries, as part of the university's long-range goal of microfilming manuscripts tucked away in monastic libraries in Europe and Africa for the last 1,000 years.

Challenge to Old Views

As scholars pore over the writings that have already been microfilmed, which cover subjects including music, astronomy, military tactics and medicine in addition to the tomes of theology, views of the Christian past and of the Middle Ages are being challenged.

Since 1965, more than 50,000 manuscripts have been microfilmed, catalogued and filed in uniform, numbered rows in a wing of the university library under the guidance of a staff of scholars and librarians.

While most of the Christian world was disrupted by the Seventh Century Islamic invasions around the rim of the Mediterranean, Ethiopia went unscathed. Therefore, Father Diekmann said, "the hun-

project, steers a delicate course in his attempts to convince abbots and others in charge of monastic libraries that the benefits of making copies of the manuscripts far surpass any liabilities. "Some think it is cultural exploitation," Dr. Plante said in his library office. "They're afraid to lose control over their own heritage. My point is that we are helping to preserve their heritage."

Through tact and assurance that the documents will be treated with utmost care, the project staff has won permission to photograph materials in 18 nations. In the most extensive project, in Austria, 30,000 manuscripts, the known total, were filmed in seven years under the supervision of the Rev. Oliver Kapsner, a St. John's monk who has been a professional librarian since 1925.

With heavy support from foundations the project spent $3 million in its first 10 years. The working pace has steadily picked up, and each week 30 new rolls of film arrive to be catalogued.

Sorting the manuscripts is often a slow, painstaking job. At present, for example, Dr. Hope Mayo, a medieval scholar who catalogues Western manuscripts, is in the early stages of a yearlong effort to classify the contents of the Herzogenburg monastery in lower Austria. The collection, from the 15th century, is fairly typical of those found in the region, and consists mostly of sermons, biblical concordances, limited word dictionaries and treatises on church law.

As the microfilm collection grows, an increasing number of scholars come to St. John's to conduct research. About 100 researchers are expected to arrive this year to study a wide variety of topics. Among those this week was Merritt Nequette, an instructor at the College of St. Thomas in St. Paul, Minn., whose doctoral thesis on the music of Melk monastery in Austria was based on the availability of all the relevant manuscripts at St. John's.

GENERAL ARTICLES ON RACISM IN THE CHURCHES

THE CHURCH OF ETHIOPIA

A PANORAMA OF HISTORY

AND

SPIRITUAL LIFE

1970

bringing with him the Ark of the Covenant, which he had obtained by subterfuge. From then on, Judaism was practised in Ethiopia. It is said by some authorities that the Falasha tribe of northern Ethiopia, who practise a form of Judaism to this day, are descendants of the Israelites. The form of Judaism professed is apparently a development of a pre-Talmudic type of worship.

2. THE INTRODUCTION OF CHRISTIANITY

St. Frumentius and the Conversion of Ezana c. 330 A.D.

Although Christianity became the official religion of the Aksumite kingdom in the fourth century, the religion had been known in Ethiopia since a much earlier time. In the *Acts of the Apostles*, VIII: 26-40, we are told of a certain Eunuch, the treasurer of Queen Candace of Ethiopia, who went to Jerusalem to worship the God of Israel. There he met Philip the Deacon and was baptized by him. Ethiopian tradition asserts that he returned home and evangelized the people. In his Homily on Pentecost, St. John Chrysostom mentions that the Ethiopians were present in the Holy City on the day of Pentecost. Later, when the Apostles went out to preach the Gospel, Matthew was allotted the task of carrying the good news to Ethiopia, where he suffered martyrdom. Ethiopian sources, such as the *Synaxarium*, make no mention of this, however; on the contrary, Ethiopians believe that they received Christianity without shedding Apostolic blood. Nevertheless, Christianity was certainly known in Ethiopia before the time of Frumentius, being the faith practised by many of the merchants from the Roman Empire settled in the Aksumite region. In important cities, such as Aksum and Adulis, these Christian merchants had their prayer houses and openly practised their religion.

The introduction of Christianity as the State religion of Ethiopia came about not as the result of organized evangelical activity from outside the country, but because it was the desire of the King. The story of the conversion of the Aksumites has come down to us in the work of the contemporary Church historian, Rufinus (d.410 A.D.). Meropius, a philosopher from Tyre, set out to visit India accompanied by two young relatives, Frumentius and Aedesius. Apparently they

FLAME 1997

RESPONDING TO THE REALITY OF CHANGE

THE FLAME is a publication
of the
West Indies School
of Theology

PENTECOSTAL ASSEMBLIES OF THE WEST INDIES

Alvin O. Thompson

Change is everywhere within the Caribbean, but we shall only consider two broad categories, the first has to do with ethics and morality; the illegal use of drugs, sexual promiscuity (including the spread of homosexuality and prostitution), abortions, casino gambling, money laundering, mail fraud, etc. We are part of the wide scenario in which many of the values once held sacred are becoming (and some have already become) profane. The advance of materialism, secularism and formalism have made Christian precepts and practices seem at best only peripheral to human life.

The other broad area of change is the increasing questioning by our young people as to why our theology seems to be so "white oriented". Arguably, much of it is based implicitly, and sometimes explicitly, upon the notion of a white God and a black devil, as demonstrated, for instance, in photos, films, skits, etc. The view of James I of England (1603 - 1625), in his book Demonologies, that witches' covens were usually presided over by a black person who was the devil, still prevails in some of our present day theology. Highly questionable is the theological soundness of a well-known song which goes in part: "My heart was black with sin until the Saviour came in His precious blood I know has washed me white as snow".

Nowhere in the Bible is sin referred to as black. The point is important because our youths, who often have a highly developed sense of racial pride, find it difficult to relate to such a theology. They sometimes see this as a form of discrimination by God against black peoples. All images perhaps need to be abolished from our churches, so that no one will bow down and worship them.

Christianity was born in Asia and spread to Africa before reaching Western Europe. However, almost nothing is taught about African Christianity, except in the context of the Church Fathers in Alexandria, who are seen as part of the Western European Church. Even less is said, or indeed known, about their history of the church in the Indian subcontinent.

We need to make it very clear that God is no respecter of persons and that whoever will seek Him will find Him. We need to make it equally clear that black peoples like other peoples, have played an important role in the history of the church universal. In this respect we need to move away from the limited exposure which we give our Bible students to Western church history wrongly referring to it simply as "Church History".

Religion fraught with racism

The Sunday Gleaner, April 9, 1989

By Conrad Lindo

Other columnists have dealt with the race issue from political and economic perspectives. The constraints of this column, however, dictate that I look at the question from a religious perspective. Furthermore, contrary to what some might think, the question of race is not just a political and economic one but it is also related to religion.

The truth is that religion has perhaps been the most effective psychological tool used to keep Blacks in their place. This is not to say that religion does not have its merits, and in some instances is not a source of inspiration and liberation for Blacks.

However religion, particularly certain forms of Christianity, has been a very effective cloak not only for the spreading of racism but for dulling racial consciousness. So much so that converts to some of these Christian expressions are duped into believing that race does not matter, and that they should only be happy for "salvation".

Descendants of Ham

The irony is that some of these overtly racists religions have taken root in Jamaica and have been able to win converts, mostly Blacks. I remember talking to a white Mormon expatriate in Jamaica a few years ago. I asked him about the status of Blacks in the Mormon Church, particularly to explain the fact that Blacks were excluded from the priesthood of the church up to 1978. This Mormon first tried to assure me that the Mormom Church is not racist. He then went into a long explanation about the history of the black man from his Mormon perspective.

In the 1950s and '60s, many Black Jamaican migrants to Britain discovered to their shock, that their black presence was not welcome in churches. They quickly realised the wisdom of forming their own churches or finding churches which made them "feel at home". Even today it comes as a revelation to some local Christians to learn that churches in the United States are largely segregated — white churches and black churches.

Many local evangelicals do not know that much of evangelical Christianity in the United States is fraught with racism. Few local evangelicals are aware that whenever neighbourhoods in certain cities of the U.S.A. become "too black" in population, the evangelical church is usually among the first institutions to move out. This was affirmed to me some time ago by a prominent white evangelical from the U.S.A., who among other things, said how he felt freer to associate with blacks in Jamaica than "the ones in America". The "racial harmony" that exist in Churches in Jamaica was a "joy to him". He felt comfortable because the form and style of worship he found in many churches in Jamaica were similar to what he had back home.

The observation of this white, American evangelical is not strange, since many Jamaican Christians are only exposed to the white side of Christianity. Generally there is ignorance of what Black Christians are saying and even a lack of awareness that Black Christians can create and write their own story. This ignorance is perpetrated and reinforced because that foreign guest speaker at church conventions or crusades is usually white. The image or painting of Christ displayed in churches and homes is also white.

BISHOP ABDULAH

Page 4 TRINIDAD GUARDIAN, Saturday, February 5, 1983

Anglicans vote against ordination of women

THE ANGLICAN Church of Trinidad and Tobago has voted against ordination of women as priests. Anglican Bishop Clive Abdulah revealed this yesterday at a Press Conference at the Bishop's residence, Hayes Court. He gave details of the 28th Synod of the Church of the Province of the West Indies held in Belize.

The Synod was held over five days. The Bishop said the ordination of women gained a "no majority consensus at the Synod. Three Caribbean countries Jamaica, Barbados and Antigua voted in favour while the others voted like Trinidad against the proposal.

Explaining the Trinidad and Tobago stand, he said the Anglican sector of this country was not prepared to accept women in the priesthood. They were not ready for women to take the responsibility in the administrative and functional role in the Church.

According to the Bishop, while women already held top positions in

change was.

He said women held very responsible positions in the Anglican church and there was no discrimination against women for top positions in the Church.

He would have to know that the Church would only accept women because of the so-called "women's lib." Women in the Anglican Church did not hold a higher or lower role than the men, but instead were involved in different functions.

BORDER DISPUTES

Bishop Abdulah said countries such as the United States, and Canada had agreed to have women ordained as priests while the United Kingdom and Africa did not. Trinidad and Tobago did not necessarily follow the pattern of the United Kingdom but acted its own.

A communique agreed upon at the Synod stated: "We regret that there exists in the Caribbean area many threats to the realisation of peace, both within the political and socio-economic systems as they operate, and those generated by

the Presbyterian Church, he woundered how successful the external forces."

The communique also said that while it was aware of the territorial claims by Venezuela and Guatemala against Guyana and Belize respectively, it was hoped that there would be a just and peaceful solution in each case.

The communique stated: "We are aware of the reports of the serious curtailment of the freedom of expression as well as that of the media in some territories. The development we greatly lament. On the other hand, we challenge the media whether privately or Government-owned that in the exercise of this freedom, they should recognise their duty and responsibility to create and preserve the freedom inherent in the concept of democracy.

"We are concerned that in some places relationships between State and Church have deteriorated with counter productive results in those countries. There has come to our notice, for example, the withdrawal and refusal of work permits to clergymen and others for reasons which suggest that there is a manipulation of the process, which causes us much uneasiness.

Women in Ministry debate

ANGLICAN

The Bible a barrier to ordination

By Ian Boyne

Gleaner January 11·1997 Jamaica

MUCH OF the argument against the ordination of women to the priesthood/Christian ministry arise from rank prejudice, bigotry, ignorance and a history of sexism.

Gender discrimination and patriarchal oppression are among the great evils of Western "civilisation" and the Christian church, itself an important purveyor of racism, classism and imperialism, has been an important ally in the sexist's cause.

Arguments that seek to bar women from the priesthood based on ability, temperament, emotional make-up or their ability to get pregnant are pathetically misguided. Yet the attempt to prove that the Bible allows for the ordination of women to the ministry is absolutely futile. Confused? Let me explain my "contradictions".

If we leave the Bible out of the discussion, or take the view that the Bible is culturally and historically limited and that its authority is not transcultural, there can be no objection to women's ordination. However, there is no way to hold a conservative view of Biblical authority and maintain the ordination of women. No sound hermeneutical or exegetical principle can be adduced to get around the timelessness of 1st Timothy 2:11-15, 1st Corinthians 14: 33-35 and 1st Corinthians 11: 2-9.

Various attempts have been made by evangelical feminists to churches which practice proof-texting and have a naive view of Biblical inerrancy (including the dictation theory) have women bishops when the Pauline writings say women should be silent and should not authoritatively teach in the congregation. And some priests who are liberals on Scripture and hold that it is historically limited and even deny some fundamental tents like the Virgin birth etc, are madly opposed to women's ordination.

Liberal feminist

Some Anglican priests are hopping mad over the recent ordination of four women to their priesthood. It is important that the issue be approached rationally, not emotionally. Liberal feminist theologians say openly that the Bible itself is the greatest barrier of women's full liberation. They say there is no way to rescue the Bible by means of hermeneutics and exegesis from the charge that it does not allow functional equality between the sexes in ministry. Elizabeth Schussler Fiorenza's book In memory of Her: A feminist Theological Reconstruction of Christian Origins, is an excellent introduction to the liberal thinking. This theological approach is internally consistent, unlike the positions put forward by supposedly conservative Baptist theologians.

"The Bible", Fiorenza says unblushingly, "is not just interpreta-

text or to make it pliable to the tasks of modern feminism. Either one accepts the notion that the Bible authoritatively and inerrantly contains the universal, transhistorical propositional truths such as male headship of the home and the church, or one takes an historical and existential approach to Biblical exegesis. Says Mattera, "Fiorenza insists that feminist scholarship cannot adopt an approach to Scripture that tries to distil a transhistorical theological centre from the 'accident' of Scripture's patriarchal historical formation."

For example, attempts to show that Paul in Timothy was giving a command for that time fails utterly to note that Paul grounds his objection to female authoritative teaching in the church on the ground of the creation order, rather than present circumstances. In 1st Corinthians 14: 34 he makes reference to "the law", not historical exigencies. Arguments about "new creation order" rather than "order of creation" are semantical games and the Galatians 3: 28 text frequently invoked as a paradigm for accepting female ordination is one of the worst examples of sloppy Biblical interpretation.

The view that Jesus only chose women because of a concession to a sexist society ignores the fact that Jesus broke a number of traditions in his time, including some having to do with relations with women in pub-

Women in Ministry debate

The New Testament supports the idea

Gleaner January 11, 1997

By Rev. Michael Friday

THE NEW Testament supports the idea of females in ministry. It regards all Christians, male and female, as ministers, both generally and specifically. First Peter 2:9 declares that all believers are "a royal priesthood". Why, then, would God exclude females from the ordained ministry, simply because of their sex? What could allow both sexes into ministry, generally, yet disallow females from the ordained ministry?

There is no scriptural nor theological basis for debarring females from the ordained ministry, simply because of their sex.

The passages about man being woman's head (I Cor. 11:3) and women learning in silence (in church) (I Tim. 2:11) cannot be faithfully interpreted without the following being taken into account: (a) the culture of the writer and reader (b) the specific problem the writer was addressing (c) that 'women' in these cultures often means "married women". Any attempt to superimpose these passages upon today's reality and culture without the proper filter of textual and other criticism will trivialise the issue.

The arguments for females as ordained ministers are manifold. Firstly, there is the argument from history. The Scriptures record that there were prophetesses in Old

For Christ's message to have been palatable, he had to, as a human being, work within the strictures of his cultures, which relegated women to particular roles (just as, though he was God, he was limited by his physical body).

It is highly improbable that Christ, had he continued, physically, into today's culture in the western world, would have excluded women from his inner circle. He has, however, continued in the world through the person of the Holy Spirit, and has, through the ministry of that Spirit, removed the obstacles debarring women from ordained ministry.

Western cultures

This leads us to the argument from culture. The times have changes, and, in western cultures, the place of women has grown far beyond the home. Women have been able to demonstrate their intelligence, competence and talents. How can God be said to be against this tremendous resource being available for His ministry?

This leads, fourthly, to the argument from spiritual gifts. Joel (2:28) prophesies that God, in the last days, would pour out his Spirit on all flesh (male and female alike). I Cor. 12:7-11 teaches that each believer is given some gift or gifts of the Spirit (among which the gifts usually identified as pre-

the one serving Holy Communion than for the one receiving it? Or for the one baptising than for the one being baptised? Or for the one preaching from the pulpit than for the one sharing one's faith (also preaching) over dinner? And are we saying that this greater measure of grace is given exclusively to males? May it never be!

Fifthly, the argument from creation. God, in Genesis 1:27 "created man in His own image, male and female he created them". It is both male and female which are created in the image of God. Can anyone make a case for God excluding from ministry, that which is in his own image, simply because of her sex? Further, in Galatians 3:28, Paul unequivocally declares that there is no distinction between male and female in Jesus Christ, since all are one in Christ.

Concomitant with this, is, finally, the argument from the nature of God, in which, in the final analysis, but one can determine that God has a sex and what that might be. In fact, there are references in Scripture from which it might be inferred that God is s much female as male, though, in most references, he is more "Other" than male of female.

There is the assumption that since God is male and his Son, male and all his major prophets and priests, male and his Son's disciples, male, then his ordained servants today must

Anglicans ordain
first women deacon

Herald [Jamaica] Feb 7. 1994

Three women were ordained as deacons of the Anglican Church yesterday in a history-making ceremony indicating the changing view of gender roles affecting the church.

Judith Daniel, Patricia Johnson and Sybil Morris became the first Jamaican women elevated to the Holy Order of Deacons in the Anglican Church in a ceremony witnessed by a congregation packed into St James' Cathedral in Spanish Town.

The historic ceremony was performed by Lord Bishop of Jamaica Rt Reverend Neville deSouza who in his sermon said the occasion marked a new era in which women were being accorded equal status in the church as men.

Bishop deSouza said the Anglican Church was guided by four considerations in making its decisions. These were the Holy Scriptures, the teaching of the Church, the historical traditions of the Church and the contemporary situation.

The Lord Bishop quoted from Galatians chapter 3 in the Bible where the Apostle Paul said all people were one in Jesus Christ. He said the priesthood of Jesus bridged the gap between Heaven and Earth, and between humans.

Bishop deSouza said some sons argued that women could mirror Christ because Christ to masculine image while he wa Earth. The bishop pointed ou the Bible says neither man woman alone can represent C because Christ mirrored both and female components. He the patriarchal era of history based on the story that God cr the first woman Eve from the the first man, Adam. He said ever that both man and womar the same genesis.

"The leadership battle bet the sexes is really nonsensi Bishop deSouza said emphas that "differentiation did not division". He said the dominar any one of the sexes meant d for all. The Bishop challenge newly ordained deacons to the integration of the Church level of the ministry. He sai women would bring their "inl and innate gifts" to the work church while men with their u gifts would "complement and plete" the ministry.

Bishop deSouza challe the church to personalise the ministry of Jesus.

'I Suffer Not a Woman to Teach'

Baptist Group Reserving The Pulpit For Men

THE WASHINGTON POST

THE WASHINGTON POST SATURDAY, JUNE 10, 2000 B9

By Bill Broadway
Washington Post Staff Writer

In 1984, Kelly Sisson became the first woman to preach in the chapel at New Orleans Theological Seminary, one of six graduate schools run by the Southern Baptist Convention.

The next Sunday, a local pastor pronounced the chapel's pulpit demonically possessed because a woman had preached there. The next month, delegates, or "messengers," at the annual meeting of the Southern Baptist Convention passed a resolution discouraging the ordination of women for pastoral functions and leadership roles.

Sisson, pastor of Glade Baptist Church in Blacksburg, Va., doesn't think there is a direct connection between her preaching at the seminary and the convention's action that summer.

But the Rev. Bill Merrell, spokesman for the Nashville-based convention's executive committee, said that "there's nothing new here." Most Southern Baptists, he said, support the Apostle Paul's assertion, "I suffer not a woman to teach, nor to usurp authority over the man, but to be in silence."

The issue is not one of ordination, because women are free to be ordained to "the gospel ministry and serve in such positions as youth pastor, minister of music and education director, he said. "We believe that the office of pastor is reserved to men as qualified by Scripture."

But the pastor's objection to her preaching, plus a campus protest critical of her pulpit appearance, reflected the thinking that now dominates the country's largest denomination.

Next week, some 16,000 delegates attending the convention's 2000 meeting in Orlando are expected to approve a revision of a major belief statement that, in essence, will codify the doctrine that only men should be pastors.

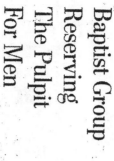

"Look what the message is for little girls," said the Rev. Kelly Sisson, of Blacksburg, Va. " . . . God is doing something in their lives."

BAPTIST — Bill Broadway

Dissent Among Illinois Baptists

Several Illinois Southern Baptist leaders have voiced concerns about a proposal to reorganize the staff of the denomination's state organization because they say it would place two women in positions of authority over male ministers.

Bob Wiley, executive director of the Illinois Baptist State Association, has announced plans to make one woman an associate executive director and another the facilitator for the service-ministry team. Both women currently are working in other capacities for the organization.

But nine ministers from the Franklin Baptist Association in southern Illinois wrote a letter to the editor of the Illinois Baptist, a newspaper, citing Bible verses that say women should not be in authority over men, reported the Baptist Press, the official news service of the Southern Baptist Convention.

Two of the letter-signers, Jim Endsley and Jim Kerley, explained their positions in an interview with the Illinois Baptist.

"We need to remain people of the Book," said Endsley, pastor of North Benton Baptist Church, referring to the Bible, "and the Book says in many places that women are not to be in authority. I don't know that I like that, but I can't do anything about it. I can't change the Scripture."

Wiley said the women in the new positions would not have authority over men. "The whole purpose of the restructure is to take away positional authority," he said.

— Religion News Service

You Can Live Forever in Paradise on Earth

Publishers   Copyright, 1982, by
WATCHTOWER BIBLE AND TRACT SOCIETY
OF NEW YORK, INC.

JEHOVAH WITNESS   GOD'S VISIBLE ORGANIZATION   195

"Now as they [the apostle Paul and his companions] traveled on through the cities they would deliver to those there for observance the decrees that had been decided upon by the apostles and older men who were in Jerusalem. Therefore, indeed, the congregations continued to be made firm in the faith and to increase in number from day to day." (Acts 16:4, 5) Yes, all the congregations cooperated with what that body of older men in Jerusalem had decided, and they grew stronger in the faith.

THEOCRATIC DIRECTION TODAY

13 God's visible organization today also receives theocratic guidance and direction. At the headquarters of Jehovah's Witnesses in Brooklyn, New York, there is a governing body of older Christian men from various parts of the earth who give the needed oversight to the worldwide activities of God's people. This governing body is made up of members of "the faithful and discreet slave." It serves as a spokesman for that faithful "slave."

14 The men of that governing body, like the apostles and older men in Jerusalem, have many years of experience in God's service. But they do not rely on human wisdom in making decisions. No, being governed theocratically, they follow the example of the early governing body in Jerusalem, whose decisions were based on God's Word and were made under the direction of holy spirit.—Acts 15:13-17, 28, 29.

DIRECTING A WORLDWIDE ORGANIZATION

15 Jesus Christ gave an idea of the size of the organization that God would have on earth during this time of the end when he said: "This good news of the kingdom will be preached in *all the inhabited earth* for a witness to *all the nations;* and then the end will come." (Matthew 24:14) Think of the tremendous amount of work needed to tell earth's thousands of millions

JEHOVAH WITNESS   MAKING A SUCCESS OF FAMILY LIFE   239

HOW GOD CREATED THE MAN AND THE WOMAN

⁴ Anyone can see that Jehovah did not make men and women the same. It is true that in many ways they are alike. But there are obvious differences in their physical appearance and sexual makeup. Also, they have different emotional qualities. Why the differences? God made them that way to help each to fulfill a different role. After God created the man, God said: "It is not good for the man to continue by himself. I am going to make a helper for him, as a complement of him."—Genesis 2:18.

⁵ A complement is something that matches or goes well with some other thing, making it complete. God made woman as a satisfying match for man to assist him in carrying out the God-given instructions to populate and care for the earth. So after creating the woman from a part of the man, God performed the first marriage there in the garden of Eden by 'bringing her to the man.' (Genesis 2:22; 1 Corinthians 11:8, 9) Marriage can be a happy arrangement because the man and the woman were each made with a need that the other has the ability to fulfill. Their different qualities balance one another. When a husband and a wife understand and appreciate each other and cooperate in accord with their assigned roles, they each contribute their part in building a happy home.

THE ROLE OF THE HUSBAND

⁶ A marriage or a family needs leadership. The man was created with a greater measure of the qualities and strengths required to provide such leadership. For this reason the Bible says: "A husband is head of his wife as the Christ also is head of the congregation." (Ephesians 5:23) This is practical, for when there is no leadership there is trouble and confusion. For a family to be without headship would be like trying to drive an automobile without a steering wheel. Or, if the wife were to compete with

4. (a) What differences are there between men and women? (b) Why did God create such differences?
5. (a) How was woman made a "complement" to man? (b) Where did the first marriage take place? (c) Why can marriage be a really happy arrangement?
6. (a) Who was made the head of the family? (b) Why is this proper and practical?

such headship, it would be like having two drivers in the car, each with a steering wheel controlling a separate front wheel.

[7] However, many women do not like the idea that a man should be head of the family. One main reason for this is that many husbands have not followed God's instructions on how to exercise proper headship. Nevertheless, it is a recognized fact that for any organization to operate well someone needs to provide direction and to make final decisions. Thus the Bible wisely says: "The head of every man is the Christ; in turn the head of a woman is the man; in turn the head of the Christ is God." (1 Corinthians 11:3) In God's arrangement, God is the only one who does not have a head. Everyone else, including Jesus Christ, as well as husbands and wives, need to accept direction and to submit to decisions of others.

[8] This means that to fulfill their role as husbands, men must accept the headship of Christ. Also, they must follow his example by exercising headship over their wives just as he does over his congregation of followers. How did Christ deal with his earthly followers? It was always in a kind and considerate way. Never was he harsh or short-tempered, even when they were slow to accept his direction. (Mark 9:33-37; 10:35-45; Luke 22:24-27; John 13:4-15) In fact, he willingly gave his life for them. (1 John 3:16) A Christian husband should carefully study Christ's example, and do the best he can to follow it when dealing with his family. As a result, he will not be a domineering, selfish or inconsiderate family head.

[9] On the other hand, however, husbands should consider this: Does your wife complain that you really do not act as head of the family? Does she say that you do not take the lead in the home, planning family activities and exercising the responsibility to make final decisions? But this is what God requires you, as a husband, to do. Of course, it would be wise for you to

7. (a) Why do some women not like the idea of man's headship? (b) Does everybody have a head, and why is God's arrangement of headship a wise one?
8. (a) Whose example are husbands supposed to follow in exercising headship? (b) What lessons should husbands learn from that example?
9. (a) What complaint do many wives have? (b) What should husbands wisely keep in mind while exercising headship?

be open to the suggestions and preferences of other members of the family and take these suggestions into consideration as you exercise headship. As husband, you clearly have the more difficult role in the family. But if you make a sincere effort to fulfill it, your wife most likely will feel inclined to give you help and support.—Proverbs 13:10; 15:22.

FULFILLING THE WIFE'S ROLE

[10] As the Bible says, the woman was made as a helper to her husband. (Genesis 2:18) In keeping with that role, the Bible urges: "Let wives be in subjection to their husbands." (Ephesians 5:22) Today female aggressiveness and competition with men have become common. But when wives push ahead, trying to take over headship, their action is almost sure to cause trouble. Many husbands, in effect, say: 'If she wants to run the household, let her go ahead and do it.'

[11] However, you may feel that you are forced to take the lead, since your husband does not do so. But could you do more to help him to carry out his responsibilities as head of the family? Do you show that you look to him for leadership? Do you ask for his suggestions and guidance? Do you avoid in any way belittling what he does? If you really work on fulfilling your God-assigned role in the family, your husband will likely start to assume his.—Colossians 3:18, 19.

[12] This is not to say that a wife should not express her opinions if they differ from those of her husband. She may have a correct viewpoint, and the family would benefit if her husband listened to her. Abraham's wife Sarah is given as an example for Christian wives because of her subjection to her husband. (1 Peter 3:1, 5, 6) Yet she recommended a solution to a household problem, and when Abraham did not agree with her God told him: "Listen to her." (Genesis 21:9-12) Of course,

10. (a) What course does the Bible urge for wives? (b) What happens when wives fail to heed the Bible counsel?

11. (a) How can a wife help her husband to take the lead? (b) If a wife fulfills her God-assigned role, what effect is this likely to have on her husband?

12. What shows that wives can properly express their opinions, even if these disagree with their husband's?

October 10, 1987   Washington Post Newspaper

Women Belong at Home, Mormon Leader Asserts

Religious News Service

SALT LAKE CITY—A woman's place is in the home with her children, while husbands and fathers should be breadwinners, said the president of the Church of Jesus Christ of Latter-day Saints during its general conference here last weekend.

In sessions attended by 6,000 people and viewed by many more via satellite, Mormon President Ezra Taft Benson praised obedient Mormons for staying true to their faith in the face of purported discoveries of documents, subsequently proved to be forged, that cast doubt on early church leaders.

Addressing the all-male priesthood of the 6.2 million-member church, Benson said, "The Lord clearly defined the roles of providing for and rearing a righteous posterity. In the beginning, Adam, not Eve, was instructed to earn the bread by the sweat of his brow."

Benson, U.S. secretary of agriculture during the Eisenhower administration, counseled young husbands still in school not to depend totally upon their wives for financial support—especially if there are young children in the home. At the same time, he urged young married students not to delay starting their families on account of income problems.

When husbands insist on their wives working outside the home, "not only will the family suffer," Benson said, "but your own spiritual growth and progression will be hampered. I say to all of you, the Lord has charged men with the responsibility to provide for their families in such a way that the wife is allowed to fulfill her role as mother in the home."

During the Oct. 4 session, Gordon B. Hinckley, first counselor in the church's First Presidency, said only church members "of little faith" were shaken by the forgeries produced by Mark W. Hofmann.

Hofmann began making news several years ago with revelations about alleged historical documents that were inconsistent with Mormon history, including the so-called "salamander letters," which linked the church's founder to practice of folk magic.

Hofmann is in prison after pleading guilty to second-degree murder charges in the bombing deaths two years ago of two prominent Mormon leaders who he feared were about to unmask his widespread forgeries.

Hinckley recalled that when the "discovery" of the documents—several of which the church purchased—was first announced by the church five years ago, it was said they bore little significance in church history.

"But some people of little faith [who] seemingly are always quick to believe the negative, accepted as fact the predictions and pronouncements of the media," he said.

But Hinckley added that "the vast majority of church members, all but a very few, paid little attention and went forward with their church service, living by a conviction firmly grounded in that knowledge which comes by the power of the Holy Ghost."

PAWI against idea of ordained women

by Cheryl Harewood
SUNDAY SUN

FEMALE MINISTERS in Pentecostal churches will have to wait a while longer before they become ordained ministers.

A resolution which was put forward at the 23rd Biennial General Conference of the Pentecostal Assemblies of the West Indies (PAWI) to have women ordained within this denomination was not accepted by a majority.

The result of such a resolution was recorded. "By majority vote, Resolution No. 3 was defeated."

The proposed Resolution No. 3.

The resolution, put forward on the first day of the five-day conference read. "In view of the importance of the spiritual contributions made and being made by women in the Fellowship be it resolved that this Conference agrees to the ordination of women, giving them the same status and title as men."

To date there are 15 women preachers within the PAWI ministries here in Barbados.

According to Reverend Gerry Seale, district superintendent United States.

on the Pentecostal churches in Barbados, women ministers

carry out same functions as male ministers with few exceptions. They cannot perform marriages and cannot be given executive general offices. They do all the functions but we do not give them the status.

Over the years, the question of female ordained ministers has been brought up at such meetings.

Meanwhile, Trinidadian Reverend Alvin Nicholson was re-turned as general secretary of PAWI, defeating Reverend Gerry Seale 120 votes to 68.

This is Nicholson's second term as general secretary. Reverend Emerson Boyce (Barbados) will serve as administrator for the third term and Lloyd Webb as regional commissioner of the church's crusade era.

General Executive members-at-large elected to serve for the next two years are Reverends Turnel Nelson and Alister Alexander (Trinidad), Reverend John Deice (St. Lucia) and Reverend Basil Clarke (Barbados).

This is the first time that non-Trinidadians have been elected as members-at-large on PAWI's General Executive.

The biennial conference of the PAWI brings together pastors from throughout the region as well as Canada, and the

REVEREND GERRY SEALE: women ministers carry out same functions as male ministers with few exceptions.

PASTORS from throughout the region as well as Canada, and the United States assembled at the Caribee Hotel for the 23rd Biennial General Conference of the Pentecostal Assemblies of the West Indies.

Sunday
May 27

Sun May 27, 1990 Barbados

DAILY NATION

THE DAILY NATION is printed and published by the N lishing Company Ltd, established in November, 1973.
President and Editor-in-Chief: Harold Hoyte
Senior Editor: Tony Cozier
Supervising Editors: Winston Walker, John Lovell, and
Sports Editor: Chris Gollop

May 31, 1990. Barbados

EDITORIAL
Yes, ordain women too

THE SURPRISING FAILURE by the 23rd Biennial General Conference of the Pentecostal Assemblies of the West Indies (PAWI) to approve the ordination of women ministers, could only strengthen the resolve of the women in our region who are battling for equal rights and justice.

It is a battle for which there is today a widening circle of supporters who are understandably anxious that the Church be also influenced by the positive wind of change that has resulted in women rising to the highest positions in numerous professions, including politics, diplomacy, education and medicine.

As one of the reputedly fastest growing Christian denominations in this region, at a time when the "mainstream" churches are complaining about declining congregations, the Pentecostals seem to be as insensitive to women's rights as their brethren of the Roman Catholic and Anglican faiths.

The PAWI biennial conference, which concluded in Barbados last week, was urged to approve a resolution extending to women the right to be ordained as ministers, a right that has traditionally been limited to men.

More than women's rights activists have been questioning the stubbornness of the opponents of women priests. Such opponents have often sought refuge in irrelevant dogmas and archaic traditions to perpetuate what is widely perceived as obvious discrimination against women.

Women constitute the biggest segment of any church constituency. They are known to be the most faithful worshippers and are always around to support any programme of the Church — fund-raising, spiritual renewal, counselling and others.

The PAWI statement that disclosed the rejection of the resolution for women to be ordained as ministers did not offer an explanation why the estimated 230 delegates, from 18 countries across the region, came to their negative conclusion on the matter.

We would like to believe that this concept is embraced by all segments of the Christian religion in this region where the Church, for all the criticisms it often attracts from its detractors, remains a very powerful influence in the lives of West Indians.

The contributions of the women of the Caribbean Church remain vital to the process of full human development. Justice, therefore, demands that they also enjoy all the rights and privileges, including ordination, that are normally extended to male ministers.

RELIGION

Pentecostals ordain women ministers

AS PART of the 6th Biennial Conference of the Pentecostal Assemblies of the West Indies Trinidad and Tobago (PAWI,T T), a special Ordination Service was held specifically to ordain women ministers for the first time in the history of the fellowship.

This was in keeping with the resolution passed at the last General Conference of PAWI International held at Hilton Hotel recently.

The Ordination Service was held at the Revival Time Assembly, San Fernando. The featured speaker was the Rev Alister Alexander, Chairman of the Pentecostal Assemblies of The West Indies Trinidad and Tobago.

Describing the new recruits as devout and honourable, Rev Alexander in his address spoke about the special powers God has invested in women, and utilising scriptural references from both the Old and New Testaments, he showed how God has always used women in various ministries as they worked along with the men of God from both eras.

He mentioned that women have the facility and potential for fulfilling God's purpose, and that among the PAWI Fellowship the pioneers of the gospel to the Caribbean had women of God in the forefront advancing the Kingdom of God.

Citing Abigail Suzanna Wesley as an example Rev Alexander then explained how God has placed in women an ability to develop their initiative and own thinking to influence others positively as was done to her two sons, Charles and John Wesley, founders of the Methodist Church.

At the service each lady minister to be ordained was called forth by her District Superintendent and presented to the Chairman and the Assembly as a suitable candidate for ordination.

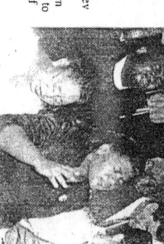

THE LAYING on of hands on the new recr Rev Ann Devinish, Rev Brenda Quanina, Re Raymond, Rev Ruth Ev

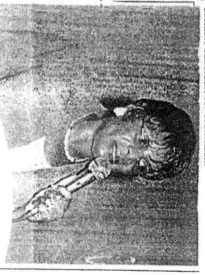

REV JOYCELYN NELSON, wife of the General Superintendent of PAWI addressing the gathering.

NEWSDAY December 1 1998

JAMAICA THE DAILY GLEANER, SATURDAY, SEPTEMBER 24, 1988

Pope rules against women as priests
Cites males as apostles

VATICAN CITY, Sept. 23

POPE JOHN Paul, in an eagerly expected personal document on women, says categorically they cannot become priests because Christ chose only men as his apostles.

A Spanish translation of the Pope's apostolic letter expected to be officially released by the Vatican next week, was obtained through Church sources on Thursday.

The Pope says the Church admires and cherishes women as mothers, sisters, wives, and nuns and adds that women, like men, were created in God's image and should enjoy equal human dignity.

The 125-page document, called "Mulieris Dignitatem" (The Dignity of Woman) is a highly theological work, with hundreds of Biblical references.

The Pope calls the style of the document "a meditation", and announces the future publication of another document on women in the Church and Society based on the conclusions of a 1987 Synod of Bishops in Rome.

The most significant part of the document is a chapter called "The Eucharist" in which the Pope defends the Roman Catholic Church's ban on women priests, saying it was willingly instituted by Christ.

"Christ called as his apostles only men, he did this in a totally free and sovereign way," the Pope says. "and he did this with the same freedom with which his behaviour displayed the dignity and vocation of a woman, without adapting to the custom and tradition endorsed by the legislation of his time.

Method of working

"Because of this, the hypothesis that he called men as apostles because of the widespread mentality of his time does not completely reflect Christ's method of working," he said.

way to the priestly service of the apostles, it is legitimate to think that in this way he desired to express the relationship between man and woman," he says.

Some Catholic groups have demanded that women be allowed to become priests but the issue has not been as divisive or explosive in the Roman Catholic Church as it has been in other christian denominations.

Last July, the Church of England Synod voted in favour of ordaining women priests. The issue is one of the major obstacles to eventual reunion of Catholics and Anglicans.

In the document, the Pope touches only briefly on the specific role of women in the Church and society, apparently because these issues will be the subject of the second document he announces in the letter.

Dignity of woman

In the document's introduction, called "A sign of the times", the Pope says: "The dignity of the woman and her vocation, a constant object of human and christian reflection had assumed a very popular importance in these recent years."

He holds up Mary, the Mother of Jesus, as a model for women, pays tribute to women saints and extols virginity and celibacy as virtues still applicable in the modern world.

"With virginity, freely chosen (by Nuns), a woman reaffirms herself as a person...and at the same time realises the personal value of her very feminity," he says.

The 1987 Synod which the Pope says in this letter will be the basis for his second, more specific document, called for more study on the role of women in the Church and society.

A8 SUNDAY, SEPTEMBER 6, 1992

Bishops' Draft: Male Priesthood 'Willed' by God

Associated Press

NEW YORK—A new draft of a Roman Catholic bishops' teaching document on women continues to denounce sexism "as a moral and social evil," but takes an even more conservative line than previous versions against female priests.

"The fact that the call to ministerial priesthood is addressed only to men is not arbitrary, nor is it rooted in a view that women are inferior as persons," according to the document's fourth and newest version.

A male priesthood is "willed by the Lord," in the Vatican's judgment, says the draft.

Because priests represent Christ they are "to give themselves to the baptized as the divine bridegroom gave himself for his bride," the church, the draft says.

The pastoral letter has been in the works for nine years. Bishops are to consider the latest draft in November.

"It is far worse [than previous drafts] in that they've added, like, 15 pages and most of that is extremely conservative—old, bad theology, sociology, anthropology," said Ruth McDonough Fitzpatrick, national coordinator of the Women's Ordination Conference.

"The new tactic they have gone to is, because we've proven theologically and historically there were women priests and bishops, they're saying even if the pope wanted to, he could not ordain women because God doesn't want him to."

The revision was drawn up by a five-bishop committee headed by Bishop Joseph Imesch of Joliet, Ill.

Women and the Church

Q A couple of weeks ago you answered the question of Mary's mediatorship but I feel you could have said more. Also I would like you to comment on 1 Tim 2:9 ff about women's behaviour in church assemblies.

Ask Me Another

By ARCHBISHOP ANTHONY PANTIN

A You are right: I could have written much more about the mediatorship of the Blessed Virgin Mary so let me begin by quoting the Vatican II document on the Church:

"...The Blessed Virgin is involved by the Church under the titles of Advocate, Auxiliatrix, Adjutrix (Helper) and Mediatrix. These however, are to be so understood that they neither take away from nor add anything to the dignity and efficacy of Christ the one Mediator.

"For no creature could ever be classed with the Incarnate Word and Redeemer. But, just as the priesthood of Christ is shared in various ways so also the unique mediation of the Redeemer does not exclude but rather gives rise among creatures to a manifold co-operation which is but a sharing in this unique source.

"The Church does not hesitate to profess this subordinate role of Mary."

Many, many people (myself included) have enjoyed a wonderfully deep relationship with our mothers.

When we remember that Mary was the only source of Jesus' human nature, since she conceived through the power of the Holy Spirit (Luke 1:35), it is more than reasonable to presume that there must have been a very close relationship between this Mother and her divine Son.

There is no doubt that no one knows Jesus better than Mary and Mary's only role is to lead us to Jesus. True Devotion to Mary can NEVER lead us away from Jesus. Just look at all the great Saints who have been as devoted to Jesus: Mary played a big part in their lives.

It was God who ordained that His Son would come to us through Mary and there is no way that going to Mary will lead us away from Jesus. On the contrary!

With respect to Paul's admonition to women, we must remember that the apostles were part and parcel of the social atmosphere of those times.

Particular details given by the apostles were never meant to be for always and forever.

For example St Peter writes: "Slaves must be respectful and obedient to their masters, not only when they are kind and gentle but also when they are unfair." (1 Pet 3:18).

That certainly does not mean that Peter approved of slavery. So we have to take the admonitions of the apostles in accordance with the customs of the days on which they were given.

In fact, other parts of the New Testament show clearly that some women had important roles to play in the early Church.

Here are some examples: Phoebe who was a deaconess of the church at Cenchrae (Rom 16:1-2); Priscilla and Aquilla whom Paul calls "my fellow workers in Christ Jesus." (Rom 16:3).

Women could prophesy, once she wore a veil (1 Cor 11:5). Priscilla and Aquilla "took an interest in him (Apollos) and gave him further instruction in the way." (Acts 18:26).

There are certain elements in the Church's discipline that can never change the articles of faith. But there are other elements which belong to the Church and do not come from divine authority and these the Church can change, has changed and will continue to change according to circumstances.

Women priests why not?

asks Father Clyde Harvey in a letter to the editor

—CATHOLIC NEWS - Sunday, February 13, 1977 · Page 5

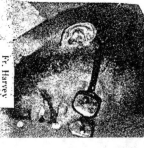

Fr. Harvey

DEAR FATHER PETER, This is just a short note to express my disappointment with your front-page editorial of Sunday, February 6. The document, on the ordination of women merited more than just a re-statement. It calls for critical comment.

While I may be able to agree with the decision not to ordain women at this time, it is extremely difficult, if not impossible, to argue that the Church cannot, at some time in the future, decide to ordain women. To say that she is not authorised to do so is false. Her own Scripture scholars have already made it clear that there is no scriptural evidence preventing her from doing it. A negative decision is purely pastoral and must be based more on cultural, sociological and psychological reasons than on Scripture or theology.

TO SAY THAT "Christ is a man" is not enough. Our present understanding of human sexuality shows us quite clearly that such clearcut divisions between male and female are not real. Christ was first and foremost a human being and it is as such that he saves us. He took upon himself our human nature. To portray his manhood as over and against womanhood is to belittle the mystery of the Incarnation and Redemption. It smacks of that kind of culture in which women were saved through men and, therefore, had either to be married or remain subject to their fathers — giving way to the worst kind of male chauvinism.

The document also notes that only a man can effectively symbolize the relationship between Christ and his Church, that of Bridegroom and the Bride. While many symbols are precious, no symbol is absolute in itself. The reality of the marriage symbol vis-a-vis the Church is that of the always faithful, ever-forgiving love of Christ for the Church with strong overtones of Hosea. If one wishes to draw an analogy between Christ and the priest, it is that reality which

THE TRADITION of the church clearly has not accepted the ordination of women. However as we now know so well, that tradition in matters of discipline is not and never has been unchanging. It has always been at the service of the effective preaching of the Good News. Some female theologians have shown very persuasively how that tradition has been anti-female, like its eminent place of Mary. To rely on such a tradition in an age when the Church has herself admitted the need for greater recognition of women can only lead to the continuation of that anti-female bias. This may well be an institutional sin. No self-respecting female will be able to accept this. Small wonder that fewer and fewer intelligent women are willing to dedicate themselves to the full service of the Church today.

A YOUNG FRIEND of mine once said in a discussion on woman priests — "You people make Christ a male chauvinist pig." It is very important that we clarify where our genuine reasons lie. In this case, it would seem that Christ himself did not ordain women, not because of his own attitude towards them, but because the people of the

time just would not have accepted it. Yet he tried in very subtle ways to bring them around to a new understanding of and appreciation for women, by his own example. The reasons today for not ordaining women are with us, not with Christ. If any epithets are to be addressed, let them be addressed to us, not to Christ.

I am quite willing to accept that this may not be an 'opportune moment for the universal Church to sanction the ordination of women to the priesthood. In many areas of the world, it would probably hamper the evangelisation of people, notably in Asia and Africa — although we may well ask if the Church does not have a prophetic role in this regard. But let us say this clearly and not befuddle the issue with arguments that only destroy the Church's credibility especially with our young people. The Holy See has the right to decide on these issues, even contrary to her own scholars. But she also has an obligation to be credible in the eyes of her own faithful.

THE CHURCH ALSO has an obligation to educate both men and women towards a more truly human attitude towards women in our society. Propagating devotion to Mary is not enough. That can very easily go hand-in-hand, in the lives of many men, with the oppression of their real mothers and wives. We need to educate people to truly accept women as man's equal and helpmate, towards the day when we will be able to accept them fully as ordained priests. Then we will be able to proclaim in word and deed that in Christ, there is neither Jew nor Greek, male nor female, we are all one in Him.

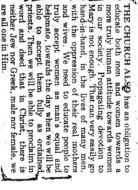

The irony of religious male power

By Clifford Longley, Religious Affairs Correspondent

Two thirds of an average church congregation in Britain is likely to be female, while males have almost a monopoly of power and influence in the church. That could be paradoxical and a sign of injustice; or it could be cause and effect. There are substantial differences in religious attitude between men and women.

That difference has received little study though the subject must hold valuable insights into what makes religion "tick" (or not tick). Those who want to make it tick faster have neglected an obvious source of guidance for their policy-making.

What is the more remarkable, is that such evidence as is available shows that women, are more likely than men to go to church, and are more critical of the church. They are most critical indeed, of its attitude to them.

A report by the Laity Commission of the Roman Catholic Church of England and Wales, published earlier this year, showed women were often quite bitter and angry towards the male-dominated leadership of that church, both at parish level and higher up.

A recent collection of essays by Anglican vicars' wives, written in response to Mrs Rosalind Runcie's article in *The Times* last year called "Clergy Wives and People Too", has many echoes in it of that Roman Catholic study. In neither case are the people whose views are expressed, far-out feminists. They complain, but they do not rationalize their experiences into an ideology of women's oppression.

Nevertheless they tend to authenticate what the conscious feminists have been saying about church and about religion: there are clearly not two classes of women involved, a contented vast majority and a tiny minority of angry militants. Nor, in either of these two case studies, is the issue of the ordination of women to the fore. The issue, rather, is that there appear to be not two classes in the church, the clergy and the laity, but three, the clergy, the male laity, and the female laity, in that order of precedence.

Feminism in the secular world has not surprisingly rejected church religion as being some kind of ultimate case of feminism's arch enemy, patriarchy. Religious feminism makes much the same objection, but wishes to deal with it by asserting the claim to equality within the church, particularly equality of religious experience.

The "experience" of being called to be a priest is only one element in that wider field; most women do not want it for themselves, and those who want it for others seem to see it primarily as a means towards this wider equality. If some clergy were female, being a lay woman would cease to be second or third class, so the theory goes. In the Free churches which have women clergy, however, the theory is yet to be vindicated.

A further recent collection of essays, which again echoes the two studies previously mentioned, suggests that the problem is more subtle than can be solved by power sharing between the genders. Each contributor was asked to write very personally about her spirituality, her experience of herself at the level of ultimate meaning. And that female spirituality, in spite of the diversity that collection bears witness to, has one common element in an experience of being other-than-men, other-than-powerful, not a patriarch.

The feminist's critique of male power, and especially the feminist theologian's critique of male church power, generally advances the view that there is such a thing as pure natural womanhood which male power aims to exploit and corrupt; in religion, therefore, space has to be made for pure natural womanhood's distinctively female religious expression.

"Why can't a woman be more like a man? the Laity Commission, 38 Eccleston Square, SW1; 50p; *Married to the Church;* Triangle, £1.95; *Walking on the Water;* Virago, £3.95.

Seventh-day Adventists reject female ministers

Trinidad Guardian July 7. 1995

THE SEVENTH-day Adventist Church has rejected the ordination of women, the church announced Thursday during its world congress in the Netherlands.

"Women can be ordained to be elders (in church) but not as ministers," said a church spokesman Cees van der Ploeg.

The women's ordination request came from the church's North American division, which asked that ordination be allowed specifically in its North American churches.

Ordination is not allowed for women in Adventist churches worldwide.

"Gender inclusive ordination, while perhaps not appropriate in some places, will be helpful in North America," said Alfred C. McClure, president of the Adventist Church in North America, in a presentation before the Wednesday vote.

"There is a generation of bright and devout young people coming on the scene — tomorrow's leaders ... the majority of whom believe it is right, and who will be seriously disillusioned by a negative vote," he said, according to a church statement.

In the opposing camp was Dr Gerard Damsteegt, associate professor of theology at Seventh-day Adventist Theological Seminary, who suggested that women are "different in functional roles."

The Bible does not allow "spiritual headship" of women in the family or in the church, he said in the pre-vote discussion, adding that women ordination runs counter to Adventist interpretation of the Bible.

Fewer than one-third of the delegates attending the church's 56th world congress this week voted in favour of ordination of women. Most of those in favour were from Europe and North America, while the bulk of the opposition came from Central and South America, Africa and Asia.

1974 TRINIDAD GUARDIAN December 11.

White racism greatest pollution PM tells Chinese community

PRIME MINISTER Dr. Eric Williams told the Chinese community on Monday night that he intends to use his position on the Council of the United Nations University to get rid of white racism throughout the world.

Dr. Williams, the only Head of Government to be appointed to the 24-member Governing Council of the university, which will have its headquarters in Tokyo, Japan, was speaking at a function organised by the Chinese Association concerning his recent visit to China and Japan.

He told the large gathering that the greatest pollution in the world today was racism — white racism.

Dr. Williams went on to praise the Japanese Government for its contribution of $100 million over a five-year period towards the establishment of the UN university.

The Prime Minister's lengthy discourse was packed with historical data on the achievements of China and Japan from the 10th century.

Describing the members of the Chinese community as the "law-abiding representatives of people of Asian ancestry," he described his visit to the two countries as "one of the most enriching experiences in all my adult life."

"I am not for any reduction in oil prices at all. Let them stay as they are for as long as possible."

Rejecting a reference made by the Chairman of the function to China as the "motherland," Dr Williams stressed that the only place he considered as "motherland" was Trinidad and Tobago.

He pointed out, however, that it was "perfectly legitimate" for one to have an interest in the country of his ancestry, especially if such interest could indicate a total repudiation of the entire philosophy spawned by Europe that the people in this part of the world had come from an alien, insignificant culture.

"We have come from people who have contributed and are contributing to the totality of world culture, as demonstrated by the Government of Japan in respect of the UN University," he declared.

He said one of the most ironical aspects of human history was the fact that a backward European country, Portugal, should have led its equally backward forces and gone all around Africa, and South East Asia at the very time China was moving westward and had reached as far as the East African coast.

He pointed out that by the time Columbus set out to discover America, the leaders in the sphere of navigation for three to four centuries were the Chinese.

The magnetic compass ap-

peared in China in the 10th century and one Chinese ship of the 12th century was more than four times the cunning of the three ships that sailed with Columbus.

Dr. Williams said the Chinese had everything they needed — particularly the capacity to produce the ships — to discover the New World.

Concerning the China of today, Dr. Williams said: "Whatever you see in China you would not see any influence of drug addiction. You look at Peking and you see that you are in a completely new society.

"And with all the statistics quoted on China you would not see statistics of the female form. It's a completely different society — no pollution in Peking because there are no motor-cars.

A PREDICAMENT

"You get a picture of a society, the dominant feature of which is austerity. There is an atmosphere of complete friendliness — quite different from western society with its sexuality and personal conduct. Food is adequate in both quantity and quality and there are no signs of malnutrition."

Dr. Williams pointed out, however, that the Chinese were now facing a predicament which the Japanese were in the midst of now.

The city of Johannesburg moved yesterday to eliminate the final remnants of "petty apartheid." A black woman rode with whites on a bus after all public places were opened to all races.

Associated Press

New York Times September 28 1989

Johannesburg Acts to Ease Segregation

By CHRISTOPHER S. WREN
Special to The New York Times

JOHANNESBURG, Sept. 27 — The city of Johannesburg opened swimming pools and recreational centers to all races today and proceeded with plans to desegregate buses.

The city's action came after the Johannesburg City Council decided Tuesday night to eliminate the final remnants of what is called "petty apartheid" here. The council voted after a survey conducted among the city's 271,000 white voters showed general approval for such a move.

At a news conference today, Jan Burger, the leader of the National Party councillors who control the council, said President F. W. de Klerk had been informed of the decision and had raised no objections. Mr. Burger said the repeal of the segregation laws was consistent with Mr. de Klerk's promises of evolutionary change.

Restaurants, hotels and sports stadiums in Johannesburg and other major cities have opened to all races in recent years, but most public accommodations had remained technically closed to nonwhites.

A train stop for whites only not far from Cape Town. South Africa

Indians in Durban prepare to take a segregated bus to their townships

Colored families disembark from a rail car reserved for nonwhites

Racial mixing is becoming more common, but still not on trains.

Toronto Star Newspaper October 12, 1985

Slowly nibbling away at apartheid

In the small towns, the boycott by blacks of white stores is so effective, blacks and whites are talking

Associated Press

The Rev. Allan Hendrickse, a South African Cabinet minister, with his son Peter, at left with arm raised, as he led supporters into the surf at a whites-only beach in Port Elizabeth yesterday in a protest against apartheid.

Cabinet Official Defies
Apartheid Law

By ALAN COWELL
Special to The New York Times

JOHANNESBURG, Jan. 4 — A mixed-race Cabinet minister led supporters today onto a whites-only beach in Port Elizabeth for a swim to protest apartheid.

The Cabinet member, the Rev. Allan Hendrickse, one of two nonwhite ministers in President P. W. Botha's Government, declared, "This is God's beach," as he and about 150 followers attending a party congress took to the waters.

Police officers and whites opposed to racial mixing on South Africa's beaches looked on but took no action against Mr. Hendrickse and his supporters, who, under apartheid's definitions, are classified as colored.

Racial restrictions at beaches have become a major issue in recent days. The City Council has, however, removed the "whites only" signs at all but one of Port Elizabeth's beaches.

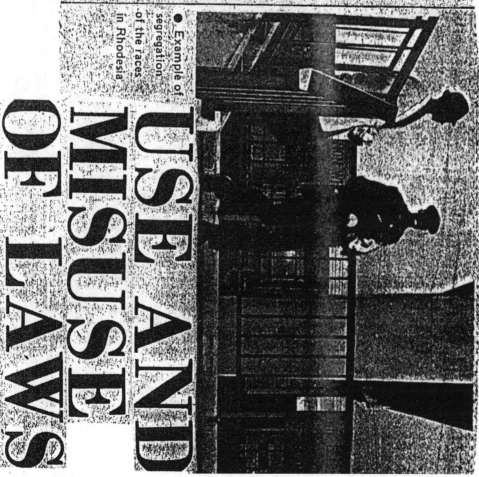

RACE SEGREGATION -RHODESIA(Zimbabwe)

Side by side—but separate. The principles of racism extend even to the water-taps. WORLD HEALTH Magazine of the World Health Organisation, United Nations, July 1975. (Southern U.S.A.)

Things You Didn't Do, Boy

One by one beginning with the *Brown* v. *Board of Education* decision in 1954, which outlawed school segregation, reaching on through the Civil Rights Acts of 1957, 1964, 1965 and 1968 — the barriers against blacks in the South have come tumbling down. But it is shocking to recall how high they were in 1954, and in many cases much later than that. By statute, ordinance or custom that had the force of law, blacks in most parts of the eleven states of the Confederacy, plus some Border states and Washington, D.C., did not:

Serve on juries.

Send children to white public schools.

Drink from a "whites only" water fountain.

Use a "whites only" rest room.

Rent a room in a white hotel, motel or apartment building.

Try on clothing in a store.

Sit down in a white restaurant.

Sit on the main floor of a movie theater, concert hall or other public arena.

Sit in the front of the bus.

Visit a white public park, beach or swimming pool.

Marry a white or even whistle at one. (Emmett Till, 14, from Chicago, was beaten and shot to death in Mississippi in 1955 for such a "crime," and other blacks were routinely beaten for "reckless eyeballing," *i.e.*, looking at a white female.)

To most Southern whites, blacks were not entitled to normal courtesies. In courtrooms, black witnesses were usually called by their first names or "uncle" or "gal." In some Southern towns, blacks were obliged to step off the sidewalk into the street to make room for passing whites. In some areas they were warned to be out of town by sunset. The few black policemen could not arrest whites.

A SEAT APART IN THE OLD DIXIE

A DRINK UNDER SEGREGATION

FINANCIAL DISCRIMINATION IN THE CHURCH, ECCLESIASTICAL GRANTS-GOVERNMENT FUNDS TO THE CHURCHES

THE HISTORY OF THE WEST INDIAN ISLANDS OF TRINIDAD AND TOBAGO
1498-1900

by

GERTRUDE CARMICHAEL

Lately Librarian to the Trinidad and Tobago Historical Society and Assistant Librarian, Imperial College of Tropical Agriculture, Trinidad, W.I.

ALVIN REDMAN
LONDON

XXXI

Trinidad (89)
17th December, 1844.

AN ORDINANCE

No. 16, 1844.

For the better regulation of the duties of the Clergy of the United Church of England and Ireland in this Colony and for ensuring the more effectual performance of the same.

WHEREAS Her Most Gracious Majesty Queen Victoria was pleased to grant Letters Patent under the Great Seal bearing date at Westminster the twenty-first day of August in the sixth year of Her Majesty's Reign, which Letters are to the tenor and effect following, that is to say :

Victoria by the grace of God of the United Kingdom of Great Britain and Ireland, Queen Defender of the Faith to all whom these presents shall come greeting.

Summary

The preamble comprises references to the following Acts, which are herinafter revoked with the exception of those of William IV, 4th March, 1831, and Victoria, 1841 :

George IV, 24th July, 1824.   Constituting Barbados, Grenada, St. Vincent, Dominica, Antigua, Montserrat, St. Christopher, Nevis, the Virgin Islands, Trinidad, Tobago and St. Lucia a Bishop's See entitled " The Bishopric of Barbados and the Leeward Islands " and appointing William Hart Coleridge Bishop for life.

George IV, 2nd April, 1825.   Creating two Archdeaconries, respectively of Barbados and Antigua, the former to embrace Barbados, Grenada, St. Vincent, Trinidad, Tobago and St. Lucia, and the latter to embrace Antigua, Montserrat, Dominica, St. Christopher, Nevis and the Virgin Islands.

FINANCIAL DISCRIMINATION IN THE CHURCH, ECCLESIASTICAL GRANTS-GOVERNMENT FUNDS TO THE CHURCHES

George IV, 11th May, 1826.	Proclaiming Demerara, Essequibo and Berbice to be parts of the See of Barbados and the Leeward Islands.
William IV, 4th March, 1831.	Constituting the above mentioned settlements on the Coast of S. America one Colony to be known as British Guiana.
1831.	Creating an Archdeaconry of British Guiana subordinate to the See of Barbados and the Leeward Islands.
Victoria, 24th September, Victoria, 1841.	Legalizing an increase of the number of Bishoprics and Archdeaconries within the territorial limits of the existing Sees of Jamaica and Barbados and the Leeward Islands.

In the preamble, reference is next made to the resignation of Bishop Coleridge on 6th April, 1842, leaving the See of Barbados and the Leeward Islands vacant.

The purpose of the Ordinance is then declared to be to create a new See to be known as the Bishopric of Barbados, with two subordinate Archdeaconries, namely of Barbados and of Trinidad. The new See shall include the City of Bridgetown and the Island of Barbados and the Islands of Trinidad, Grenada, St. Vincent, Tobago and St. Lucia. The Archdeaconries shall include respectively, Barbados, St. Vincent, St. Lucia and Trinidad, Grenada and Tobago.

The parochial church of St. Michael in Bridgetown, Barbados, is ordained a Cathedral Church and Bishop's See and the Town of Bridgetown is proclaimed a City.

The Hon. Thomas Parry, D.D., formerly Archdeacon of Barbados, is nominated Bishop of Barbados for life, subject and subordinate to the Archepiscopal See of Canterbury and " the most Reverend Father in God William by Divine Providence Archbishop ", an oath of due obedience to whom he and his successors shall, at their consecration, take.

The Bishop and his successors shall perform the functions peculiar to their office, within their Diocese, according to the Ecclesiastical Laws in force in England.

The " Bishop of Barbados " shall be a body corporate and may own property, may use a corporate seal, may plead and be impleaded in all manner of Courts and shall have perpetual suc-

428

cession. The Bishop and his successors shall for ever hereafter be called and known by the title of "Lord Bishop of Barbados".

Of the sum of money payable out of the Consolidated Fund as the salaries of Bishops and Archdeacons, the sum of £2,500 per annum is assigned for the maintenance of Thomas Parry and his successors and the sum of £500 per annum for the Archdeacon of Barbados and the sum of £250 per annum for the Archdeacon of Trinidad. The sum of £2,000 per annum is assigned to the Bishop to apportion among the Ministers, Catechists and School Masters of his Diocese, subject to the approval of the Commissioners of the Treasury or the Principal Secretary of State.

Witness Ourself at Westminster the twenty-first day of August in the sixth year of Our Reign.

By the Queen Herself.

. . . .

The sense of 39 amplifying clauses enacted by Lt. Governor in Council follows:

Summary

1. The Ecclesiastical Laws of England to be in force in the Colony and the Judges of the Supreme Courts to assist in carrying processes into execution.

2. As regards the Established Church of England, the Colony shall be divided into the following Sixteen Parishes, namely:

Holy Trinity, town of Port of Spain, and Suburbs, with the Quarters of La Ventille, Tragarete, St. Ann's and Maraval.

St. Paul, town of San Fernando and the Quarter of North Naparima.

St. Michael, the Quarter of Chaguaramas, Carenage, Diego Martin, and Mucurapo, with the Islands of the Bocas.

St. Mary, the Quarters of Tacarigua and Arouca.

St. Jude, the Quarters of Arima and Guanapo, with the settlements of Cuare, Touroura and La Seiva; and such parts of the Quarter of Caroni as lie to the eastward of the junction of the Caroni and Tacarigua Rivers.

St. John, the Quarters of Cimaronero, Acarigua, Santa Cruz and St. Joseph and such parts of the Quarter of Caroni as lie westward of the junction of the Caroni and Tacarigua Rivers.

St. Thomas, the Quarter of Chaguanas.

St. Andrew, the Quarters of Carapichaima, Barancon, Cascajal and Couva.

St. Philip, the Quarter of Savonetta.

St. Peter, the Quarter of Pointe-a-Pièrre.

St. Luke, the Quarter of South Naparima.

St. Stephen, the Quarter of Savanna Grande.

St. Matthew, the Quarters of Oropouche, Le Brea and Guapo.

Christ Church, the Quarters of Cedros, Icacos, Erin and Irois.

St. Mark, the Quarters of Moruga and Guayaguayare.

St. Batholomew, the Quarters of Mayaro, Nariva, Toco and the settlement of Manzanilla.

3. The five several Parishes of the Holy Trinity, St. Paul, St. Mary, St. Stephen and St. Luke shall be constituted into five several Rectories, and the Parishes of St. Andrew and St. Philip shall be constituted into one Rectory, to be called the Rectory of the United Parishes of St. Andrew and St. Philip.

4. If the need arise, in a Parish which is not attached to a Rectory, the Government may allow an Island Curate, who shall be licensed to officiate there under the direction of a neighbouring Rector.

5. The patronage of every Rectory and Island Curacy shall be vested in Her Majesty.

6. For each Rectory, it shall be lawful for the Governor in Council to allow a Curate as Assistant to the Rector; such Curate to be licensed by the Bishop of the Diocese on the nomination of the Rector and approved by the Governor.

7. There shall be allowed to the Archdeacon and the Rectors, Island Curates and Assistant Curates appointed under this Ordinance, from the Colonial Treasury, the following stipends payable quarterly:

To the Archdeacon, £500 per annum.
To the Rector of the Parish of Holy Trinity, £600 per annum. And to every other Rector, £350 per annum.
To the Island Curate, who shall be appointed to act for the Parish of St. Michael, £300 per annum.
To every other Island Curate, £150 per annum.
To every Assistant Curate, £100 per annum.

8. The Governor in Council may, on the decease of any Archdeacon, Rector, or Island Curate, alter the annual stipend attached to any such Archdeaconry, Rectory or Island Curate.

9. For each Church or Chapel, duly consecrated or licensed, there shall be allowed a Clerk and Sexton who shall be paid from the Colonial Treasury, an annual salary of £20 16s. 8d. payable quarterly.

10. Where Churches shall be built, a convenient house shall be built at the common charge; and the Rector, except the Rector of the Parish of the Holy Trinity, shall keep the Rectory house in good repair, for which purpose an annual sum of £20 shall be allowed him; and the Archdeacon shall once in each year, inspect each Rectory house in the Island, and shall certify to the Government the state of repair of the same.

11. To each Rectory house, except that of the Parish of Holy Trinity, shall be given 3 acres of land.

12. The present Rectory house of the Parish of Holy Trinity shall be kept in repair at the expense of the Colonial Government.

FINANCIAL DISCRIMINATION IN THE CHURCH, ECCLESIASTICAL GRANTS-GOVERNMENT FUNDS TO THE CHURCHES

13. Every Rector and Island Curate shall reside in his parish, unless otherwise permitted by the Bishop.

14. It shall not be lawful for any Rector or Curate to act as attorney in the management of any estate or plantation, or as receiver of any Court in this Island or any Estate on any pretence whatever.

15. It shall not be lawful for the Bishop to permit any Incumbent to absent himself from his duties without an approved Locum Tenens; and the Bishop shall not permit any Incumbent to absent himself for more than one year together; or the Governor may declare the Rectory or Curacy to be vacant.

16. Any Incumbent irregularly absent from his Parish for more than three months in any year may forfeit a proportionate amount of his salary.

17. Empowers the Bishop to replace an Incumbent incapable of officiating and defines procedure.

18. Empowers the Governor to suspend salary or proceed to deprivation of an Incumbent whose competence or conduct may be proved unsatisfactory to his Vestry.

19. Registers of baptisms, marriages and burials shall be made and kept by the Rector or officiating Minister of every Parish, in well bound books, to be provided at the expense of the vestries of the respective Churches and Chapels, in which every officiating Minister shall record in a legible hand the several particulars and sign the same; and in no case, unless prevented by unavoidable impediment later than within three days after any such ceremony shall have taken place.

20. The Registry Books in the several Parishes shall belong to every such Parish and shall remain in the custody of the Incumbent of such Parish, and the said books shall not be removed from his custody.

21. A certified copy from the Registry Books shall be admitted in all Courts as legal evidence.

22 to 31. Deal with the election, duties and proceedings of the Vestry to be established in every Church and Chapel.

32. The two wardens, appointed respectively by the Incumbent and the Vestry, shall be treasurers and receive the pew rents for which they shall account to the Vestry, and shall have the same power as any church warden has by the Law of England.

33. The Church Wardens shall be allowed to retain to their own use a commission, at the rate of six per cent, on the amount of monies actually received by such Church Wardens respectively.

34. Of every church in any Parish under this Ordinance, one-fifth part of the seats or sittings shall be free seats for the use of the poor; and the remaining seats may be let out. Provided always that seats free of rent be set apart in the Church of the

Holy Trinity, for the Governor and his family, and the Arch-deacon and his family, and in each Church or Chapel for the Incumbent and his family and for strangers.

35. The Vestry shall have authority to settle and alter the rates at which the rented seats shall be let.

36. The amount of rents received in respect of the sittings shall be divided into two equal portions, one portion to be applied to defray church expenses, and the other portion shall form a building fund, to be applied to the keeping the body of the Church in repair.

37. All sums due for pew rent may be recovered before any competent Court, by an action in the name of the Church Wardens.

38. The several fees mentioned in the schedule to this Ordinance shall be paid to the Rector, Curate or officiating Minister and Clerk, for the several services performed in the Church or Chapel; and none others shall be demandable by them.

39. Authorizes the Incumbent to appoint clerks and sextons.

Passed in Council this second day of December in the year of Our Lord, 1844.

JAMES PORTER,
Acting Clerk of Council.

Bishops of Barbados and the Leeward Islands
William Hart *Coleridge*   1824 to 1842
            Parry   1842 to 1872
Bishops of Trinidad
Richard *Rawle*   1872 to 1888
James Thomas *Hayes*   1889 to 1904

XXXII

The Roman Catholic Church, Trinidad

In the early days the whole of the West Indies had been included in the Roman Catholic See of Santo Domingo, but later when some of the islands became British Possessions, so far as the Roman Catholic Church was concerned they came under the spiritual jurisdiction of the Roman Catholic Bishop of London, whose Vicar-General up to 1815 was the Abbé Planquais. Trinidad, however, was still regarded as being under the jurisdiction of the Bishop of Guiana. In 1820 the Rt. Rev. James Buckley was created Bishop of Olympus and 1st Vicar Apostolic with jurisdiction over Trinidad and the Lesser Antilles. On his death he was succeeded as follows :

1828   Daniel MacDonnell, 2nd Vicar Apostolic. Assumed duty June 21st, 1829.

FINANCIAL DISCRIMINATION IN THE CHURCH, ECCLESIASTICAL GRANTS-GOVERNMENT FUNDS TO THE CHURCHES

1844	R. Patrick Smith, 3rd Vicar Apostolic.
1850	R. Patrick Smith, 1st Archbishop of Port of Spain.
1855	Vincent Spaccapietra, 2nd Archbishop of Port of
1860	Ferdinand English, 3rd Archbishop of Port of Spain.
1863	Louis Joachim Gonin, 4th Archbishop of Port of
1887	Patrick V. Flood, 5th Archbishop of Port of Spain.

Note : During the period 1828 to 1887 three Apostolic Administrators held temporary office at Port of Spain, viz. from
1852 to 1855 Michael Monaghan, Bishop of Roseau,
Dominica; 1859–1860 James Etheridge and 1862–1863
François Cuenat.

Roman Catholic Establishment, Trinidad, 1899

Archbishop.
Vicar-General.
Parish Priests 42. Assistant Curates 5.
Jurisdiction of the Archbishop extended over St. Lucia, St.
   Vincent, Grenada, Trinidad and Tobago.
1 Cathedral.
67 Churches.
Archbishop's Residence.
Cathedral Presbytery, also one attached to each church.
Schools 59, with 7,686 children enrolled.
Formerly the Roman Catholic Clergy were paid salaries directly
from the Treasury and were entitled to pension. This was
changed and a grant made from the Treasury to the Arch-
bishop in aid of the Roman Catholic Church.

THE HISTORY OF THE WEST INDIAN ISLANDS OF TRINIDAD AND TOBAGO

1498-1900

by

GERTRUDE CARMICHAEL

Lately Librarian to the Trinidad and Tobago Historical Society and Assistant Librarian, Imperial College of Tropical Agriculture, Trinidad, W.I.

APPENDICES

I   1783

The Royal Cedula on Colonization of ~~1879~~ X

I, THE KING.

Whereas by my instructions of the 3rd September, One Thousand Seven Hundred and Seventy-Six, to Don Manuel Falquaz, Captain of Foot, who was then appointed Governor of my Island of Trinidad to Windward; and by the Commission which I afterward gave Don Joseph de Abalos, appointing him Intendent-General of the Province of Caracas, I thought proper to establish regulations, and to grant various privileges for the population and commerce of the said Island; I have now resolved, on the representation of the said Intendent, and at the instance of certain colonists already established in the said Island, and others who request permission to settle therein, to establish complete instructions in the following articles :

Article 1st. All foreigners, the subjects of powers and nations in alliance with me, who are desirous of establishing themselves, or who are already settled in, the said Island of Trinidad, shall sufficiently prove to the Government thereof, that they are of the Roman Catholic persuasion, without which they shall not be allowed, to settle in the same; but the subjects of these my dominions, or those of the Indies, shall not be obliged to adduce such proof, because no doubt can arise as to their religion.

Article 2nd. All foreigners who shall be admitted, agreeable to the foregoing article, to reside in the said Island, shall take, before the Governor thereof, the oath of fealty and submission; by which they shall promise to obey the laws and general ordinances to which Spaniards are subject; and immediately there shall be granted to them, in my Royal name, gratuitously for ever, the lands proportionally mentioned according to the following rules.

Article 3rd. To each white person, of either sex, four fanegas and two sevenths; and the half of that quantity of land for each Negro or coloured slave, which the settlers shall induce; the lands to be so distributed, that everyone may participate of the good, middling and bad; the assignments of lands to be entered in a book of registry, with insertion of the name of each settler, the day of his or her admittance, the number of individuals composing his or her family, their rank, and from whence they came; and copies of such entries shall be given to them, to serve as titles to their property.

FINANCIAL DISCRIMINATION IN THE CHURCH, ECCLESIASTICAL GRANTS-GOVERNMENT FUNDS TO THE CHURCHES

shall be allowed to procure them from foreign islands belonging to the Powers in alliance with me, subject to the same duties as the flour and meal.

Article 24th. I have likewise ordered that two secular or regular priests, of known erudition and exemplary virtue, and skilled and versed in foreign languages, shall be appointed to reside in the said Island to serve as new parish priests to the settlers, and I shall assign to them the necessary stipends to enable them to live in the decent manner which their character requires, without being any charge on their parishioners.

Article 25th. I permit former and recent settlers to propose to me, through the medium of the Governor, such ordinances as shall be most proper for the regulating the treatment of their slaves and preventing their flight; and at the same time, to point out such rules as the Governor shall observe relative to this article, and the reciprocal restitution of fugitive slaves from other islands belonging to foreign powers.

Article 26th. I also enjoin the said Governor to take the utmost care to prevent the introduction of ants into the island, which have done so much injury in the Antilles; and for that purpose, to cause the equipage and effects of the settlers arriving at the said Island to be severally examined; and as the inhabitants are the persons most interested in the execution of this order, they shall propose to the Government two of the most active and proper persons to examine the vessels, and zealously watch over the observance of this point.

Article 27th. When the crops of sugar become abundant in the said Island of Trinidad, I shall allow the settlers to establish refineries in Spain, with all the privileges and freedom from duties which I may have granted to any natives or foreigners who shall have established the same; and I will allow in due time the erection of a Consular Tribunal to increase and protect agriculture, navigation and commerce; and I have charged the Governor in his private instructions, and the other judges of the said Island, to take care that all the inhabitants, Spaniards and foreigners, be well and humanely treated, and justice equitably administered to them; so that they may not meet with any molestation or prejudice, which would be greatly to my Royal displeasure.

Article 28th. Lastly I grant to the former and recent settlers the privilege whenever they have questions to ask me worthy of my Royal consideration, of directing their representations to me through the medium of the Governor and the Chief Secretary of States for the Indies; and if the matters are of that nature that require a person to be sent on their account, the inhabitants shall request permission to effect and I will grant the same, if just.

Journal
of
CARIBBEAN
STUDIES

Coral Gables, Florida, USA, 33124

Volume 2   Autumn/Winter 1981   Nos. 2 & 3

CARL CAMPBELL/238

RALPH WOODFORD AND THE FREE COLOUREDS: THE TRANSITION FROM A CONQUEST SOCIETY TO A SOCIETY OF SETTLEMENT, TRINIDAD 1813 - 1828

Carl Campbell

'I do not fear contradiction when I aver, that they have suffered more affronts and more injuries during his (Woodford's) government, than they have experienced since the commencement of the annals of the colony'[1]

The entire basis of the developmental plan was the availability of fertile unsettled land for commercial agricultural production. The most important document governing the distribution of th eland between 1783 and 1797, was the famous Cedula of the 24th November, 1783.[2]

According to this Cedula any national of a state friendly to Spain, being a Roman Catholic, who went to the island, and took the oath of allegiance to Spain, would be entitled to free land. If a white male or female, the personal allotment was 10 quarrees,[3] with an additional 5 quarees for each slave imported into the island. Free black and free coloured settlers were entitled to half the entitlement to land given to whites. The land granted was without cost and could be held forever, provided the grantees settled in the island for at least 5 years. Children and other relatives, or even friends, could inherit the land, if they resided or came to reside in the island; and even if they chose to stay away, provided they were Roman Catholics, they could sell the land inherited or remit the proceeds abroad after paying specified duties. Political privileges were offered to foreigners and their children after 5 years of residence: they were then entitled to be naturalized as Spaniards and were eligible for civil service posts and positions in the militia according to their rank and abilities. A more liberal and thoughtful document was hardly ever framed for a colony which had attracted so little thought or attention in previous times.

FINANCIAL DISCRIMINATION IN THE CHURCH, ECCLESIASTICAL GRANTS-GOVERNMENT FUNDS TO THE CHURCHES

Sources of
West Indian History
compiled by
F. R. AUGIER
and
SHIRLEY C. GORDON

LONGMANS
1964

Sources of West Indian History

under control. . . . ous habits are stimulated by the prospects of success, while the . . . . ial and agricultural condition of the island alike indicate steady b . . . . rogress. To Sir John Peter Grant no small share of the credit of th . . . state of things is due, nor has he lacked the assistance of able and zealous co-workers.

7. The payment of the Anglican clergy from public funds was criticised by members of other churches. In Trinidad and St. Lucia Catholic clergy were also paid from public funds.

a. Baptist objections in Jamaica

Speech by Knibb in England, 7 June 1845

I believe in free trade, not merely in sugar, but in religion too. I would never cast such a slur upon the episcopalians who tell us . . . that they number all the talent, that they possess all the energy, and have engrossed all the wealth of the church, as to suppose that they loved their religion so little that they did not like to pay for it. Others may say so if they please, and may assert that unless Christianity is supported by the state it will fall. I believe no such thing. . . . I do not say that feeling will not sometimes rise that these striplings should step in when we have been twenty years toiling for the poor slaves, and were binding up their broken hearts when they were scarcely born, or if they were born, were playing at marbles at Oxford or Cambridge. . . . But do not suppose, Christian friends, that our people are caught; not at all, our congregations still stand, fair, clear, and numerous.

b. A Governor points out that the Established Church is maintained at the expense of members of other denominations

Governor of the Windwards to Secretary of State, 13 January 1857

They can scarcely be satisfied with a system under which their food and other necessities are taxed for the support of the clergy of the Church of England, while they have to pay their own clergy either by voluntary effort, as in the case of the Wesleyans and Moravians, or by fees as in the case of the Roman Catholics. . . .

There can I think be no doubt that the influence of the Church of England, in the several West India legislatures is greater than among the people at large, and in view of all the circumstances, my own conviction is that the wisest policy which the authorities of that church can pursue is to submit cheerfully to the decisions of the respective legislatures regarding ecclesiastical grants and especially to avoid any controversy, which will bring prominently forward for discussion the merits of the existing system.

c. The contribution from public funds made to Anglicans and Catholics in Trinidad contrasted

De Verteuil, *Trinidad*, 1858

The majority of the population are Catholics in several of the British West India islands, viz. in Dominica, Saint Lucia, Grenada, and Trinidad; but, in every one of them, the Church of England has the lion's share. In Trinidad, where the catholic religion is now, and has, since the capitulation in the year 1797, always been supported from the general funds of the colony, the church of 45,000 catholics cost the colony £4,500, and that of 17,000 episcopalians, £5,500, besides extra allowances. For the last thirty-four years the catholic bishop had been in the receipt of £1,000 per annum as his stipend: our present governor, . . . has, by the advice of a protestant committee, and with the aid of an irresponsible council, reduced that sum to £500 sterling.

d. The Governor of Trinidad deprives a Catholic bishop of the stipend and official recognition because he is not a British subject

De Verteuil, *Trinidad*, 1858

The present administrator of the diocese being an alien, the governor has withheld the entire stipend; and even refuses to recognise the bishop's authority *in matters of church hierarchy*. The withholding of the administra-

FINANCIAL DISCRIMINATION IN THE CHURCH, ECCLESIASTICAL GRANTS-GOVERNMENT FUNDS TO THE CHURCHES

THE COLONY OF TRINIDAD AND TOBAGO.

ESTIMATES FOR THE YEAR 1938.

OF

REVENUE AND EXPENDITURE

— *As passed by the Legislative Council on the 12th November, 1937.*

53

ESTIMATES, CIVIL SERVICES, 1938.   Head 10.

HEAD 10—ECCLESIASTICAL.

	1938.	1937.	In-crease.	De-crease.	Explanations.
	$	$	$	$	
Roman Catholic Church	25,282	25,282	—	—	
Church of England	18,000	18,000	—	—	
Methodist Church	2,347	2,347	—		The grant of $50,880 is apportioned on the basis of population of the various denominations according to the latest Census returns.
Moravian Church	1,176	1,176	—	—	
Presbyterian Church	2,525	2,525	—	—	
Baptist Church *LONDON*	1,550	1,550	—	—	
TOTAL .... $	50,880	50,880	—	—	

FINANCIAL DISCRIMINATION IN THE CHURCH, ECCLESIASTICAL GRANTS-GOVERNMENT FUNDS TO THE CHURCHES

ECCLESIASTICAL GRANTS GIVEN TO THE ROMAN CATHOLIC CHURCH
AND CHURCH OF ENGLAND (ANGLICAN) 1936-1988 DONATED BY
GOVERNMENT OF TRINIDAD AND TOBAGO

From 1986 to present, ecclesiastical grants given by government has
actually tripled in figures for some denominations,

ROMAN CATHOLIC   TOTALS

1936 - 1954	: $25,282.00 per year	$480,358.00
1955 - 1965	: $25,690.00 per year	$282,590.00
1966 - 1973	: $49,100.00 per year	$392,800.00
1974	: $147,300.00	$147,300.00
1975 - 1979	: $49,100.00 per year	$245,500.00
1980 - 1983	: $49,100.00 per year	$196,400.00
1984 - 1986	: $49,100.00 per year	$147,300.00
1986 - 1988	: $141,248.00 per year	

Grand Total $1,919,248.00

Total Receipts for Roman
Catholics between 1936-1986 = One Million nine
hundred and Nineteen thousand two hundred and
forty-eight dollars.

CHURCH OF ENGLAND (ANGLICAN)   TOTALS

1936 - 1954	: $18,000.00 per year	$ 342,000.00
1955 - 1975	: $18,058.00 per year	$ 198,638.00
1966 - 1973	: $28,700.00 per year	$ 229,600.00
1974	: $86,100.00	$ 86,100.00
1975 - 1979	: $28,700.00 per year	$ 143,500.00
1980 - 1983	: $28,700.00 per year	$ 114,800.00
1984 - 1986	: $28,700.00 per year	$ 86,100.00
1986 - 1988	: $62,950.00 per year	

Grand Total $1,200,738.00

Total Receipts for Anglicans between
1936-1986 = One Million two hundred

FINANCIAL DISCRIMINATION IN THE CHURCH, ECCLESIASTICAL GRANTS-GOVERNMENT FUNDS TO THE CHURCHES

(Independent) TRINIDAD AND TOBAGO ESTIMATES OF EXPENDITURE FOR THE YEAR 1963 Page 176, Head 26 ECCLESIASTICAL

Roman Catholic	$25,690
Church of England	$15,058
Methodist	$ 1,875
Moravians	$ 954
Presbyterian	$ 2,679
Baptist *LONDON BAPTIST*	$ 1,626
Hindu	$16,524
Muslim	$ 3,694
	$71,100

REPUBLIC OF TRINIDAD AND TOBAGO DETAILS OF OTHER CHARGES 1976 PAGE 159, HEAD 26 ECCLESIASTICAL

	1974	1976
Roman Catholic	$147,000	$49,110
Hindu	$ 93,600	$31,200
Anglican	$ 86,100	$28,700
(Church of England)		
Muslim	$24,300	$10,100
Presbyterian	$15,900	$ 5,300
Methodist	$ 9,000	$ 3,000
Seventh Day Adventist ...	$ 6,300	$ 2,100
Baptist Spirtual	$ 4,200	$ 1,400
Baptist Orthodox *LONDON*.	$ 5,100	$ 1,700
Moravian	$ 3,000	$ 1,200
Pentecostal	$ 1,800	$ 600
Jehovah Witness	$ 4,800	$ 600
Church of God	$ 1,200	$ 400
Gospel Hall	$	$ 200
Pilgrim Holiness	$ 600	$ 200
Brethren		$ 200
Ethiopian Oethodox		$ 100
	$400,800	$136,100

FINANCIAL DISCRIMINATION IN THE CHURCH, ECCLESIASTICAL GRANTS-GOVERNMENT FUNDS TO THE CHURCHES

ESTIMATES OF EXPENDITURE, 1994

Head 13 - OFFICE OF THE PRIME MINISTER

Sub-Head / Item / Sub-Item Description	1992 Actual $	1993 Estimate $	1993 Revised Estimate $	1994 Estimate $	Increase $	Decrease $	Explanation
005 Non Profit Institutions							
RELIGIOUS BODIES							
01 Roman Catholic	85,793	115,724	57,861			57,861	
02 Hindu	63,867	85,157	42,580			42,580	
03 Anglican	38,682	51,575	25,790			25,790	
04 Muslim	30,246	40,326	20,160			20,160	
05 Presbyterian (C.M.)	19,830	26,440	13,220			13,220	
06 Methodist	7,611	10,146	5,071			5,071	
07 Seventh Day Adventist	13,206	17,607	8,802			8,802	
08 Baptist (Spiritual)	9,936	13,246	6,620			6,620	
09 Baptist (Orthodox)	12,705	16,940	8,470			8,470	
10 Moravian	2,691	3,589	1,790			1,790	
11 Pentecostal	18,810	25,080	12,540			12,540	
12 Jehovah Witness	3,606	4,808	2,400			2,400	
13 Church of God	2,418	3,225	1,610			1,610	
14 Stewards (Christian Brethren)	672	896	450			450	
15 Pilgrim Holiness	363	482	240			240	
16 Ethiopian Orthodox Church	366	488	240			240	
17 Non Profit Institutions	-	-	-			-	
Total Non Profit Institutions	311,802	415,729	207,844	415,729	415,729	207,885	

43

LONDON

1994

ECCLESIASTICAL

FINANCIAL DISCRIMINATION IN THE CHURCH, ECCLESIASTICAL GRANTS-GOVERNMENT FUNDS TO THE CHURCHES

Pallackdharrysingh

MP: Grant should be for all churches

NAPARIMA Representative Raymond Pallackdharrysingh has questioned the ecclesiastical grant made in the 1988 Budget to certain established churches.

Speaking during the Budget debate in the House of Representatives on Thursday, Pallackdharrysingh maintained the grant should be "ecumenical" and for all religions.

He noted that the grant had been cut by Dr Eric Williams in 1971 after a Caribbean church conference criticised existing injustices and decided participants should not "associate with the status quo."

He stressed that religious bodies should become more "integrated in secular programmes."

The Naparima Representative also called on the government to "monitor fly-by-night religions" through which money was sent abroad, and to appoint a commission to work out codes and norms of practice for religions.

FINANCIAL DISCRIMINATION IN THE CHURCH, ECCLESIASTICAL GRANTS-GOVERNMENT FUNDS TO THE CHURCHES

Barbados Advocate (News)

SATURDAY, OCTOBER 13, 1984

Church and cash

According to Bishop Drexel Gomez the Anglican Church has serious cash flow problems. It is an experience that is not unique to the Anglican Church at this time. But what aggravates the situation for the Anglicans is that there are pressing financial needs and the Church is apparently not in a position to do very much to help itself at this stage.

Bishop Gomez said that some 27 churches and rectories in the Anglican diocese are in need for repair or replacement. That requires money which the Church cannot raise in a hurry. Apart from these needs there has had to be a rebuilding programme for three large Anglican churches — St. Philip's Parish Church, St. Peter's Parish Church and St. Leonard's Church — which were destroyed by fire in a four-year period.

The income of the Anglican Church has not been keeping pace with these financial requirements. The Bishop outlined the Church's main sources of funds as contributions from various parishes to the Diocesan Fund, income from investments such as stocks and bonds, rents from properties, an annual subvention from the Government of Bds$30 000, and contributions from overseas sources.

When the Anglican Church was the established Church it did not have to worry about its housekeeping as is now the case. The State provided most of the funds required and so no heavy demands were placed on the congregations. Today it is a different story. The Anglican Church has been disestablished but the attitudinal change of many of its congregations has not been forthcoming to ensure a greater sense of financial responsibility towards their Church.

This change of attitude was never a factor which a number of other denominations, with fewer people among their memberships, had to face. These churches from the start had had to rely on the enthusiastic financial support of their members to carry on their work. For many in the Anglican Church it came as a new experience for them to be told that more monetary contributions would have to be made.

The Anglican Church has never insisted on tithing, which has enabled a number of other denominations to realise the financial support required to meet their needs.

At the same time where there is a united Church it is always easier for the clergy and the members to face their problems, financial and otherwise. The impression at the moment is that the Anglican Church is not as united as it could be. In the circumstances enthusiasm will vary throughout the diocese as pleas are made for the required support. It is not unlikely that formerly staunch Anglicans might even turn away and seek spiritual guidance elsewhere because of their annoyance with such a state of affairs.

BARBADOS ADVOCATE

Saturday, April 15, 1989

Anglicans must be prepared to give $$

Barbados Advocate April 15, 1989

ROBERT BEST
Best on Saturday

Barbados' estimated 80 000 Anglicans are in the midst of a drive to raise some Bds$3 million through pledges. The money is needed to enable the church to press on with its work in the community and to meet outstanding debts, apart from meeting the cost of needed repairs and refurbishing of a number of its churches.

With such a large estimated following, reaching the Bds$3 million should not be too great a challenge. But while the figures of church membership are impressive from the last census statistics, these figures cannot guarantee "commitment" and it is "commitment" that will make all the difference.

the years. It is now some 21 years since the Anglican Church was disestablished but it is a case, for many Anglicans, of old habits dying hard. In this case the "old habit" is that of not giving generously to their church.

In the days when the State provided the wherewithal for the Anglican Church as the State Church to meet its expenses, it did not matter too much what was provided by the congregations or practising Anglicans. The picture changed, however, with disestablishment but for many Anglicans the old attitude of not digging too deeply into their pockets did not change.

It is these church members who are now being called upon to pull their weight financially to assist their church. The pledges requested will give an early indication of what the church can expect from the drive when the money is eventu-

a place of worship. One felt a sense of inspiring awe in such an environment. And then a heavy rain came and one felt let down.

The wedding guests had to be bobbing and weaving from the raindrops which came in from the roof and through the windows on one side even when they were supposed to be closed. The bride and the groom, while kneeling in the chancel, had no such privilege. There they knelt with the water dripping down on the bridal gown and with the groom receiving the more than occasional drop in his head like some Chinese water torture.

It helped to regard the situation as one where the raindrops were the result of

Bds$3m needed by the Church

I do not know how many other Anglican churches are leaking from their roofs in this way but the majority of them are old structures and time will take its toll.

It is not as simple a problem, in some cases, as raising money for a few galvanise sheets. The repairs required are more extensive and since the buildings go back to more spacious days when the cost of material used in building, was not as expensive as today, the repairs to be done often must be as elaborate as the work that was orginally put in to make that particular

day to day costs. Apart from this, the tithe has the psychological effect of making church members committed to financial support of their church.

Anglicans have never had to make this type of commitment in terms of tithing. It has always been left to their discretion and to tell the truth, this is often lacking.

One idea that Anglicans could do well to borrow from other houses of God is the idea of tithing. This is one way that other denominations raise money for the Lord's work.

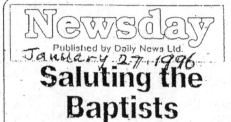

Newsday

Published by Daily News Ltd.

January 27, 1996

Saluting the Baptists

YESTERDAY'S announcement in Parliament that March 30 (in perpetuity) had been declared a public holiday — Spiritual Baptist Shouter Liberation Day — was a symbolic addressing of the imbalance of history, which had seen African slaves and their descendants who practised their religion or a blend of it with Christianity, persecuted and/or simply dismissed.

Discriminatory laws under the Shouter Prohibition Ordinance which had made it an offence for Spiritual Baptists or Shouters to practise their religious beliefs were only repealed on March 30, 1951 following on a vigorous clamour by former Government Minister, Albert Gomes and labour hero, Tubal Uriah Butler.

Butler had been involved with the Baptist movement and had founded the Butlerite Moravian Baptist Church in the 1930s.

Police raids against the Spiritual Baptists and Shouters were a common feature in the 19th century and the first half of this century.

Even as we offer kudos to the Government on giving the Spiritual Baptists and Shouters their holiday, we urge them to go yet further and part-fund the construction of a cathedral the Baptist have long asked for.

Although we do not advocate a policy of dependency, the Baptists, who had been persecuted for their religious beliefs, and had literally been dispossessd for more than 150 years, deserve a kick start.

Had the Baptist movement been always persecution free and had been permitted by the State to develop as the other religions had, then clearly they would have long had a cathedral of their own.

An argument in favour of State financial assistance in the construction of a cathedral for Spiritual Baptists is that State aid had been granted to the Roman Catholic Church, first under the Spaniards in the 18th century and then under the British in the 19th century. The Roman Catholic Archbishop of Port-of-Spain received a stipend from the State for several decades.

The Anglican Church received State aid as well and both churches were tax exempt from day one.

FINANCIAL DISCRIMINATION IN THE CHURCH, ECCLESIASTICAL GRANTS-GOVERNMENT FUNDS TO THE CHURCHES

Inflicting religious terror

Page 12 NEWSDAY Sunday October 17, 1999

THE BRITISH employed their Police and their military, along with slavemasters to force African slaves to turn to Christianity and away from their Orisha religion; the Canadians would later use the lure of education to proselytise Hindu and Muslim indentured labourers, while, in 1685, the French had made the Roman Catholic conversion of African slaves an Article of their Code Noir.

But the British, not content with terrorising their slaves to convert them, took it a step further and placed economic pressure on French settlers in Trinidad, Dominica, St Lucia and Grenada clearly to abandon their Roman Catholic faith and turn to the Anglican Church.

While, admittedly, the argument of conversion of the French was never officially advanced, the intent could not have been otherwise.

Dr Louis de Verteuil wrote in 1858 that "in several of the British West Indian islands, viz. in Dominica, St Lucia, Grenada and Trinidad although the majority of the population were Catholics, "in everyone of them the Church of England has the lion's share." He pointed out that although in Trinidad the Catholic Church had

45,000 members it received 4,500 pounds sterling, the 17,000-member Episcopalian church received 5,500 pounds sterling.

A British Governor reduced the stipend the Catholic Bishop received from 1,000 pounds annually, to 500 pounds.

The Ecclesiastical Ordinance enacted in 1844 made the Church of England (the Anglican Church) the established or official Church of Trinidad.

Fourteen years later, according to Dr de Verteuil, the Governor of Trinidad withheld the entire stipend.

The Canadians worked among the Indian indentured labourers to convert them to Christianity and in 1868 set up primary schools in Trinidad, the idea being to convert them to the Canadian Mission (or Presbyterian) faith.

Many of the Indians who sent their children to these schools and their children to be Christians very often professed themselves for the benefit of the Canadian Mission authorities, while practising their religion at home, or at the temples and mandirs.

The majority of indentureds, however, resisted this proselytising, and in 1911, 43 years after the CM's opening of schools, mainly in Central and South Trini-

dad, as many as 97 percent of Indian descendents here were illiterate.

It was a terrible price that they had to pay to retain their religious beliefs, and this was a contributory factor in many being unable to access better paying jobs, as well as to become doctors, lawyers, educators etc.

The missionaries persisted and their first real breakthrough came in the 1890s, when Lal Behari took his vows as a Minister of the Presbyterian faith.

I had referred earlier to the Code Noir, Article 2 of the Code Noir stated, "All slaves in our islands shall be baptised and in-

GEORGE
ALLEYNE

structed in the Catholic religion, Apostolic and Roman. We instruct the colonists buying newly arrived slaves that they should inform the Governor and Intendant of it within one week at the latest on pain of a summary fine, and they shall give the necessary orders to have them instructed and baptised in due course."

It is ironical that the teachings of Jesus, known to his followers as "The Christ, reached Africa, East Africa that is, long before it reached England and France and indeed Europe, with the exception of perhaps Rome.

A powerful Kushite, who served Queen Candace of Kush (later to be described in the Bible as Ethiopia) had been baptised by the Apostle Philip, who had met him on the road to Gaza, in Egypt.

The man described in the Acts of the Apostles 8:27 as "a eunuch of great authority under Candace, Queen of the Ethiopians—who was over all her treasure" had been reading from the book of the prophet Isaiah, when Philip met him.

Kush had been a great civilisation that had traded with India, China, Asia Minor and (other) parts of North Africa. It has been described by the British author, Basil Davidson, in his book Old

Africa Rediscovered

FINANCIAL DISCRIMINATION IN THE CHURCH, ECCLESIASTICAL GRANTS-GOVERNMENT FUNDS TO THE CHURCHES

Italy-Vatican Pact to End Subsidies for Clergy

By E.J. DIONNE Jr.
Special to The New York Times

ROME, Nov. 17 — Italy and the Vatican signed a protocol this week that will eliminate state subsidies for the clergy's salaries and tighten tax benefits for church institutions.

The protocol was an addition to the Concordat signed by the Government and the Vatican last February that ended Roman Catholicism's role as the state religion of Italy.

The agreement, along with the Concordat, symbolized the abating of the church-state conflicts that have wracked Italian political life since the middle of the last century, when Italy was reunited in a process known as the Risorgimento.

It also signaled major changes that have taken place in the Roman Catholic Church's attitudes toward church-state relations since the Second Vatican Council of 1962-65.

"We can now say that today, at last, the troubling vicissitudes of the Risorgimento and post-unity periods involving the regulation of church property have found a solution," said the Vatican's Secretary of State, Agostino Cardinal Casaroli, who signed the agreement for the Vatican on Thursday.

Prime Minister Bettino Craxi, whose Socialist Party was historically identi-

fied with anticlericalism, said the agreement "definitely turns a page" on the church question. Mr. Craxi signed the accord for the Government.

For individual clergymen, the agreement will not be without its costs. The accord calls for an end to state subsidies for the clergy's salaries in 1988. At that point, Italy's bishops will pay salaries from funds contributed by the faithful. The subsidies cost the Government about $165 million a year.

The agreement, however, provides generous tax credits — up to about $1,100 a year — for Italians who contribute to such funds.

Some Italian bishops have expressed concern that an end to state subsidies for salaries might force some priests into poverty, and the Vatican newspaper, L'Osservatore Romano, today acknowledged the concerns of priests.

"Every reform inevitably troubles those who are involved," the paper said. But by freeing clergymen from subsidies it said, the accord allows the priest to regain all his dignity within the ecclesiastical community.

On the thorny question of how church property should be taxed, the new agreement provides that churches continue to enjoy tax benefits, provided they are open to the public. Church institutions such as seminaries will also be free of taxes.

But charities formed by lay people will have to be recognized by the Vatican to be eligible for tax benefits.

FINANCIAL DISCRIMINATION IN THE CHURCH, ECCLESIASTICAL GRANTS-GOVERNMENT FUNDS TO THE CHURCHES

Governor unveils new organ at AME Church

Trinidad Guardian March 7, 1987

50 YEARS AGO

YESTERDAY evening the Governor unveiled the new pipe organ at the A.M.E Church, Woodbrook Street, Port-of-Spain. *Woodford St*

The new organ was bought by the Rev Dr Mayhew, M.D., Pastor of the Church, while he was in the U.S.A. recently.

Its erection was completed by a local organ-builder. The tone is rich and melodious.